INDICTMENT

D1595730

INDICTMENT

FROM THE PARTY OF LINCOLN AND REAGAN, GOP DEVOLVEMENT INTO THE PARTY OF TRUMP

BRANT J. MOORE

ARCHWAY
PUBLISHING

Archway Publishing books may be ordered through booksellers or by contacting:

Archway Publishing
1663 Liberty Drive
Bloomington, IN 47403
www.archwaypublishing.com
844-669-3957

ISBN: 978-1-6657-0779-4 (sc)
ISBN: 978-1-6657-0780-0 (hc)
ISBN: 978-1-6657-0781-7 (e)

Library of Congress Control Number: 2021911272

Print information available on the last page.

Archway Publishing rev. date: 10/28/2021

CONTENTS

PREFACE

I HAVE WRITTEN this book to help clarify and explain my journey from a lifelong Republican (regular campaign donor, campaign volunteer, and professional campaign manager) to the status or station of Never Trumper. In some ways this was a difficult decision. It resulted in strained relationships with some friends and family. For about three years for the most part, I avoided the topics of Donald Trump and the Republican Party in social situations and family settings. When others brought up the subjects, I would share my opinion, but generally I was reluctant to engage in too much verbal sparring. Most of my conversations about our forty-fifth president were with my wife, Louise; my son, Matt; and before her death in 2018, my mother, Paula. Without those conversations, I would have felt alone and adrift.

Fortunately, I occasionally met and found other like-minded people (independents and Republicans) who felt they could never support the Trumpist takeover of the Republican Party. While golfing in Orlando, Florida, in 2017, I was paired with a man about ten years younger (a real estate project manager from New York). On the back nine, a short, but severe thunderstorm hit and caused us to leave the course and stop at the bar for a snack and a beer. President Trump (and I use the word *president* loosely) appeared on the television. This man blurted out his total disgust for the character and actions to date of the president. It was a cathartic moment for each of us as we shared our profound fears for our country and our sadness for the state of the Republican Party. We each agreed on the spineless cowardice we were witnessing from elected officials, but neither of us could come to terms with people we knew and cared about who seemed to rationalize, spin, justify or deny behavior by President Trump they never would have accepted from a politician of the other party. We finished, said our goodbyes, and expressed our hopes that this dark period facing our country and the world would be short-lived.

I have also written this book to show the sad, corrosive impact this thoroughly awful presidency has had on our nation and the consequences for our future. It is not a pleasant book to read, but it is full of substance and honesty for those who are willing to face reality. My fear is that those Trumpists who need to read this book and other books and articles about the Trump years will not. However, my hope is that enough other people will read it and realize the depth and depravity of the Trump presidency and be unafraid to share their thoughts with those Republicans that worship and cling to Donald Trump in an emotionally, spiritually, and intellectually unhealthy way. This book and other books by much more well-known authors will make the case for the Faustian bargain many Republicans have made with their "Dear Leader." Many will remember in one of the debates during the primary contests, Trump bragged that he could shoot someone in broad daylight in Times Square and that his people would still stand behind him. Just a few days ago, he incited insurrection and domestic terrorism on the Capitol, and many of his supporters cannot even now own up to what a depraved, manipulative sociopath they have sponsored. Too many people in the Republican Party have nearly sold their souls to this abomination of a human being.

It will not be a book filled with detailed policy positions and large numbers of statistics. Instead, it will be more of an indictment of a president, his family, the Republican Party, and its supporters.

I am writing this foreword after the defeat of Donald Trump in the November 2020 election. In my opinion, enough Americans were repulsed by the lies, deceptions, misinformation, and ugly kooky conspiracy theories spread by President Trump and his minions, and this led to a defeat for the president and his supporters. I hope and pray that the Trumpist movement is a tragic historical aberration that our country eventually recovers from for the sake of future generations. To recover our dignity, our spiritual health, and our leadership in the world, the people who supported this malignant narcissist in 2016 and 2020 must be held accountable.

Those who voted for Trump only in 2016 can be more easily understood and accepted. They were strongly against Hilary Clinton, and they saw Trump as a disruptor and potential reformer. At least these voters woke up and recognized what a disaster four years of the Trump administration had been.

The voters who voted for him twice, however, deserve no respect. Personally, I will speak up, and I will not tolerate their spewing of revisionist history about the Trump presidency. I also will give them an earful if I hear any of them try to distance themselves by saying they never liked Trump but supported him in both runs for the presidency because they liked some, most, or all his policies. What a crock!

I respect and gratefully thank anyone who opposed this presidency, but especially the Never Trump Republicans. This group of people is comprised of patriots who put their country above themselves. Some have lost friendships. Some have lost career opportunities in Republican circles. Some have even had their lives threatened by Trump's most extreme supporters. At least the Never Trumpers can look themselves in the mirror and smile.

Trumpists, who propagandized for him, believed his ridiculous conspiracy theories, and spread his misinformation and outright lies cannot escape the harsh light of truth. They own him and his policies and beliefs (summarized below) until they admit their mistake and pledge to themselves and others that they will never again support a candidate so outside the bounds of human decency and basic American values.

➤ His racism, his corruption, his dysfunction, his nonstop deceit, his stream of mendacious lies.

- His jarring lunge toward fascist authoritarianism.
- His complete disregard for the rule of law and basic human decency.
- His treachery and traitorous acts including his demeaning of our war-dead, demeaning of prisoners of war like John McCain, and demeaning of our troops in the field.
- His twisted subversion of the Military Code of Justice.
- His slavish devotion to dictators, and his attempts to undercut our allies around the world.
- His unwillingness to confront Vladimir Putin over intelligence reports of the Russians paying bounties on the death of American troops in Afghanistan.
- His decision to separate over six hundred children from their parents at the US border when the parents were sent back to their home countries, governed by tyrants and ruined by drug gangs, despite pleas for humanitarian refugee status.
- His bribing his voters to trade decency and honor to worship at the altar of tax cuts and coveted Supreme Court seats. While I am a person who believes in the sanctity of life, it means more than just promoting alternatives to abortion. It means showing love and support to people in trouble, people wrestling with life-changing issues, and people who need kindness, love, protection, and justice.
- His racial dog whistles and the acceptance and promotion of White supremacists (remember our president's comments about good people on both sides of the march in Charlottesville after those splendid human beings in hoods carrying torches murdered a counter protester).
- His encouragement of armed thugs at rallies in state capitals and the chants at Trump rallies to lock up the governor of Michigan, Gretchen Whitmer, literally days after the FBI uncovered a plot to kidnap and murder her.
- His wink and a nod to the Proud Boys: "Stand down but stand by."

- His astonishing incompetence, misinformation, and outright lies concerning the coronavirus.
- His superspreader events at the White House and his rallies.
- His presidential ad campaigns, the most malicious and deceitful that I have ever witnessed in the history of modern politics. Supported and financed by Trump's campaign, the Republican Party, and independent political action committees, these ads stated that President-Elect Biden (ouch, that must hurt) wanted to defund the police and military and supported wealth taxes. They were so patently untruthful they should have caused their creators and believers to swallow their own tongues, metaphorically speaking.
- His unwillingness to cooperate in a peaceful transition of power after his election defeat in November 2020.
- Finally, his open invitation to his thug army of Trumpist traitors to invade the Capitol of the United States of America.

In my mind, the only way Trumpists ever regain even a modicum of credibility is for them to admit their tragic mistake, apologize for it, and never again support someone so thoroughly unfit to lead our nation. Do I think that will happen? Could it be when pigs fly? This bootlicking devotion of Trumpist world reminds me of the worst cult of personality our nation has ever seen. Hard-core Trump supporters need deprogramming, and they need to experience completely and thoroughly a sense of shame. In the absence of sincere, deep recanting of Donald Trump, they should not be taken seriously in the rebuilding of this country. While I hope and pray that they can find it within themselves to admit fault and seek forgiveness and grace, I am less than optimistic about their chances. Introspection is something I see sadly lacking in most Trumpists. While most of my rhetorical venom is directed at the worst of the worst promoters and enablers of Donald Trump, I must state for the record that this does not exonerate the many Republicans who voted for Donald Trump, either.

This pathetic movement's willingness to subvert our values on such a massive scale is not something I ever expected to see in the

United States. Some of the parallels with the early days of the rise of European fascism in the 1930s are quite chilling. Hopefully, the election result is the beginning of the end for "Know Nothing Party II." For those who remember nineteenth century American history, the Know Nothing Party, was the populist anti-immigrant political party that split the Whig Party. Both wings/parties soon went out of business from a political standpoint and were replaced by the Republican Party. That, in and of itself, is so rich with historical irony.

In a November 4, 2020, article in the *Atlantic*, "A Large Portion of the Electorate Chose the Sociopath," by Tom Nichols, is a frightening description of what is happening to our society and our withering democracy.

> But no matter how this election turns out, America is now a different country. Nearly half of the voters have seen Trump in all his splendor—his infantile tirades, his disastrous and lethal policies, his contempt for democracy in all forms—and they decided they wanted more of it. His voters can no longer hide behind excuses about the corruption of Hillary Clinton or their willingness to take a chance on an unproven political novice. They cannot feign ignorance about How Trump would rule. They know, and they have embraced him.
>
> Sadly, the voters who said in 2016 that they chose Trump because they thought "he was just like them" turned out to be right. Now by picking him again, those voters are showing that they are just like him: angry, spoiled, racially resentful, aggrieved, and willing to die rather than ever admit that they were wrong.[1]

In writing this book, including this preface, I kept asking myself if I was being too unkind or too harsh to Trump supporters, but my conclusion was that if anything, I was being too easy on them. Each day our country witnesses new assaults on our democracy, new assaults on truth, and new assaults on honor and goodness. Today, I watched a news report on CNN discussing the action of the Arizona Republican Party. This dysfunctional group of traitors masquerading as a political party voted to censure Doug Ducey, the governor of Arizona; Jeff Flake, a retired former senator of Arizona; and Cindy McCain, the widow of former Senator and 2008 GOP presidential candidate John McCain. This act against honorable, truthful, patriots is beyond disgraceful. Particularly, attacking Cindy McCain, the wife of a war hero and former presidential candidate, because she had the audacity to endorse and vote for Joe Biden rather than a man who would later foment an insurrection against our government that resulted in the death of several people, is an affront to basic human decency unparalleled in American history.

A political party that stoops this low is a political party that deserves to die. Whether it happens relatively quickly or relatively slowly, the Republican Party is a horrid, savage, withering political tribe dedicated only to maintaining power. It does the bidding of White supremacists, kooky conspiracy fanatics, and insurrectionists. It claims the mantle of patriotism while worshipping perhaps the greatest traitor in American history—Donald John Trump. It puts the blue MAGA Trump flag above the American flag. It spits on its fellow citizens by clinging to and spreading the greatest lie in American history—that the 2020 election was stolen. It cares nothing about serving Americans, nothing about preserving national honor and international leadership, and nothing about serving the law and the US Constitution. It seems to care less about the death of thousands of Americans and less about pulling together to conquer coronavirus than it does about propping up their version of "American Mussolini." It serves no other purpose than proselytizing for a narcissist and a traitor and a putrid wannabe dictator. Without grace, without conscience, and totally without honor, this self-serving group of people has gravely underestimated the strength of the rest of the American people. This political party will lose its campaign funding from corporate America, as well as any future majority status with the country at large. Other than winning legislative seats in pockets of red states, it will not be capable of winning future presidential elections for a long time, if ever. While its adherents seem incapable of shame for the Republican Party's actions, the rest of the country feels shame and embarrassment for them.

On January 6, 2021, the president (lame-duck) urged his swarm of followers to attack our Capitol. Despite the violence, the damage, and the actual deaths, despite the potential deaths of the vice president, House members, and senators, and despite their oaths of office to protect and defend the Constitution of the United States, forty-five Republican senators abdicated their honor and their duty by voting against having an impeachment trial (the second for Trump). Five senators—Susan Collins, Lisa Murkowski, Ben Sasse, Mitt Romney, and Pat Toomey—lived up to the standard of public servants. The other forty-five deserve nothing but contempt for their cowardice and their lust for power. If inciting a seditious insurrectionist riot at our Capitol is not grounds for impeachment, then what could possibly ever be grounds for impeachment. Trump and his violent supporters made our country look like a banana republic. They disgraced themselves before God; they disgraced their families; they disgraced their country, and they disgraced themselves.

Notice, I did not mention that they disgraced their political party because their political party is so far past disgrace, it is hardly worth mentioning. The conduct of most Republican senators and representatives has been abhorrent, and so plain for all to see.

Most Americans hope to never see again what happened on January 6. Only those clinging to remain within the cult, and those with deeply flawed character and judgment, accept and excuse what happened. Those who did not participate in the atrocities of January 6 still bear some responsibility for the heinous results. By countenancing the lies of Donald J. Trump over the last four years (especially the lies about the election being stolen) and by not fighting against those lies, they own the results. Until Trump supporters face this harsh truth and separate themselves from this evil man and his legion of enablers in the Republican Party, they will not be again welcomed by other Americans back into our civic life. Republicans used to believe in responsibility and accountability. Despite their lame demands to move on from this evil, sad chapter in our history, in the name of national unity, Republicans like Kevin McCarthy will never again be taken seriously by most people other than those die-hard Trump loyalists. Unless or until the Republican Party takes responsibility for the Trump-fomented insurrection on the American people in our Capitol, the Republican Party has no right to ask for our forgiveness or our votes. Because not enough Republican senators voted to convict Donald Trump in his second impeachment trial, the Republican Party deserves neither forgiveness nor access to significant political power ever again.

The one saving grace regarding Donald Trump's second impeachment trial is this: although he was acquitted by a minority vote, he will forever be remembered by most Americans as a vile traitor who inspired an insurrection against the United States of America. Some of the Republican senators who ultimately voted to excuse his crimes against his country will pay a price in future elections (maybe not in primary elections, but more likely in general elections). Those that manage to survive politically will be forever branded as weak cowards. Their votes to acquit the worst demagogue imaginable will seal their pathetic verdict in history. They will be digging the collective grave of the Republican Party, and they will have to answer to their grandchildren when asked about what they did and where they stood on the question of the impeachment of Donald J. Trump. Their loyalty to party over country will be higher than Trump's loyalty to either. Donald Trump will hold over their heads the prospect of a third political party: the MAGA Patriot Party. This party, if it ever does come to pass, will be neither MAGA nor Patriot. Trump will also hold over their heads the possibility of primary challengers. I say bring it on. Enough Americans will be repulsed by a Trump-dominated Republican Party or a Trump-inspired third party. The weak-minded decisions of Republican leaders will not benefit them but will haunt them forever.

A particularly revolting example of how far this party has fallen from grace was the recent appearance of Nikki Haley on Laura Ingraham's show on Fox News. Haley opined on how tough the second impeachment was going to be on Donald Trump and how it would harm efforts at unifying the country. She showed more concern for poor Donald Trump than for Capitol Police Officer Brian Sicknick, who was beaten to death by Trump's riotous mob. When leaders of a political party are more worried about their political futures than their constitutional duties, they deserve contempt. Her misplaced loyalties to Donald Trump rather than to her shocked and grieving country demonstrate her complete and utter unfitness for future office. This degree of sycophancy to Donald Trump quite frankly makes me want to vomit. Abraham Lincoln and Ronald Reagan would roll over in their graves if they were able to hear her and others try to escape from the damage done to our democracy by one self-absorbed wicked man and his army of traitors and collaborators.

On Inauguration Day, the Capitol was unable to host a celebration, a turning of the page from national incompetence and treachery to a return to competence and true patriotism. Rather than let a duly elected man assume control of the executive branch of government and allow the country to have the time-honored tradition and celebration associated with a just and legal transfer of power, the Republican Party owns the guilt and shame of having to witness the placement of twenty-five thousand National Guard troops around the Capitol to prevent further attacks from traitorous hordes of subhumans.

Why did this have to happen? It happened because a huge number of Americans fell for the constant gaslighting of Donald Trump. Rather than use their brains and hearts as God intended, they listened to Trump's repetitive lie about the election being stolen. This constant refrain by Donald Trump, this constant dangerous call to action, resulted in death and destruction, not only at our Capitol, but potentially irreparable harm to our democracy and our civic affairs. Trump's constant incivility infected too many of his supporters. It turned some of them into traitorous criminals. It turned others into sad, selfish collaborators. It wounded our democracy and our republic.

Whether the wound is mortal remains to be seen. One thing is certain: without acceptance of responsibility by the Republican Party and political punishment of Donald Trump, the wound will fester and could become fatal. Donald Trump can never be allowed to run for office ever again.

As for the Never Trump movement, our options might be to help recover and rebuild a Republican Party that never again accepts and promotes a sociopath as its leader. I fear this will be a difficult if not impossible task.

It might mean the building of a new moderately conservative political party, and working through it, to defeat and destroy vestiges of the ossified Republican Party. Again, I fear this will be a tough, but not impossible, challenge.

Finally, it might be a realignment with the Democratic Party. The addition of patriotic Republicans to the other party might result in a less tribal, a less blood-sport approach to the entire nation's politics. It could unify, rebuild, and strengthen our values and our resolve. It might strengthen and expand the Democratic Party and allow it to compete more effectively throughout the country. It might also be much more attractive to younger people. This could facilitate making the Democratic Party a more moderate party, capable of winning elections for generations to come. It could help return us to the lectern on the stage of world leadership and make our foreign and military policy stronger and more bipartisan. It might also make more Americans quit hating each other.

None of this is possible, however, without a full accounting of responsibility. Republicans, need to recant. They need to apologize for Donald Trump. They need to act like grownups. They need to disown him. They need to make sure that he never holds public office ever again. They need to show the rest of the country that they learned a lesson from this tragic mistake. Without that, they will remain a large, nomadic political tribe, albeit a minority one, with shriveling political power, and shriveling respect from the rest of the country. With or without contrition by Republicans, the country will move on.

In examining Donald Trump's words, actions, and inactions, the record shows much overlap between topics. In other words, many of the things he did or attempted to do could be categorized in more than one topical area or chapter. For instance, his actions claiming fraud, trying to undermine the election results and planting seeds of doubt in the minds of his followers, could be put in the chapter "Lies, Misinformation, and Conspiracy Theories," or the chapter "Traitor in Chief," or the chapter "Threatening the Peaceful Transfer of Power." Much of what Donald Trump has done has been harmful in multiple ways, making it difficult to precisely categorize. As a result, some of the lies and destructive actions will be mentioned more than once in more than one place throughout the book.

I hope this book adds to the discussion we Americans must have with each other. We will not reclaim our heritage, our goodness, and our leadership if we fail.

ACKNOWLEDGMENTS

A MAN OF honor that I hold in high esteem, Charlie Sykes, will be quoted extensively in this book because he has always done what he thinks is right, not what is expedient. Moreover, his analysis of the rise of Donald Trump and the takeover of the Republican Party by the Alt Right is the most thoughtful, penetrating analysis on this period of recent American history I have ever read. So anyway, thank you, Charlie Sykes. I also want to thank Max Boot and David Rothkopf for their insights as well. Both are quoted extensively too.

I have read numerous articles and opinion editorials. Each of the writers offered real insights and helped clarify my thoughts on the various topics presented in this book. Thank you one and all.

I would also like to thank my wife, Louise, for her suggestions and patience during the past few months while writing this book. She offered great suggestions and helped with footnoting and editing. I would also like to thank my son, Matt, who also encouraged me in this endeavor. I love you both very much.

Finally, I have to say a few words about our little dog, Kensi, who passed away in late November 2020. She was a sweet female Cavalier King Charles spaniel, who was born with congenital kidney dysplasia. She only lived four and a half years, but she was a blessing to each of us. I missed having her in the office with me as I wrote much of this book.

I know this book has been hard on Trump voters, but I also know it needed to be. I hope in time they will recognize what a truly horrible person they placed their faith in and how detrimental a force he has been to our country's values and shared ideals.

CHAPTER 1

TRAITOR IN CHIEF

THE CHARGE THAT someone is a traitor is not something to be expressed casually or carelessly. It requires evidence, and it must clear a high bar to be taken seriously. A person involved in espionage (primarily for money) by providing state secrets or critical military information to an enemy country without explicit permission of our government is obviously guilty of criminal treason. A traitor, however, can also be someone who takes actions or speaks falsely about his country to harm its status in the world and to destroy or to cripple its values and institutions. There are many actions or public statements that could be categorized as traitorous even if those actions or public statements do not meet the strict definition of punishable criminal treason.

Documentation for some of the most egregious and ugly examples of treacherous words and deeds of our forty-fifth president, Donald Trump follows.

DISRESPECTING OUR ADMIRALS AND GENERALS

In their book *A Very Stable Genius*, Carol Leonnig and Philip Rucker describe a meeting in the Pentagon in the summer of 2017 with top administration officials and the Joint Chiefs of Staff to discuss US alliances and military posture and readiness that devolved into angry rants by President Trump, who accused our highest senior officers of incompetence. Trump then called Afghanistan a "loser war" and scolded them by saying, "You don't know how to win anymore." Next, he chided them for the cost of ongoing military operations overseas. He stated that the United States should have gotten payments in oil from the allies it assisted in the Middle East.

Trump then said, "I wouldn't go to war with you people. You're a bunch of dopes and babies." According to others in the room, Secretary of State Rex Tillerson defended the military leaders and told the president that his criticism was "totally wrong." This exacerbated a growing rift between Tillerson and President Trump, which resulted in Tillerson's dismissal in March 2018.[2]

This tirade by the president directed at the top military officers of the United States is without question one of the most morale-destroying rants in US history. A man who never served in our military had the audacity to dress down the very men and women our nation depends upon for its safety and security. These senior officers, who have given so much to the service of our country, were treated with a profound and sad disrespect by a cruel, deceitful man ill-equipped intellectually, morally, or spiritually to be their commander in chief.

SUCKERS AND LOSERS

In a September 3, 2020, article titled, "Trump: Americans Who Died in War Are 'Losers' and 'Suckers,'" in the *Atlantic*, Jeffrey Goldberg reported the president had repeatedly demeaned and disparaged American soldiers, sailors, and airmen by questioning their intelligence and sacrifice. In addition to demeaning active-duty service members, he asked that wounded veterans be kept out of military parades. According to Goldberg, this article relied on multiple sources and was independently verified by several other news organizations, including Fox News reporter Jennifer Griffin.

When President Donald Trump canceled a visit to the Aise Marne American Cemetery near Paris in 2018, he blamed the last-minute decision on rain, saying helicopters could not fly there, and the Secret Service didn't want to drive there. Neither of these claimed excuses by the president was true. The truth was that the president did not want his hair to look disheveled and that he did not feel it was important to honor our war dead.

According to a conversation with senior staff members on the morning of the scheduled visit, Trump said, "Why should I go to that cemetery? It's filled with losers." In a later conversation on the same trip, the president referred to the more than eighteen hundred marines who lost their lives at Belleau Wood as "suckers" for getting killed. The battle at Belleau Wood was crucial in World War I because it stopped the German advance toward Paris in the spring of 1918. [3]

Also, on this trip, Trump asked his aides, "Who were the good guys in this war?" Finally, he said he did not understand why the United States would intervene on the side of its Western European Allies. Are you kidding me, Mr. President? What is wrong with you? Is this how an American president is supposed to act toward our brave war dead who gave their last full measure? If he had been president during either World War I or World War II, could you imagine how those wars would have turned out?

DEMEANING JOHN MCCAIN'S PRISONER-OF-WAR STATUS

The late senator and former presidential candidate John McCain spent more than five years in the harshest captivity after his plane was shot down over Hanoi in 1967. He was tortured by his Vietnamese captors and refused an early release in 1968 because it would have meant leaving before the other men. Trump said while running for the Republican nomination in 2015, "He's not a war hero," and "I like people who were not captured."

There has been no other example in American history of this

contemptible, cruel attack on an American patriot. The shameful, disgraceful behavior on the part of President Trump continued after John McCain's death from brain cancer in 2018. When McCain died, Trump told his senior staff, "We're not going to support that loser's funeral." Trump also became enraged when he saw flags lowered to half-staff, and he said, "What the fuck are we doing that for? Guy was a fucking loser." Trump also referred to former President George H.W. Bush as a loser for getting shot down during World War II over the Pacific.[4]

TRUMP VISIT TO ARLINGTON NATIONAL CEMETERY WITH DEPARTMENT OF HOMELAND SECURITY SECRETARY JON KELLY

Also reported in the same article on Memorial Day 2017, President Trump and General John Kelly visited the grave of John Kelly's son, Robert Kelly, who died while serving in Afghanistan in 2010. While there, Trump said to General Kelly, "I don't get it. What was in it for them?" Kelly, who later became Trump's chief of staff, did not initially understand what Trump was trying to say. He thought it was a clumsy reference to the selflessness of America's all-volunteer armed forces. Later he came to the realization that Donald Trump did not understand anything other than purely transactional life choices.

Eventually, Marine Lieutenant General John Kelly resigned from his position as White House chief of staff. In an article dated October 16, 2020, by Marina Pitofsky in *The Hill*, John Kelly called Donald Trump the most flawed person he had ever met. In this article, John Kelly is quoted as saying, "The depth of his dishonesty is just astounding to me. The dishonesty, the transactional nature of every relationship, though it's more pathetic than anything else. He is the most flawed person I have ever met in my life."[5]

Trump is a wealthy, entitled, spoiled brat with no comprehension of the true meaning of service or patriotism. He has picked fights with

Gold Star families. He has used the military for his own political purposes when convenient, including photo ops. In the 1990s, Trump said efforts to avoid contracting sexually transmitted diseases constituted his "personal Vietnam." Trump is a selfish, petty, and viciously cruel human being. It is no wonder that a survey of 1,018 active-duty troops conducted by the *Military Times* in partnership with the Institute for Veterans and Military Families at Syracuse University between July 27 and August 10, 2020, found that 43.1 percent of respondents said they were voting for Biden while only 37.4 percent said they were voting for Trump.

The real mystery is why Republican voters have, for the most part, ignored his behavior toward the military. If these attitudes had been expressed by Barack Obama or any other American president, these postures and statements would have been disqualifying. Apparently, remaining in the Trump Republican cult and getting your tax cut is more important than revering American traditions, values, and war heroes.

PROTECTING WAR CRIMINALS AND UNDERMINING THE UNIFORM CODE OF MILITARY JUSTICE

This might be one of the most perplexing series of events discussed in this chapter. In a *New York Times* article by Dave Phillips dated December 27, 2019, entitled "Anguish and Anger from Navy Seals Who Turned in Edward Gallagher," men in his unit described their leader in the ghastliest terms.

Chief Petty Officer Eddie Gallagher had many incidents during his career that could easily have been career-ending. These included alleged drug use, alleged theft, and possible murder. *New York Times* reporter Dave Phillips struggled to get anyone in the military to give him much information on the record as to why Chief Gallagher appeared to be untouchable despite a trail of serious allegations. What came out from a series of off-the-record interviews was that navy commanders were afraid if they tried to punish Gallagher, President Trump might reverse the punishment and then fire the military leaders who ordered it.

Combat video, text messages, and confidential interviews with members of Seal Team 7 revealed frightening details about the conduct of Chief Eddie Gallagher. When his own men revealed that he committed horrible war crimes, the navy chain of command was forced to deal with those dreadful allegations. Members of his unit told navy investigators that Gallagher was a reckless leader with a troubling hunger for violence. They told investigators that they spent much of their time protecting Iraqi civilians from their violence-prone chief instead of going after ISIS.

In a released video, Gallagher is shown kneeling beside an injured, defenseless ISIS captive moments before Gallagher allegedly plunged a knife into the prisoner's neck. Most of the men were reluctant to break the Seal code of silence and were aware of the extreme blowback to their careers. But they said they were driven to come forward to try to rid the Seals of a chief they felt was unfit to lead.

Sadly, conservative commentators on Fox News, News Max, and One America News all painted the picture of Gallagher as an experienced warrior who made difficult decisions in the confusing fog of war. His own men, who were there, suggest the killing was premeditated, not a split-second decision under extreme duress in the heat of combat.

The Gallagher case created a real and lasting divide between top military leadership and President Trump that has never healed. Top military officers tried to persuade the president to avoid involving himself in the Gallagher case on the side of a deeply troubled, dangerous soldier, but the president ignored their advice. This subversion of the Uniform Code of Military Justice has upset the balance between the military's need for discipline and the US Constitution's requirement of civilian rule.

By publicly intervening in this court-martial case, the president attempted to steer the verdict, and he was partially successful. Gallagher was not convicted of murder even though he also was suspected of being involved in the controversial killing of a young Iraqi woman in 2010. However, he was convicted of photographing and posing with the dead corpse of the fifteen-year-old boy under his care and custody. In an unusual twist, Corey Scott, the SEAL medic, testified that he killed the wounded captive by cutting off his air supply. The medic has reached out to other members of the platoon to talk. None have responded to his request.

As typical with any federal official who crosses the president, Richard Spencer, the secretary of the navy, was fired for writing an op-ed in the *Washington Post* arguing against presidential involvement in the case. Pete Hegseth, a guest host on *Fox and Friends*, continues to praise the president for his involvement in the Gallagher case and urges the president to pardon other service members convicted of war crimes. The navy wanted to expel Gallagher from the SEALs, but Trump, with the unrelenting support of his cable news pundits, blocked the military from disciplining Gallagher.

One purpose of the Uniform Code of Military Justice is to seek justice for victims, even enemy combatants. Our military has always been held to the highest standards. The UCMJ specifically mandates that our service members must not follow or carry out illegal orders. When a leader like Donald Trump breaks this sacred bond of trust, it destroys unit moral and gives propaganda ammunition to our enemies. Instead of holding our soldiers to honorable standards, he is giving permission for them to commit and/or to cover up atrocities. This is not who we are! We are better than that! In a very real sense, his intrusion into this court-martial weakens our nation's resolve and puts our soldiers, sailors, and airmen at greater risk, if any of them suffer captivity. Oh, that's right: he doesn't care because they are "suckers and losers."[6]

KISSING UP TO DICTATORS AND THUGS AROUND THE WORLD

President Trump's pathological need to be not only accepted by but to be admired by the dictators and authoritarian governments around the world is truly one of the saddest and most disturbing legacies he will leave for himself and his sycophants in the Republican Party. He has forfeited the moral high ground for himself and his party.

One of the most prominent examples occurred during a joint press conference with Vladimir Putin in Helsinki, Finland, in 2018. During the press conference while on foreign soil, Trump attacked his Democratic opponents and our FBI. When he was asked about 2016 election meddling by the Russians, he stated that he held both countries accountable for the previous state of their relationship. By setting up this false moral equivalence, he put us, from a public relations standpoint, on the same moral level as a devious, duplicitous dictatorship. Despite being told by key US intelligence officials, including Director of National Intelligence (and former senator of Indiana) Dan Coates that Russia was clearly involved in mounting a major electoral disinformation effort against social networks in the United States, Trump cited Putin's "strong and powerful" denials of such interference.

In a July 16, 2018, *Business Insider* article titled "An Absolute Disgrace," written by Allan Smith, several key Republicans described Trump's performance as "shameful," "an absolute disgrace," and "moronic."

Senator Ben Sasse of Nebraska issued a statement calling Trump's comment that both countries were responsible for the state of US-Russia relations "bizarre and flat-out wrong."

"The United States is not to blame," Sasse said. "America wants a good relationship with the Russian people, but Vladimir Putin and his thugs are responsible for Soviet-style aggression. When the President plays these moral equivalence games, he gives Putin a propaganda win he desperately needs."

Representative Justin Amash of Michigan tweeted that someone could be in favor of improved relations with Russia and of Trump meeting Putin "and still think something is not right here."

Senator Jeff Flake of Arizona, who has frequently disagreed with President Trump, described the remarks as "shameful."

"I never thought I would see the day when our American President would stand on the stage with the Russian President and place blame on the United States for Russian aggression," he said. "This is shameful."

Even Senator Orrin Hatch of Utah, a close Trump ally, said in a statement that "Russia interfered in the 2016 election."

"Our nation's top intelligence agencies all agree on that point," he said. "From the President on down, we must do everything in our power to protect our democracy by securing future elections from foreign influence and interference, regardless of what Vladimir Putin or any other Russian operative says."

Representative Liz Cheney of Wyoming, the daughter of former Vice President Dick Cheney, tweeted the following:

> I was deeply troubled by President Trump's defense of Putin against the intelligence agencies of the United States & his suggestion of moral equivalence between the US and Russia.

Senator Bob Corker of Tennessee, who has often bristled with Trump, said, "I do not think this was a good moment for our country."

Senator John McCain of Arizona (before his death), who has also not agreed with President Trump on many domestic and national security issues, said this about the press conference. "This was one of the most disgraceful performances by an American president in memory."

Representative Trey Gowdy of South Carolina, the chairman of the House Committee on Oversight and Government Reform, said this in a statement: "Russia attempted to undermine the fundamentals of our democracy, impugn the reliability of the 2016 election, and sow the seeds of discord among Americans" and that he hoped Trump administration leaders "will be able to communicate to the President it is possible to conclude Russia interfered with our election in 2016 without delegitimizing his electoral success."

House Speaker Paul Ryan of Wisconsin said in a statement:

There is no question that Russia interfered in our election and continues attempts to undermine democracy here and around the world.

The President must appreciate that Russia is not our ally. There is no moral equivalence between the United States and Russia, which remains hostile to our most basic values and ideals. The United States must be focused on holding Russia accountable and putting an end to its vile attacks on democracy.

Finally, a former chairman of the Republican National Committee, Michael Steele, even said that Donald Trump was acting as if he were an "asset" next to his handler."[7]

Another clear example of our president putting relations with a dictatorship ahead of America's interests is his failure to confront Russian President Vladimir Putin over reported bounties placed on the death of American soldiers in Afghanistan. Officials in the Trump White House insisted that he was not personally informed of the alleged plot by the Russians. What a total crock! Reports tell a different story. He was provided, at a minimum, a written briefing earlier in 2019. He clearly did not confront Russian President Vladimir Putin over this issue raised by our intelligence services. This information was uncovered by our intelligence networks operating in Afghanistan while negotiation efforts to end the nineteen-year war in Afghanistan were taking place and while President Trump was currying favor to improve our relations with the Russians. Bounty-gate was reported by the *Washington Post*, the *New York Times*, and the *Wall Street Journal*. Of course, the Russians and the Taliban denied the story, but US operatives found large stashes of US currency in a location controlled by the Taliban. What president learns of this information, does nothing to confront our enemy, ignores the US intelligence community, and does nothing to protect our troops in the field from this provocative act of war by the Russian GRU (Russian military intelligence)? The answer is simple: a self-serving *traitor*.

Another example of Donald Trump placing his interests above our country's interests concerns his request at a state dinner in China in 2017. As reported in former National Security Adviser John Bolton's book *The Room Where It Happened*, Trump stressed to President Xi the importance of farmers and increased purchases of soybeans and wheat in the electoral prospects of President Trump. He specifically pleaded with President Xi to buy more US agricultural products to help ensure his 2020 electoral victory.[8] Again, what type of president would so brazenly and selfishly beg a foreign leader on foreign soil for actions to aid in his reelection?

Another sad example was the president's relationship with Kim Jong Un, the dictatorial leader for life of North Korea. The brutal leader, responsible for the murder of relatives and political opponents, knew exactly how to appeal to President Trump's vanity. As most people who follow the news know, the two leaders met for their 2019 summit to discuss denuclearizing the Korean peninsula at a meeting across the Demilitarized Zone at the border village of Panmunjom.

As reported in *National Security* in an article entitled "As Kim Wooed Trump with 'Love Letters,' He Kept Building his Nuclear Capability, Intelligence Shows" written by Joby Warrick and Simon Denyer on September 30, 2020, prior to this meeting, they exchanged numerous letters describing their budding "bromance." Kim wrote in one letter, penned in December 2018, which the president shared with the public, "Future meetings with your excellency would be reminiscent of a scene from a fantasy film." Even as he was stroking our president's ego, the North Korean military were busy working at six military bases digging a system of tunnels and bunkers to move mobile missile launchers so as to be undetected and capable of launching quickly and without sufficient warning before launch. At the same time, southeast of Pyongyang, new facilities were being built to process uranium for up to fifteen new nuclear weapons as reported by current and former US and South Korean officials as well as a report by a United Nations panel of experts. While the North Koreans have refrained from any new testing of their most advanced weapons systems, they never stopped working on them. Kim Jong Un got to strengthen his military's offensive capability while our president got them to only stop doing things (nuclear testing) that hurt the president's standing during daily news cycles.

In 2019 our defense secretary, Mark Espers (recently fired after Trump lost the election to Joe Biden), announced that joint military exercises with South Korea would be suspended indefinitely as an "act of good will" toward North Korea. This was done despite these joint exercises being the most important and realistic means of keeping our troops stationed near the DMZ combat-ready on short notice. Trump called these joint exercises a waste of money and a provocation to North Korea. With our then soon-departing president, it appeared everything in the international arena (our national security and the national security of our allies around the world) was simply transactional. Shortsighted and ignorant of history, this president fortunately will not be laying waste to the international connections and cooperation the world desperately needs to recover from his extreme misjudgment and tragic mistakes.[9]

THREATENING TO LEAVE NATO AND BECOMING A DYSFUNCTIONAL AND UNRELIABLE ALLY

After Joe Biden's win over President Trump in the recent presidential election, it is obvious how much our Western allies appreciate this changing of the guard. Congratulations from presidents and foreign ministers from Canada, Germany, and France make the point about how much better our relations with key allies will be under a new administration.

A *New York Times* article, "Trump Discussed Pulling US from NATO, Aides Say Amid New Concerns Over Russia," by Julian Barnes and Helene Cooper, dated January 14, 2020, stated clearly that there are not many things more desired by Vladimir Putin than the weakening and eventual disintegration of NATO (the North Atlantic Treaty Organization). This military alliance among the

United States, Canada, and Europe has deterred Soviet and Russian aggression for seventy years. Last year, President Trump suggested a move that would be the death-knell of NATO: the full and complete withdrawal of the United States. The president's repeatedly expressed desire to withdraw from NATO also worried national security experts particularly because of his also expressed desire to keep his phone calls and meeting with Putin secret from even his own aides and an FBI counterintelligence investigation into the administration's Russian ties. Retired Admiral James Stavridis, a former supreme allied commander of NATO, said withdrawal from this alliance would be "a geopolitical mistake of epic proportion." Russia's meddling in our elections and its efforts to keep former satellite states such as Latvia, Lithuania, and Estonia from joining NATO have aimed to weaken the alliance that is viewed as the "enemy next door." A NATO without the United States, unfortunately, would no longer be the counterweight to Russian expansionist goals. Putin could behave without restraint. No one should be surprised by Trump's publicly repeated ambition to withdraw from our commitments, both military and economic. Trump constantly complained that most European governments were not spending enough to support the shared costs of defense, leaving a disproportionate burden to the United States. He fails to grasp the details that spending levels are set by the individual parliaments of member countries. Donald Trump's skepticism about NATO seems to be a core belief, like his often-expressed desire to expropriate Iraqi oil. Both President Obama and President George W. Bush expressed frustration with NATO member countries not spending more of their budgets on defense. What is different about Trump is how central and fundamental central defense spending is to his opinion of NATO's overall worth. Again, for Trump, it came down to a purely dollar-valued transactional measurement. President Obama and President George W. Bush both recognized the value of shared intelligence, logistical support, and political and public relations efforts between and among members.[10]

Opinion columnist Brett Bruen, in an article titled "Trump Wrecked the International Order. It's Time to Start Thinking about what Happens when He's Gone," in *Business Insider*, dated August 2, 2020, lists the agreements the Trump administration sought to pull out of including the Paris Climate Accords, the Iran Nuclear Treaty, the Transpacific Trade Treaty, and NATO. This go-it-alone, reckless approach has sickened our allies, especially in Europe, but elsewhere in the world, as well.

By withdrawing from the Paris Accords, Trump exposes his ignorance about the science and the economics of climate change. My wife, Louise, and I were both skeptical some years back about global warming/climate change. A trip to the Canadian Rockies changed our perspective. While staying at a hotel on Lake Louise near Banff, Alberta, in 2017, Louise commented to me and several others on the trip with us about how the glacier had shrunk so much from the last time she had been there about twenty years ago. As a result of this observation and other information we have been exposed to in recent years, our perspective and attitude has changed considerably on this subject. Trump's outdated views seem wedded to the belief that climate action is way too costly and hurts job growth. This belief is no longer reality rooted as tremendous advancements in materials technology, architecture, building methods, alternative energy generation, and artificial intelligence have brought down costs and created job opportunities. According to a Yale University study, 69 percent of American voters (including 51 percent of Republicans) disapprove of Trump's decision to pull out of the Paris Accords. Fortunately, his opposition is moot. He lost to Joe Biden! The United States can reenter the agreement after our new leadership sends a request to the United Nations. It will take only thirty days after the request is reinstated.[11]

By withdrawing from the Iran Nuclear Treaty, Trump demonstrates his willful ignorance once again. In a report published in *Foreign Policy* by Colum Lynch, dated May 8, 2020, and titled, "Despite US Sanctions, Iran Expands Its Nuclear Stockpile," the regime in Tehran has cut in half the time it would need to produce enough weapons-grade fuel for a nuclear bomb. The imposition of pressure from more stringent sanctions has not caused Iran to reduce its support for regional militias or the development of its ballistic missile program. Even though the sanctions have imposed great hardship and damaged Iran's economy, it has yet to rein in its nuclear ambitions. All it has succeeded in doing is reduce our credibility among our traditional allies and increased the strain on our diplomatic partnerships around the world. Trying to lead when no one wants to follow is a strategy that will fracture relationships with allies and embolden adversaries on the UN Security Council. Negotiating treaties of this magnitude with multiple countries with multiple agendas is difficult, time-consuming work. No one gets everything they want. That is why it is called negotiating. Pulling out of previously agreed-to treaties and agreements only makes the United States look like a disrespectful brat on the international stage. It demeans the other participants and their hard work and commitment. It will infuriate our allies because now adversaries like China and Russia will immediately begin to sell materials, equipment, and arms to Iran. This unilateral move by President Trump put a fork in a ten-year effort to lower the temperature and slow the speed of Iran's nuclear program. It reduces the level of trust in US "good faith" by our allies and makes it much less easy to count on them in situations where we need them very badly. The IAEA (International Atomic Energy Agency) has made it clear that Iran had stopped its design work on atomic weapons in 2009 and was complying with its obligations under the nuclear pact until the United States reneged on the deal. Since then, Iran has restarted prohibited research and development on advanced centrifuges, which would enable it to purify its uranium at a much faster rate. Some arms control experts believe that Iran would need to overcome considerable technical constraints to weaponize and deploy a nuclear weapon. They suspect Iran's reaction to our pulling out of the agreement has not been to race toward the creation of a nuclear weapon but instead to signal in a measured way to the reimposition of sanctions. Again, the defeat of Trump and his temper-tantrum approach to foreign policy will open the doors to reestablish a sound framework to curb Iran's nuclear ambitions without destroying and further radicalizing the country's most militant factions.[12]

PULLING TROOPS, MOSTLY SPECIAL FORCES, OUT OF SYRIA

In an October 15, 2019, article in the *Washington Post*, "'I Can't Even Look at the Atrocities': US Troops Say Trump's Syria Withdrawal Betrayed an Ally" by Dan Lamothe, the headline tells you all you need to know. The Kurdish-led Syrian Democratic Forces had been one of America's closest partners in the war against the Islamic State since 2014. In combat against the terrorist group ISIS, eleven thousand Kurdish fighters have been killed. With President Trump's order to withdraw all one thousand US troops from northern Syria in the face of a Turkish offensive, those American soldiers who have served alongside those brave Kurdish allies are left wondering about our resolve and our place in the world. Again, we found our president bowing and scraping to a foreign dictator—President Erdogan—as Trump helped him achieve his bloody aims, while stabbing a loyal ally in the back. This reckless and immoral decision by our president has caused angry reactions from service members and veterans alike. Troops have reacted strongly in interviews and on social media despite Defense Department restrictions on them expressing political opinions. Some of these truth tellers are in Special Operations units, which rarely speak to the media and do not want their operators' identities revealed. Many service members in that part of the world doubted the Turks would have launched the offensive without the White House announcing its decision to stand aside. How a president of the United States could green light a decision to throw an important, loyal, effective ally under the bus in this way is devoid of conscience. Watching the atrocities by the Turks was difficult for many of our troops. The cruelty, duplicity, and cynical cowardice on display was too much for many of these honorable soldiers. No wonder Donald Trump was unable to earn most of their votes in the recent election. His wicked act will come back to haunt our nation. Because of it, America has begun the undoing of five years of blood, sweat, and toil against ISIS. It has helped strengthen the Russians, the Assad regime in Syria, the armed militias supported by Iran, and the corrupt dictatorship of Erdogan in Turkey.[13]

INVITING THE TALIBAN TO CAMP DAVID

In a September 9, 2019 op-ed in the *Washington Post* by Jennifer Rubin titled "Trump's Invitation to the Taliban was Disgraceful. So was Republican Silence about it," she demonstrated the utter hypocrisy, cowardice, and moral vapidity that has taken over the sad, pathetic, weak Republican Party. If a former Democrat president or key leader in the Democrat Party had invited the Taliban to negotiate with the president of the United States at Camp David, the Republican Party would have gone collectively apoplectic. Their heads would have exploded. They would have suggested he was unfit for office, and they would have been right. Fortunately, President Obama never did something as awful, or as unproductive, as elevating the Taliban to the same level as the president of the United States. This sinful invitation of a violent, misogynistic, stone-aged terrorist organization brought us to maybe one of the lowest points in this terribly disturbed presidency. He discounted the lives of our recent war dead and the lives of nearly three thousand Americans who died on September 11, 2001. Donald Trump should live in infamy for all the days of our lives.

When this awful invitation was announced, we did not hear any condemnation from Republican leaders. Ben Sasse, Ted Cruz, Tom Cotton, or Lindsey Graham did not renounce this affront to our collective conscience. Their cowardice, their fear of the Trump base, and their avaricious ambition to be president themselves overwhelmed them.

A special comment deserves to be made about Ted Cruz. In 2016 my wife and I went door to door while living in Hendersonville, North Carolina before the North Carolina Republican primary dropping off literature and speaking with voters. This was one of the worst political mistakes of my life. During the primary campaign, Trump called Cruz's wife ugly and corrupt, repeatedly referred to Ted Cruz as "lying Ted," and suggested that Ted Cruz's father was somehow involved in helping President Kennedy's assassin, and yet to this day, this hollow-souled political hack continues to worship at the altar of Donald Trump. We could call him the "water boy" for Donald

Trump, but even that somehow misses the point. I do not for the life of me know how he looks himself in the mirror every day to shave or brush his teeth. How the desire to remain relevant politically and how the desire to remain acceptable to a presidential sociopath and his deluded followers trumps (pardon the pun, but could not resist) feeling good about yourself, your choices, your personal honor, and your true love of country. Sadly, there are no profiles in courage among this group.

After the Taliban exploded a bomb that killed twelve people in Kabul, including an American soldier, Trump thankfully called off the peace negotiations scheduled with the terrorist group. The Taliban thought Trump was such a weak dealer that they thought they could gain even more leverage after a terrorist attack just prior to their meeting with him. Sadness cannot even begin to describe the spectacle of this attempted sell-out of our soldiers and our people and the Afghan people seeking a life free from Taliban violence and intimidation.[14]

DISMISSING AND DEMEANING OUR FBI AND INTELLIGENCE SERVICES

We all are by now familiar with Donald Trump's reflexive refrain, "Deep State." Anytime anything is said in testimony to Congress or elsewhere by spokesmen from the FBI, the CIA, or other intelligence services that conflicts with Donald Trump's views or his distorted view of reality, he dismisses it and then demeans either the speaker or the entire agency. This is why the head of the CIA, Gina Haspel, and the director of the FBI, Christopher Wray, were both in danger of being fired by President Trump in the waning days of his lame-duck, one-term, loser presidency. She had the audacity on January 29, 2019, to challenge his views on the Iran nuclear deal during Senate testimony when she stated that the Iranians were in complete compliance with the deal negotiated by the Obama administration. Fortunately, President Biden is trying to re-engage the Iranians to resurrect the

Iran Nuclear Agreement that Donald Trump walked away from. At other times about other countries, including China, North Korea, and Russia, the nation's intelligence services' testimony was often at odds with President Trump. Their knowledge and level of detail, command of the facts, and strategic perspective was so far superior to that of our former president. They deal in facts and make recommendations based on the best analytical, satellite, and human intelligence they have available. Trump lies and makes things up in his own mind, creating his own distorted or completely wrong reality. No wonder they clashed constantly over truth versus deceit.

The FBI faced the same hostility. Donald Trump does not want objective truth; he wants loyalty at all costs. Look what happened to James Comey when Trump demanded his unconditional loyalty not to our country and truth, but instead to Donald Trump. Christopher Wray was constantly in Trump's crosshairs. Trump wanted to replace him with someone he believed would not interfere with enacting his policies or going after his perceived enemies. Wray had the audacity to not support Trump on his allegations about Joe Biden's son, Hunter. Many top-level counterintelligence experts in the FBI have expressed the view that the whole Hunter Biden laptop incident smells of a Russian disinformation campaign. In addition, Director Wray has contradicted Trump on issues such as antifa, voting fraud, and Russian election interference. Trump still fumes over the Robert Mueller investigation, claiming he was completely exonerated, which is untrue. The Mueller report found ten instances of obstruction of justice. They were simply not included in the articles of impeachment against the president. Let us not forget all the convictions of Trump campaign staff and other advisers Robert Mueller was able to achieve. This investigation yielded the indictments, convictions, and guilty pleas of thirty-four people and three companies, including Paul Manafort, Trump's campaign chairman at the time.

Has there ever been a president of the United States who openly went to war with the chief federal law enforcement agency, the FBI, and most of the intelligence services? The answer, of course, is no.

RUINING THE CAREER OF ALEXANDER VINDMAN
OVER HIS IMPEACHMENT TESTIMONY:

In an opinion article in *Newsweek* titled "Trump's Firing of Vindman Epitomizes the President's most Harmful Act of All," by Shawn Turner, dated February 11, 2020, the writer says:

> No administration in modern history has so grotesquely assaulted our democratic values and so blatantly engaged in systemic disregard for the rule of law, as that of Donald Trump. In the coming decades, volumes will be written about the character of the impeached president and the abhorrent behavior that he and his allies used to intimidate foes and deceive the American people. But when historians recount the many ways this president and his acolytes have damaged the nation they were sworn to protect, none will prove more harmful than their decision to embrace the power of "otherizing" through divisive rhetoric and dog whistle politics.

> Since the start of his campaign, Trump has repeatedly disparaged and insulted people of different nationalities, races, ethnicities, and religious backgrounds as a way of deflecting attention away from his own shortcomings. And, after three years as president, it appears that he has succeeded in normalizing identity-based attacks directed at a new target. Astute observers of the impeachment process watched as the president's defenders repeatedly stooped to linking false and anti-Semitic conspiracy theories to decorated military officers like Lieutenant Colonel Alexander Vindman, career diplomats like Ambassador Marie Yovanovitch, and private citizens like philanthropist George Soros.

Now Trump has fired Vindman from the National
Security Council. Security officers marched him
and his twin brother, Lieutenant Colonel Yevgeny
Vindman, out of the White House last Friday.[15]

Alexander Vindman, a loyal army officer and US citizen who
emigrated to the United States from Ukraine as a child, after being
fired for testifying against Trump in the House impeachment hearings, decided shortly thereafter to resign from the army. Apparently,
he knew that Trump had destroyed his career. A man of strong character and a great patriot was lost to our country's service because an
ill-tempered traitor in the White House decided to assault truth and
honor to continue his parade of defamation and lies. The same thing
happened to Ambassador Yovanovitch through a whisper campaign
that spread lies started by Rudy Giuliani. On Fox News, the ruthless
promoter of misinformation, Joe diGenova, also pushed the theory
that George Soros controls the US State Department. This reckless,
deceitful campaign against George Soros could not be further from
the truth. Soros, as a private citizen, has been given credit for supporting dissidents in Eastern Europe, thus helping contribute to the end
of the Cold War. He was also involved in efforts that saved countless
lives in Sarajevo during Yugoslavia's civil war. Around the world,
his Open Society Foundations have funded nongovernmental organizations (NGOs) doing charity work supporting poor, overlooked,
marginalized people.[16]

This overtly anti-Semitic campaign to smear people and destroy
reputations was based solely on the fact that these people either testified against the president during impeachment hearings or disagreed with him publicly over policy issues. Colonel Vindman was
in the room and heard the conversation President Trump had with
the Ukrainian president, Volodymyr Zelensky, where the president
sought to bribe/coerce a US ally into investigating a political rival
under the threat of having critical security assistance withheld, while
the Ukrainians were fighting Russian soldiers on Ukrainian territory.
But instead of owning up to his gross abuse of power, the president

accused his political opponents of treason. He then doubled down on this by accusing "deep-state" operatives of manufacturing evidence. Psychologists and psychiatrists would clearly label our president's behavior a classic example of "projection." Again, the consciences and the backbones of Republicans in the Senate were nowhere to be found. They circled the wagons in Trump's impeachment trial, called no other witnesses, and exonerated this clear and present danger to our democratic republic. While the House of Representatives could easily have presented more charges against Trump, the Senate had a moral obligation to convict and remove Trump from office. The evidence presented by the House was clear and convincing, leaving no doubt as to what our president had done. Fortunately, the Senate's dereliction of duty was rectified by the voters.

Nevertheless, most Republican senators were complicit in the beginning of the downfall of our democracy and the destruction of loyal public servants who placed their honor and testimony ahead of their careers and their safety.

RACIAL AND RELIGIOUS BIGOTRY

The American people need a president and other leaders who believe in the founding principles, values, and character on which this country was established: fairness, decency, and the rule of law. Otherwise, this nation will begin to resemble the authoritarian and eventually lawless dictatorships of the European Axis powers we fought in World War II. In Germany in the 1930s, Hitler started out by setting up the Jews through whisper campaigns. Then came propaganda. Then came race-based and religion-based discriminatory laws. Then came Kristallnacht ("Crystal Night"). And finally, came war and concentration camps and mass murder. This must be stopped in its tracks! The United States cannot have other leaders and a major political party supporting this type of racial and religious bigotry. We cannot allow ourselves to lunge into darkness and madness! The Republican Party must be held accountable for this leap from a leader like Abraham Lincoln, who freed enslaved Black Americans in the Civil War, to supporting a leader like Donald Trump, who traffics in racism and religious bigotry to stir his base of supporters, foment discontent, and attempt to remain in power at all costs.

LYING TO HIS VOTER BASE AND INSTIGATING AN INSURRECTION ON THE US CAPITOL

For two months, President Trump, after refusing to accept that he lost the 2020 presidential election, encouraged his base of supporters to continue to believe his unfounded conspiracy theories that the presidential election was rife with fraud. He asked them to come to Washington on January 6, 2021, because this was the day the Senate and the House of Representatives were going to meet to count the already certified Electoral College votes from each state. Every four years this formal counting of votes is carried out with little fanfare, but this year, because of Trump's continued resistance to the truth and his unwillingness to accede to the clear results of the election, many Republicans in Congress and several in the Senate planned to offer objections to the certified Electoral College votes.

On the White House lawn, almost an hour later, Trump repeated his most moving message: "So we're going to walk down Pennsylvania Avenue; I love Pennsylvania Avenue, and we're going to the Capitol. We're going to try and give our Republicans, the weak ones, the kind of pride and boldness that they need to take back our country. So let's walk down Pennsylvania Avenue. God bless you and God bless America." Trump told the crowd of seditionists that he loved them, and then he incited the riotous mob by asking them to "fight like hell." The crowd, whipped into a frenzy by this vicious demagogue, marched on the US Capitol upon conclusion of his speech. The results were several dead people, massive property damage, and an obscene attack on our institutions and values of democracy. He lit the match, and he gave them the green light. Combine this instigation with the unruliness of the crowd, and it is no wonder what followed. We are lucky that more deaths did not occur, including the potential murder of the vice president, senators, and congressional representatives. Let us not forget the sight of the hanging gallows set up by this gang of traitors or their chants of "Hang Mike Pence." I am no fan of the then vice president. He behaved like Donald Trump's lap dog for the last four years, but he should not be subjected to threats and intimidation from a group of traitorous criminals simply for carrying out his constitutional duties during the counting of electoral votes. Also, let us not forget that this instigation of insurrection was, and continues to be, based on a filthy, disgusting lie: that the election was fraudulent and stolen. This awful attempt at manipulation through deliberate deceit is on Donald Trump, but the willingness to believe this lie is on his followers. There was no evidence of fraud because there was no fraud. Ballots were counted multiple times; voting machines were tested and audited; results were certified by secretaries of state (some of whom were Republicans and some of whom were Democrats) in all contested states; fifty-nine of sixty court challenges were unsuccessful. Anyone with a sense of decency and honor should have accepted these election results by now. Instead, too many Trump voters opted to turn the Republican Party, the party of Lincoln and Reagan, into a fascist cult. They pretended that they were patriots, when in fact, they were the worst mass group of traitors in my lifetime.

All of this played out on the national and international news. Foreign leaders from all over the world, representing allies and adversaries, witnessed this meltdown. Traditional allies were aghast, and adversaries were jubilant.

The seditious mob stormed the Capitol steps, broke windows, and assaulted some of the Capitol police all while senators and representatives were meeting to carry out their constitutional duties regarding the Electoral College counting, the ratifying of the results of the presidential election. It took hours to clear out Donald Trump's army of vermin from the US Capitol. Senators and representatives had to be led out of the building by police. Eventually, but way too late, the DC

National Guard was mobilized. The reasons for the delay were not immediately clear, but there appeared to be a reluctance by Trump and the Defense Department to authorize the use of DC National Guard troops to put down a terrorist insurrection incited by the inflammatory exhortations of the President, himself, Donald Trump, and several of his minions (Rudy Giuliani, Donnie, Jr., Congressman Mo Brooks, among others). Bombs were later discovered near the offices of the Republican National Committee and the Democratic National Committee.

Also contributing to this disgraceful day in history were the seven Republican senators and 138 Republican members of the US House of Representatives who objected to the Electoral College vote count by the state of Pennsylvania, led by Senator Josh Hawley of Missouri and Senator Ted Cruz of Texas. In addition, six Republican senators and 121 Republican members of the US House of Representatives objected to the Electoral College vote count by the state of Arizona. These objecting Republicans should hang their heads in shame. They refused to accept the fair, legal, and accurate votes of their fellow citizens. They helped spread the lies and misinformation of the president. They were also culpable for what happened on this sad day in American history.

This shameful, traitorous attempt at overthrowing our government should be viewed today, and for posterity, as deeply evil. Everyone involved in this treacherous attack on the Capitol should be treated for what they are: disgusting thugs; cult-like fascists; and disloyal, un-American, awful human beings. They should be tried and given the maximum sentences under the law for their vicious, despicable actions. The president, himself, should be held to account for this seditious revolt. He should have been removed under the Twenty-Fifth Amendment immediately by a majority vote of the cabinet and two-thirds vote of each house of Congress. Because this was not done, he should have been convicted in his second senate impeachment trial to prevent him from running for federal office ever again and to prevent him from further metastasizing our politics and civil discourse with his lies and cancerous narcissism.

Also, he should serve time in prison along with his thug army. Never in American history has such a self-centered, ill-willed, angry man been put into the presidency.

Too many Americans bought into his politics of destruction, his demeaning, his taunting, and his bullying approach to governing. The "thug army" excused, in fact welcomed, his authoritarian advances. They parroted his lies. They attempted to shred our Constitution, and they discounted their fellow citizens. They put themselves above the law and above honor and human decency. They listened to liars and fools like Rudy Giuliani, who pushed the mob forward with ex-hortations like, "Let's have trial by combat." These willfully ignorant people listened to and believed the unbelievable rants, excuses, and falsehoods spewed by Sean Hannity, Laura Ingraham, and Tucker Carlson. After helping light the tinder, these Fox News personalities spread the biggest lie of all. They claimed this riot was the work of Antifa dressed up as Trump supporters. Apparently, they seriously believed that their audience would accept this ridiculous, implausible falsehood. This was their story, and they were sticking to it (at least for the time being). They must think their audience is pitifully malleable and gullible. Sad, cynical, and weak are the adjectives that come to mind when I think of these Fox News people.

The cabinet people who have resigned do not even deserve to have their names mentioned. Normally, I would say better late than never, but in this case, I would say, were you deaf and blind for the last four years? This hollow, transparent attempt at self-preservation and reputation-saving by running away from the Trump administration at this point looks incredibly weak and selfish. You can run, but you cannot hide from history's verdict. The stench will remain for a long, long time. From the history books, this reminds me of the Nazi thugs and higher-ups who claimed that they were not bad people and that they were just following orders. Good luck with that claim.

Early in the evening of January 7, Trump popped up on televi-sion with a short statement in which he finally, well sort of, conceded defeat to Joe Biden. He lied about calling in the DC National Guard. He thanked his supporters. He threw the mob under the bus, calling them criminals, and then he acted like he was not the arsonist who lit the match on the worst insurrection since the American Civil War. He cannot be allowed to duck away from responsibility. Donald Trump and the thug army that breached the Capitol must be held to account for their betrayal of our country. Many of the dreadful people in Trump's army of Brownshirts seem to love their big, beautiful, blue Trump flags and their Confederate flags (historically carried by the Ku Klux Klan) more than their country. Hillary Clinton's comment about the "deplorables," while very offensive at the time (2016), does not seem that far off the mark now, at least for the awful demonic group we saw on television. Confederate flags, nooses, and sweatshirts promoting "Camp Auschwitz" and "6 million were not enough" cannot be overlooked or excused by anyone living in a civil society. These barbarians can never be allowed to get away with this assault on our country. When authorities have a chance to review the videotapes inside the Capitol, hopefully, more will be arrested and tried for their seditious crimes.

My prayer is that at least some of the people that voted for Donald Trump in both 2016 and 2020 come to their senses. If they bitterly cling to his lies and his traitorous acts and statements, they will never reclaim a sense of peace. I would like to return to a relationship in which we can respect each other again and speak on a basis of shared facts. We cannot continue to operate and thrive as a nation when one side of the political divide continues to proliferate falsehood as facts. Trump supporters need to admit fully and without reservation that their president is an ugly traitor, a vicious demagogue, and a man devoid of honor and character.

As for the people who attacked our Capitol, they need to be treated as the traitors that they are. Traitors and people who support traitors should never get a free pass to walk away from their vile actions or their support of these vile actions. They will never deserve to be treated with a forgive and forget attitude. Trump supporters need to step up and admit they were wrong, very wrong, about this man. People that want respect need to show respect for others. They should not be able to claim that their votes were more important than everyone else's votes. They need to take a serious look within themselves and ask these two questions: Are some of our grievances legitimate? Are some of our grievances largely imaginary?

Many decent people, worthy of respect, are asking this key question: When are Trump supporters going to renounce Donald Trump? Until that happens, Trump supporters, fairly or unfairly, are going to be associated with supporting a president who is an unabashed traitor and a racist and White supremacist. Trump supporters need to make this personal decision. Are they going to be lumped together as stubborn dead-enders, or are they going to renounce a truly evil, malignant narcissist who drove this country down a dangerous road toward a civil war? Most Americans sincerely hope they choose wisely.

A SUMMARY OF TRUMP'S TRAITOROUS ACTS

While Donald Trump might not be prosecuted as a traitor, his traitorous acts will not be forgotten by history. In this opening chapter, I have discussed in some detail several of Donald Trump's most egregious acts against our country and its values. In his book *Traitor: A History of American Betrayal from Benedict Arnold to Donald Trump*, author David Rothkopf provides a comprehensive list of Trump's traitorous assault on the values, traditions, and character of our nation.

- Obstruction of justice
- Attacks on the rule of law
- Assault on the freedom of the press
- Pathological lying
- Unfitness for office
- Incompetence
- Corruption
- Attacks on our allies
- Violations of our international treaties and agreements
- Embrace of our enemies

- Undermining of our national security
- Nepotism
- Attacks on federal law enforcement and intelligence communities
- Fiscal recklessness
- Degradation of the office and public discourse
- Support of Nazis and White supremacists
- Indifference toward the death of Americans from coronavirus and disasters like the hurricane in Puerto Rico[17]

The overwhelming scope of his traitorous actions in some ways served as a buffer, preventing Americans from remembering everything and holding him accountable for anything. The four years of chaos, the constant feeding of misinformation and unfounded conspiracy theories, and the unwillingness of his supporters to seek truth rather than embrace falsehood enabled him to continue his reign of terror against his country for four years.

CHAPTER 2

COVID, COVID, COVID

LATE IN THE 2020 presidential campaign, former President Obama, while campaigning for Joe Biden, mocked President Trump by saying: "More than 225,000 in this country are dead. More than one hundred thousand small businesses have closed. Half a million jobs are gone in Florida alone; think about that. And what's his closing argument? That people are too focused on COVID. He's jealous of COVID's media coverage." Shortly thereafter, President Trump chanted "COVID" ten times in a row at a rally in Lansing, Michigan. Earlier in the day at an appearance in Orlando, Florida, Joe Biden suggested that Trump was more concerned with his TV ratings and media coverage than he was with combating the ongoing coronavirus pandemic. While Trump did not refer to former President Obama's comment, he did criticize the media's constant focus on the COVID-19 virus.

At this rally after chanting COVID ten times, Trump said, "You ever notice they don't use the word *death*, they use the word *cases?*" Trump continued: "And you know why we have so many cases? Because we test more. We're testing everybody; in many ways I hate it."

Tom Frieden, a doctor who served as director of the Centers for Disease Control and Prevention (CDC) under President Obama, told CNN that the increase in case numbers is not just because of increased testing. "Hospitalizations, which follow case increases by a week or two, are also increasing. What's more, the proportion of tests that are positive has increased, and this correlates with increased spread of the infection. The most reliable information is positivity, and this increased in all regions of the country."[18]

The mismanagement and dereliction of duty by President Donald J. Trump in his handling of the greatest public health pandemic in a century is so staggering, so troubling, so political, and so divisive that it is hard to imagine anyone other than the worst Trump apologists defending it. In an op-ed written by Michael Gerson in the *Washington Post*, dated October 27, 2020, he discusses interviews with senior officials who asked him to maintain their anonymity because of fear of retaliation. They offered the picture of a largely functional government betrayed by a deeply dysfunctional leader. Their testimony outlined four failures of judgment and leadership that have worsened the speed and trajectory of the pandemic in the United States.

The first was a sin of omission—the failure to act when clear duties arise. The federal government's response to Covid-19 got off to a rocky start in early February when the Centers for Disease Control and Prevention (CDC) produced a test for the virus that was contaminated and initially useless. Obviously, no country can develop and implement an adequate pandemic response without some idea of the location and extent of the early infections. Errors often occur in early stages of great national struggles, be they war, natural disaster, or pandemic. Successful leadership adapts quickly, shifts course, and rises to the challenge. There were readily available solutions to be had including utilizing the effective World Health Organization (WHO) test or allowing independent labs to develop and use their own tests. Weeks passed as the federal health bureaucracy floundered.

The cost of this testing disaster was immediate and alarmingly high. In February, plans were suggested for random testing in emergency rooms around the country. According to a senior administration official, "It never happened. We would have learned weeks earlier that this was out there in the country. We lost at least a month." While it is doubtful that this would have enabled a comprehensive test-and-trace model like that employed in South Korea, doing testing right initially would have curbed the spread of the virus more quickly and saved many lives. The White House had the ultimate responsibility to make this work. Instead, they fumbled the ball near their own goal line.

The second error was a sin of commission, the direct dereliction of duty. As events were moving quickly, the Trump administration actively and deceptively played down the extent and severity of the crisis. In his recent book, *Rage,* and on his taped conversations with President Trump that were the basis of that book, Bob Woodward documented the clear intent to mislead the American people. As the danger of the coronavirus became undeniable, the president and other spokesmen for the administration stubbornly denied it. President Trump said, "It is going to disappear. We have it well under control."

The proper sense of the emergency that was befalling the nation was not communicated to the American people. Nor was a sense of emergency and the need for extraordinary focus communicated throughout the administration. This careless attitude resulted in the view within the Trump administration that Covid-19 should be treated primarily as a political problem that could be managed by a public relations response. The White House focused on damage control, not disease control. They tried to rename the virus, the coronavirus, the 'Wuhan virus' in a clumsy attempt to shift responsibility away from the president and onto China.

This made no sense as a political strategy because the reality of the mounting number of infections, mounting number of hospitalizations, and mounting number of deaths would collapse this political, public relations strategy. This utterly incompetent political response rests on the doorstep of the president himself. Trump hated to hear from those who gave him bad news. He could not deal with uncomfortable truth. One senior administration official told Michael Gerson, there is "punishment for delivering bad news." This created a climate of "happy talk" and a dangerous and debilitating framework for an alternate but false reality. No major crisis could be managed successfully if the leader in charge refused to acknowledge bad news.

The third major error was the Trump administration's early

decision to shift the management burdens and the resulting blame to the individual states. By April, the administration strategy to hand off responsibility for the pandemic response to the states, and thus be done with the problem, was well under way. On May 11, 2020, the White House declared victory by stating: "We have met the moment and we have prevailed." With a death toll approaching sixty thousand, the Trump administration handoff to the states included some federal guidelines for the safe and careful reopening of states that had shut down schools and businesses to fight the pandemic. Trump agreed to the CDC's guidelines in an April 15 meeting, and they were announced the next day. A senior administration official told Michael Gerson, "If they had been adopted universally, it would have saved tens of thousands of lives."

On April 17, 2020, Trump tweeted to his legions of supporters, "LIBERATE" Michigan, Virginia, and Minnesota. One senior official was shocked that Trump was ignoring the CDC guidelines just released the day before and joining in with the populist critics (some of whom were armed and massing around various state capital buildings) of some of the state governors. Trump began to criticize state governors for lacking the courage to reopen their states' economies quickly as he tossed aside a second round of more detailed implementation guidance from the CDC. Blaming the states gave Trump an exit ramp from responsibility and a good excuse for not having his own comprehensive national plan for fighting the pandemic.

Gerson, in this cited article, said that by sabotaging the reopening standards, Trump politicized public health efforts throughout the country. In this highly charged polarized environment, reckless behavior by Trump supporters became viewed by them as patriotism. When the country desperately needed leadership recommending behavioral changes like wearing masks and social distancing, Trump treated this behavioral change as a sign of weakness. A senior administration official said the following: "It was increasingly destructive. It led to the death of thousands."

The fourth mistake was the administration's constant undermining of scientific and public health expertise. This manifested itself in Trump's public statements promoting a quack cure like hydroxy-chloroquine. Even more ridiculous, Trump riffed on about injecting cleaning and disinfecting products into the bodies of coronavirus victims and about treating them with ultraviolet light. This, of course, became fodder for comedians, but it also wasted time and resources that could have been applied to fighting the coronavirus.

Another problem with Donald Trump's mishandling of this crisis centered around his irrational trust in certain people, who were not experts in public health or infectious diseases, such as Peter Navarro and Scott Atlas. Navarro pushed for rapid reopening, while Atlas pushed a theory on herd immunity. Their consistently bad advice and their attempts to sabotage the advice of real experts were nothing but counterproductive. Trump, who not only wanted to surround himself with "yes-men," also wanted to use those "yes-men" to discredit people with strong reputations in their fields, the truth tellers. Trump was always difficult to argue with and convince for two reasons pointed out by Michael Gerson: first, his difficulty distinguishing between factual evidence and anecdotes, and second, his political needs always outweighing science.[19]

The writer, Michael Gerson, points out in his article that the past few months have not been without some successes in the fight with coronavirus. Doctors and nurses have been able to get the death rate down because of improvements in treatment. Also, progress on vaccines has come very quickly. Health-care workers could begin getting their shots within a couple of months.

As we approached the holiday season, the United States was seeing shocking increases in the rate of infection throughout the country. With more travel, holiday gatherings of family and friends, and lower temperatures, the United States was in a dangerous phase of trying to contain this virus. While facing this sad reality, Donald Trump, in the last couple of months of his losing campaign, kept insisting at his rallies that we were "turning the corner on this disease." Going into Thanksgiving, we were not "turning the corner," as we had over 250,000 Americans dead from coronavirus.

What this pandemic has revealed about Donald Trump is more

than noteworthy. He has no leadership skills whatsoever. He lacks talent and judgment, even at a superficial level. He is outmatched by many foreign leaders, and he is constantly looking to shift the blame for his clear and demonstrable failures. His lack of wisdom and judgment have cost this country dearly.

At least, it has cost him the election. Unfortunately, as a lame duck president, he went from just incompetent to completely missing in action. He was AWOL in this fight to contain the virus. All he seemed to care about was making dangerous and false claims about the election being stolen and playing golf. History's judgment is going to be more than harsh! He will go down, in my opinion, as the worst president in our nation's history. His dereliction of duty is without rival. [20]

In an article dated July 2, 2020, by Carl Leubsdorf in the *Dallas Morning News*, five major failures of Donald Trump's response to the coronavirus are posited. For over three years, Trump was able to enjoy the economic tailwinds of a growing economy he inherited from former President Obama. Most presidents do face a major crisis at some point during their presidency, and for Donald Trump, it was the arrival of the coronavirus that began to infect so many Americans.

Slow Start: In the first two months of the year, Trump ignored warnings from administration intelligence experts and health experts. He basically dismissed the initial indications of the pandemic and said the disease would be mild and short-lived. He relied much too much on the Chinese leadership's reassurances concerning their control efforts because of his desire to reach a major trade deal. This delay, in turn, diminished our immediate testing capability because of a shortage in inventory of domestic testing kits.

Incomplete Travel Ban: Trump, throughout this pandemic, has bragged about his strong action primarily based on his January 31, 2020, partial travel ban from China. Unfortunately, the Chinese travel ban had loopholes. More importantly, he failed to issue a European travel ban for six weeks, which left us extremely exposed to the entry of the virus into the United States. New York began to see a huge spike in coronavirus cases shortly thereafter.

Mixed Signals: Even after Trump declared a national state of emergency and ordered a national lockdown in mid-March, he communicated false signals to the American people, creating a state of confusion and doubt about the direction in which he wanted to take the country. When asked by the media about the shortage of available testing kits, he refused to take any responsibility. Instead of implementing a coordinated national response to the pandemic, he declared that actions to fight the virus were primarily the responsibility of the states, and he discouraged governors from seeking help from the federal government. Many of his supporters began aggressively protesting at state capitals around the country, demanding an immediate and complete reopening of the economy. Many of these protesters appeared at these protests heavily armed. Because he was so concerned about the domestic economy and the effect a downturn would have on his reelection prospects, shortly thereafter, Trump began pushing to restart all economic activity.

Premature Reopening: Even before his own April 30 deadline, Trump was strongly urging states to resume full economic activity. Republican governors in Texas, Arizona, and Florida were persuaded to begin their states' reopenings despite their failures to meet existing federal reopening guidelines. In another tragically symbolic move, Trump undercut his health-care experts by refusing to wear a mask. This signal to his supporters, perhaps more than any other thing he did, politicized and divided the nation at a time when it needed unity and clarity of purpose.

Ignoring Reality: As the number of infections plateaued and then rose, Trump declared a premature victory over the coronavirus and switched his focus entirely to economic revival and to the burgeoning street protests that occurred after several instances of fatal police shootings of Black Americans. Trump stopped attending pandemic task force meetings, leaving that to Vice President Pence. Dana Bash of CNN compared Pence's overly optimistic reports on progress fighting the coronavirus to the overly optimistic reports Defense Department officials gave during the Vietnam War.[21]

An example of Trump's "tin ear" and ignorance of political reality was the support of a Republican lawsuit aimed at destroying the

Affordable Care Act, the Obama administration's law that expanded health-care insurance coverage to millions of additional Americans. This attempt to undermine health-care protections to millions of Americans at a time of pandemic-caused high unemployment amounted to political malpractice. Many Americans, employed or unemployed, were deeply concerned about losing the protection for preexisting conditions embedded into the Affordable Care Act.

Polling showed that more Americans prioritized the fight against COVID-19 ahead of prematurely opening the economy. Polling also showed that Trump's heavy-handed response to the street protests demanding an end to racially motivated killings of Black Americans was not popular with most Americans. This ignorance of political reality put Donald Trump on the wrong side of the public heading into the last five months of the election campaign. While Joe Biden, the former vice president, was campaigning on a platform of uniting the country and healing division, Donald Trump was stirring the pot of racial resentment. By continuing to run a campaign aimed only at his political base, in the end, this ignorance and disregard for political realities came back to haunt Trump and helped bring about his defeat.

In an op-ed in *USA Today*, "Trump's COVID-19 record is the single biggest failure in US history. We need a new president," by Russ Travers, dated October 2, 2020, the writer made a direct appeal for Americans of all political persuasions to awake to the threat of a continued Trump presidency. Russ Travers was previously acting director of the National Counterterrorism Center. Earlier in the Trump administration, he received an award from the president for sustained extraordinary achievement, an honor only given to the top 1 percent of senior administration officials. The following year he was fired, another example of Donald Trump's mercurial, chaotic, dysfunctional decision-making and personnel management. In this article, Travers revealed that he was an independent and that he voted for John Kasich as a write-in in 2016. Travers described his experience in government as the "good, bad, and the ugly." This article was his attempt, before the recent election, to speak plainly to potential voters about the catastrophe of the Trump presidency. He stressed how other countries, particularly key figures in the governments of major allies, were rating the current global standing of the United States under Donald Trump as the lowest in their lifetimes. He referred to Trump's go-it-alone policies on climate change, trade, and international relations (including military planning and exchange of intelligence data) as reckless. He referred to those policies as "beggar thy neighbor" policies based on a "head-in-the sand" attitude.

While describing other failures of the Trump administration, Travers stressed that the overall failure in planning and executing a comprehensive federal government response to the coronavirus epidemic, was and still is, the greatest failure in American history. Travers clearly has the background and experience to discuss crisis management, or lack thereof. He testified before the 9/11 Commission and then spent the next seventeen years involved in strenuous efforts to address the failures of September 11, 2001. Again, let me stress that his well-qualified opinion was that this was the single greatest failure of the federal government in the history of our country.

With well over 250,000 Americans dead, and with cases still spiking, our lame-duck president was more interested in lying to his supporters about unsupported allegations of election fraud to besmirch our democratic values and to use his supporters' distrust as a potent political weapon should he decide to run again for president in 2024. His lack of focus, lack of judgment, and negligent leadership adversely impacted our children's education as well as the overall trajectory of our nation's economy. Travers sums up his disgust with Trump and the prospects for our future by saying, "We have gone from Ronald Reagan's shining city on the hill to the object of scorn and pity. From a leader in the world to a bit player. Given the deep-seated schisms in this country, I don't know if former Vice President, Joe Biden, can restore our status. But I know this president cannot, and for the sake of our communities, the country, and the world, we need to make a change."[22]

Written before the election, this plea did not fall on deaf ears. The American people, with their votes, removed this travesty from office effective January 20, 2021.

In an opinion editorial in *USA Today*, titled "Coronavirus response shows Donald Trump's failure of leadership," dated October 29,2020, their editorial board printed its summary view: "Trump administration is not going to control the pandemic, 'sentencing America to a hellish winter of more deaths and economic suffering.'"[23]

Early in the pandemic, Donald Trump proclaimed himself as a wartime president. Maybe in his own mind, he felt like he was fighting a winning war. Unfortunately, his lame efforts were destined to fail. Hopefully with the change in administration on January 20, the losing effort can be turned around. With vaccines on the horizon and a serious, experienced adult leader in the White House, the hope is that Americans can emerge from this nightmare without any more unnecessary death and suffering.

As the third wave of coronavirus surges across the country, White House Chief of Staff Mark Meadows threw in the towel and waved the flag of surrender, saying on CNN on October 25, "We are not going to control the pandemic." Beyond giving up on Americans and resignedly accepting without a fight the miserable winter of illness and death before the vaccine was available, the Trump administration fittingly ended its pathetic reign with the worst management performance in a crisis ever witnessed by the USA. So much for making America Great Again.

The USA has faced darkness, fear, and death in the past. Each time, the president in power (not always from the same political party), rose to the occasion, acted like a real leader, and never contemplated giving up or surrendering even in the worst moments. "Think about the challenges faced by Franklin Roosevelt, Abraham Lincoln, and George W. Bush."[24] Facing the tragedies of the Great Depression, the American Civil War, the attack at Pearl Harbor, and the terrorist attacks on September 11, 2001, the men in the office of the presidency did not give up, did not slough their responsibilities off to state governors and mayors (and then undercut them at every opportunity), or simply wish the problem would go away. They did not attempt to divide Americans from one another; they rallied Americans and fought through the darkness until they began to see sunlight. They were patriots, not tweeting, temperamental babies.

Most Americans realized, and still realize, that regardless of the person in the office of the presidency, there would be more illness and deaths from this pandemic, but they also realized that things did not have to be this bad. All but four other countries had lower death rates (measured in fatalities per one hundred thousand) than the United States. With 4 percent of the world's population, the United States accounts for about 20 percent of COVID-19 deaths. Projections are that by February 6, the anniversary of the first reported US death from the virus, the toll could exceed four hundred thousand, the number of lost Americans over four years in World War II.[25] In May of 2021, the death toll in the United States is approaching 600,000.

From the same *USA Today* editorial, a summary of the seasonal mistakes and misjudgments is shown in the highlighted sections below.

WINTER 2019

He deceived the American people from the very beginning of this extremely perilous public health crisis. After being warned by a top adviser that the coronavirus posed a grave threat to our national security and public health, Trump did not warn the American people of the grave threat. As mentioned previously in this book, in a series of taped interviews with Bob Woodward, Trump confirmed he understood the lethality of this disease, and despite this knowledge, he refused to be honest with the American people. Instead, he lied to the public by downplaying the seriousness of this virus, comparing it to an ordinary strain of flu, to avoid igniting panic among the population. A more likely explanation is that the president did not want to spook investors and lower stock prices. Donald Trump, throughout his presidency, referred to the stock market as the ultimate gauge of economic performance. Honesty by the president would have helped the American people to prepare to take actions that could have lowered the speed of the infection's spread and would have saved more lives.

Trump issued restrictions on travel from China on January 31, 2020, after forty-five other countries had already done this. For weeks, he resisted advice to ban travel from Europe, and this stubborn refusal resulted in the outbreak of the coronavirus in New York. On top of this, the federal government's (CDC's) botched efforts to create an accurate coronavirus test left public health experts initially blind as the crisis unfolded. While the virus infected thousands in February, President Trump played golf, held political rallies, and attended the Super Bowl. Through the opening months of the crisis, Trump ignored a detailed playbook left by previous administrations with step-by-step instructions to utilize his sweeping powers to communicate a national plan and then implement it immediately.

SPRING 2020

As the pandemic spread, the president refused to wear a mask and maintain social distancing. He suggested phony quack cures at press briefing sessions and on Twitter. He almost immediately lost patience with restrictions aimed at slowing the spread of the disease, and he began to fight with governors that followed his own administration's guidelines. Under pressure from his own supporters, he tweeted "Liberate Michigan" in his ongoing battle with Michigan Governor Gretchen Whitmer. After proclaiming he had the ultimate power for directing pandemic relief efforts, he quickly pivoted and left that responsibility to state governments. He was slow to implement the Defense Production Act to ensure rapid production and distribution of necessary supplies, including ventilators. He rejected any federal role in tracing and isolating victims of the disease, a mitigation tool used successfully in many other nations.

SUMMER 2020

Trump's bold and brash prediction that the virus would just fade away and disappear when warm weather arrived never proved accurate as a second wave of infections spread quickly through the South and the West. He contradicted the advice and warnings of public health agencies, sidelined CDC scientists, and blocked government experts from communicating with the American people as frequently as needed.

FALL 2020

In the two-month homestretch of the presidential campaign, Trump traveled all over the country speaking at his political rallies. He made fun of mask wearing and social distancing. On television, viewers could see for themselves that the president and many of his supporters were not taking the pandemic seriously. These political rallies became superspreader events. One of the president's most vocal supporters and a former presidential candidate, Herman Cain, attended his rally in Tulsa, Oklahoma, and he contracted COVID-19 and died shortly thereafter. Also, in the fall, President Trump held a party on the White House lawn to celebrate the confirmation to the Supreme Court of Amy Conant Barret. Again, no social distancing and few masks resulted in several people (including several US senators) catching the coronavirus. Soon thereafter, the president and his wife each caught the virus. The cruel irony of this could only be lost to the most die-hard supporters of the president.[26]

Throughout the final stretch of the campaign, the president continued to stress that the nation was "rounding the turn" on defeating the coronavirus. Nothing could have been further from the truth as now we are entering into the third and perhaps deadliest wave of the coronavirus.

The overriding and greatest mistake by Donald Trump throughout this entire public health crisis was failing to grasp that the economy could not be successfully resuscitated without first saving lives by getting control over the virus. The president always presented the crisis as a binary choice. Joe Biden, his opponent, on the other hand recognized the truth that in order "to fix the economy, we have to get control over the virus."

The only successful part of the response to this crisis came through the private sector. America's biotech and pharmaceutical companies leaped into action and developed some vaccines and other treatments. Front-line health-care workers and residents of nursing homes were vaccinated beginning in late 2020. Even with promising news on the vaccine front, Trump undermined public confidence by meddling and pressuring regulators at the FDA. Fortunately, President Biden has pushed hard to vaccinate as many Americans as possible despite distrust among a large segment of Trump supporters, particularly men. As of May 23, 2021 slightly over 39 percent of the U.S. population has been fully vaccinated according to CDC data.

The coronavirus presented Donald Trump with the greatest challenge of his presidency. A report from researchers at Columbia University took aim at the Trump administration's disastrous handling of the coronavirus. The report's authors wrote: "We estimate that at least 130,000 deaths and perhaps as many as 210,000 could have been avoided with earlier policy interventions and more robust federal coordination and leadership. Even with the dramatic recent appearance of new Covid-19 waves globally, the abject failures of US government policies and crisis messaging persist."[27]

Sadly, he failed this test so glaringly and completely that the American people fired him on November 3. Unfortunately, we needed to wait until January 20 before expecting any leadership to return to the office of the presidency.

In a November 10, 2020, article by James Hamlin, MD, in the *Atlantic* titled "How Trump Sold Failure to 70 Million People," the con man, that is and always will be, Donald Trump is exposed. Dr. Hamlin posits the idea that the psychology of medical fraud is simple, timeless, and tragic.

Given the documentable failure right in front of our eyes, the leadership vacuum at the core of the administration's failed response to the coronavirus would decide the presidential election. Polling indicated we could expect a decisive repudiation of Trump's disastrous handling of the coronavirus. The president lied by his own admission, denied the severity of the disease, and promoted false cures all while Americans watched the number of cases and number of deaths climb dramatically.

Yes, Trump lost the election, and Biden won decisively, but Trump still won over seventy-four million votes. About 80 percent of Republicans, despite overwhelming evidence to the contrary, believed the coronavirus was at least "somewhat under control" under Donald Trump. The mismanagement of the pandemic response, while obvious to Democrats and to many independents, failed to move many Republicans away from voting for Donald Trump in 2020.[28] Trump's enduring popularity with his base of voters had to do with many other factors. Nevertheless, his empty promises about the virus were not only self-serving, disingenuous, and deadly; they were surprisingly effective to a large block of voters.

His attempts to paint the scientific world and many doctors as corrupt liars was shockingly successful with his base of voters. He used the same tactics that have worked so well over the years for cult leaders, self-proclaimed healers, and wellness quacks. Apparently, when people are threatened by disease or sick themselves, they are much more susceptible to quacks and their ridiculous scams. Dr. Hamlin described this phenomenon so very well: "The quack is nothing if not a prophet: he promises access to a truth that no one else has. Unlike all the slow, doom-and-gloom scientists, he can make your problem go away now."[29]

For centuries, quacks have been able to rely on people's belief in antiestablishment hope and lofty promises. These peddlers of hope rely on what Dr. Hamlin referred to as information asymmetry, which is the relative inability to distinguish whether-or-not something works. It is relatively easy to tell if certain types of products work or not. Your automobile, your vacuum cleaner, and your washing machine all come to mind. It becomes trickier when evaluating medical products that offer cures, or beauty products that offer youthful-looking skin or hair.[30]

This same appeal to hope is what Donald Trump offered his gullible base of voters when he promised that the invisible coronavirus was "magically going to disappear." He told people what they wanted to hear. His promises included the following: "Everything will go back to normal; everyone will have amazing treatments; there will be a vaccine very soon; the disease is not that serious." Despite conflicting and erroneous claims, Trump used misdirection by pointing to another threat. Over and over, he repeated that stopping the coronavirus through complete or partial shutdowns of the economy would threaten jobs and incomes. This, of course, was a false dichotomy. The two issues, controlling the virus and maintaining the economy, are linked together very closely. "Economies collapse, when going outside and being among crowds of people, is dangerous. Economies thrive when people not only *feel* safe, but when people *are* safe."[31]

Trump, throughout the crisis, has tried to position himself as an alternative to the scientists and the doctors, forcing his followers to choose between trusting the doctors and scientists and trusting him. William Swann, a psychology professor at the University of Texas, referred to this process as "identity fusion." Once fused with their leader, people tend to believe whatever their leader says. By defining truth around a leader, people do not have to think for themselves anymore. They are comforted in uncertain, threatening times by this attachment to their leader.[32]

Most Americans fuse our identities with other things or people. We attach ourselves to our families; we attach ourselves to our sports teams, and we attach ourselves to our pets. The stakes become much higher, however, when we attach ourselves to politicians. This can cause people to sometimes vote against their self-interest. A good example of this would be the Affordable Health Care Act, passed under President Obama. Most Americans, when polled on individual elements of this health-care law, express approval (even many Republicans). Despite this fact, Donald Trump campaigned against this law and sought its repeal.

The freedom from scrutiny and criticism that Donald Trump enjoys from his supporters is reflected in an ignorance of where he stands on issues related to the pandemic. In a recent survey, cited by Dr. Hamlin, 81 percent of Trump voters who believed mask mandates should be required also believed that Donald Trump agreed with them. Trump has never supported a mask mandate, and he has rarely worn one and rarely endorsed wearing one.

While campaigning for president, Joe Biden offered voters a pledge to follow the advice of scientists and a pledge to support mask wearing and social distancing. He stressed the need for continued vigilance during the pandemic until the vaccines are readily available to everyone. If Joe Biden follows through on his plans, many lives will be saved. Biden offers Americans perseverance and logic.

Unfortunately, the appeal of quacks and demagogues will remain within a subset of the American people. After Trump leaves office on January 20, Biden can cite statistics and promote his reasoned plans for handling the pandemic, but millions of Trump voters will ignore him and cast their lot with a failed, incompetent one-term ex-president. Many Trump voters believe that Trump tells it like it is, even though he does not. They hear what they want to hear, despite overwhelming evidence to the contrary.

Dr. Hamlin wraps up this article on a positive note by stressing that there are ways a confident, optimistic leader can serve without making ridiculous false promises. He or she can promise the government will be there for them by guaranteeing that no one will go into hopeless debt because they had to go to the hospital. He can also promise that people will have enough paid sick leave and job security so that they can stay at home when it is necessary, like during a pandemic. If politicians and the public health community fail to offer realistic hope to people during trying times like this, they will see significant defections of people to demagogues, who offer hope. The lure of false promises always remains for some people.[33]

An editorial in the *New York Daily News*, "Lethal dereliction: Trump's failures in the COVID-19 pandemic," dated November 1, 2020, captured the depth and depravity of the president's failures so clearly. While I run the risk of sometimes being repetitive in this chapter, I found this editorial provided such a clear indictment of the president's failure to protect the welfare of this nation. It was published two days before the election and screamed to potential voters not to reelect this malignant narcissist. If not for the election being so close, Trump would have deserved being impeached again, this time, on the grounds of criminal neglect and malicious disregard for the welfare of the American people.

As a lame-duck president, his total abdication of even providing a modicum of care and attention to duty is beyond comprehension. He is more focused on spreading lies and misinformation about his claims of election fraud than worrying about the accelerating climb in the number of new cases of coronavirus and the resulting climb in the number of deaths attributed to it. Not long ago, America could point with pride to providing the world's best medical care, at least to those with health insurance. Despite the heroic efforts and talent of America's doctors and nurses, the chaotic mismanagement of this public health crisis by the Trump administration put us in the worst position in our history from a public health perspective.

The origin of this debacle began in 2018 when the White House disbanded a pandemic response team that had been established under President Obama in 2015. In 2019, Trump fired a CDC epidemiologist on the ground in China who was responsible for detecting disease outbreaks there. Even without those useful tools, Trump had plenty of warning to begin marshalling a strong response when the threat landed on our shores. On January 29, 2020, Peter Navarro, a Trump aide involved in trade relations, warned the president by memo: "The lack of immune protection or an existing cure or vaccine would leave Americans defenseless in the case of a full-blown coronavirus outbreak on US soil." Around the same time, Trump told Bob Woodward that the disease was "more deadly than even the most strenuous flus" and highly contagious. The president told the American people a different story: "We have it totally under control. It's one person coming in from China. It's going to be just fine."[34]

When he wasn't praising the Chinese government's response,

he was insisting, "We pretty much shut it down," saying, "it miraculously goes away," and boasting that the fifteen cases then in the United States "within a couple of days is going to be down to close to zero." On February 26, Trump said, "This is like a flu." The death rate for hospitalized coronavirus patients is five times more lethal than for hospitalized flu patients. While the number of cases were rising rapidly in the early days of the pandemic, Trump continued in his failure to husband the testing resources and establish and carry out the necessary tracing activities to stay ahead of the virus.[35]

He discouraged mask wearing by ridiculing those wearing masks, particularly Democrats and members of the media. When mask wearing was the simplest and most effective way to prevent the spread of the virus, could he have been any more foolish? Wearing a mask certainly is no guarantee of not getting the coronavirus, but it raises your odds of not contracting and transmitting the virus by about 600 percent. When combined with social distancing, it is the easiest way for people to safeguard themselves and others.

When state governors were confronted with their hospitals being overrun with coronavirus patients and were forced into implementing temporary economic shutdowns, he threw gasoline on the fire by stirring up large-scale rebellions among his followers. His tweets demanding liberation of states run by Democrats demonstrated he was not a leader trying to work with the states. He was a vicious partisan, trying to undercut these governors at a time when Americans needed calm, focus, and unity.

Since the spring of 2020, his malevolence, his irresponsibility, and his cluelessness have grown as knowledge of the virus has increased among doctors and public health experts, and the death count has risen dramatically. The White House has meddled with CDC reports. Trump disengaged from his own COVID task force and has gone to war with his government's top infectious disease expert—Dr. Anthony Fauci. One of Trump's earliest supporters and political operatives, Steve Bannon, went so far as to call for Dr. Fauci's "head on a spike."[36]

Trump held a superspreader event in the Rose Garden, infecting himself, his staff, family members, and several US senators. He used the "People's House" in a blatantly political way, clearly violating the Hatch Act. He held rally after rally, with most supporters squeezed together in tight quarters, mostly without masks. At these events and in his tweets, Trump continued to tell supporters that the nation is "rounding the corner" on the coronavirus even as his chief of staff, Mark Meadows, admitted that "we are not going to control this epidemic."

This editorial summarizes the tragedy by saying: "Donald Trump's actions and inactions were directly responsible for the sickening and death of thousands of Americans. To reward him with a second term would be to spit on their graves."[37]

In an article in the *Atlantic*, titled "Trump's Indifference Amounts to Negligent Homicide," dated November 20, 2020, by James Fallows, the writer discusses the concept of negligent homicide and whether it can be applied to Donald Trump for his handling of the coronavirus outbreak. Negligent homicide, in the law, is the concept that someone died because someone else did not exercise reasonable care.

> Some common examples might be an adult leaves a loaded gun where children could find it; a motorist, while texting, runs over a pedestrian; a parent leaves a small child or a baby in the car with rolled up windows on a very hot day and the child dies. Prosecutors and juries do not consider these cases murder because the accused had no intent to kill their victims. This distinction over intent makes a big difference to the person being charged, but not to the victim. Absent the indifference to risks that should have been foreseen, the victim would still be living.[38]

Fallows wrote another article more than a year ago. In that article, titled, "If Trump Were an Airline Pilot," he said Trump would have already been removed from his job as a pilot. He speculated that anyone with a job like a CEO, an airline pilot, a submarine commander, or a surgeon would have been removed from that role if they had demonstrated "the impulsiveness, the irrationality, the vindictiveness, the ceaseless need for glorification,"[39] that constantly characterized Donald Trump. The stakes in potential lives, legal exposure, and defense status (war or peace) would have been too great to keep that person in the job. In this article, the author made the case that Trump was temperamentally, intellectually, and morally unfit for the job of president of the United States.[40]

Since then, the country and most of the rest of the world has been besieged by the coronavirus. The president does little that is helpful in the fight against this deadly virus. In fact, his actions, or in some cases inactions, directly contribute to the rising number of cases and the rising number of deaths. Some examples include:

➤ He tweets in rage about anyone that crosses him.
➤ He fires anyone suspected of disloyalty when usually they are just doing their job.
➤ He encourages endless lawsuits that are tossed out of court one after another, doing cumulative damage to confidence in elections and democracy.
➤ He stalls efforts to begin the transition process for the incoming president.

Next, Fallows puts forward some potential analogies in attempting to capture the essence of Trump's reckless disregard for the American people during this public health crisis.

➤ Is it like Nero fiddling while Rome burns?
➤ Is it like the Allied generals during the grimmest trench warfare stage of World War I, sending wave after wave of young troops over the top to almost certain death from German machine guns?
➤ Is it like an armed school security guard who hears gunfire inside the building but does not go in to protect the children, not wanting to get shot, himself?

➤ Is it like an airline pilot not looking at his instruments because he is involved in a Twitter war when the plane is headed toward a mountain or into the ocean?

➤ Is it like a doctor or nurse strolling past the emergency room just as a patient goes into cardiac arrest because he or she is on break and wants to get a snack in the cafeteria or from the vending machine in the break room?[41]

These potential behavioral analogies are not something you would expect would happen from people whose job it is to provide a high standard of care and protection to those relying on it. Unfortunately, during this pandemic, our president is behaving with reckless disregard and callous indifference. Examples include: leaving states and cities and hospitals and families to their own resources while hospitals and mortuaries fill past capacity, leaving medical workers to serve endless shifts without sufficient rest and backup, and knowing that they could be next to succumb to the deadly virus, not recognizing or caring that the coronavirus is taking a disproportionate toll on racial minorities and on families that are under huge pressure from the unequal economic impacts of the pandemic, particularly in the travel, leisure, and restaurant industries.

Under these awful circumstances, a normal human being leading the country would be doing many things with a sense of urgency and mission. First, he or she would restore cooperation outside the country on early detection of new outbreaks, address lessons learned from failed and successful containment strategies, and implement coordinated travel controls and other necessary global responses to a global threat of this magnitude. Next, he or she would restore cooperation within the country so that equipment availability, quarantine and social distancing plans, vaccine rollouts, and other measures and actions would be focused and coordinated, not a free-for-all. Next, he or she would give clear, steady, truthful reports to the American people so that our population would not panic and would understand the status of containment activities now and what additional steps might be necessary in the future. Rather than having politicians giving briefings for a short period of time and then abandoning the briefings altogether, Trump could have served the people of the United States much better if he had directed Dr. Anthony Fauci to give daily briefings. Finally, he could have used his political leverage to get financial aid to businesses, families, schools, and city and state governments. Instead, the US Senate was convened to ram through judicial appointments, including a Supreme Court appointment, and then do nothing else.[42]

On December 18, 2020, several television news sources interviewed Michigan Governor Gretchen Whitmer, and New Jersey Governor Phil Murphy. Each indicated that their state did not receive their state's promised full (allotment) of the Pfizer vaccine from the federal government. Both governors are Democrats. Both have tangled with President Trump over the president's interference with their states' mask policy and economic shutdown policy. Governor Whitmer had to endure rants to "lock her up" at Trump rallies. This was right after the FBI uncovered a plot by White terrorists to kidnap her, put her on trial, and execute her. Is this a simple bureaucratic distribution mix-up or something more sinister? It remains to be seen, but this just seems like too big a coincidence for me. If this turns out to be political payback at the direction of the Trump administration, it will rank as the most evil, depraved action by a president in US history. Punishing the citizens of Michigan and New Jersey defies human imagination. What kind of a person would do such a thing? What kind of people would continue to support a person who does such a thing? If this turns out to be political payback, this action warrants criminal prosecution and hyperbolic moral outrage. Anyone who would defend it deserves the eternal shame and disgust seldom rendered by the rest of the entire country.

The careless, callous indifference toward his fellow citizens, both before the election and after his defeat, reveals a person more concerned with himself than with serving others. His rants about the election results and unproven election fraud, his talk of running again in 2024, his firing of competent senior national security personnel, including the head of cybersecurity, in the waning days of his presidency put on full display his selfish, out-of-touch narcissism. Not all, but certainly many more American lives could have been spared if he had shown the fortitude and leadership required by this severe challenge. He failed the oath of office, he was derelict in his duties, and he was responsible for negligent homicide.

For even more detailed information on Trump's failures regarding the coronavirus, the reader should reference an article in *VOX*, "A detailed timeline of all the ways Trump failed to respond to the coronavirus," by Cameron Peters, dated June 8, 2020. This article, in more detail, shows sequentially the nearly daily missteps and misstatements of Donald Trump during the first wave of the pandemic. During the second wave, all he worried about were his misinformation rallies, campaign fund-raising, and his reelection efforts. In the third phase as a lame duck, all he worried about is spreading lies about purported, unproven election fraud. As far as doing anything to stem the spread of COVID-19, Donald Trump was missing in action (MIA).

CHAPTER 3

DAMAGING THE RULE OF LAW

IN THIS CHAPTER, I will highlight the wide-ranging attempts to highjack the rule of law during the administration of President Trump. His efforts to subjugate rules and norms to benefit himself and his family in their businesses and personal lives before he assumed the office of the presidency currently are being investigated in the state of New York. His efforts to subvert legal processes and the laws themselves after he assumed office to enrich himself, politically benefit himself, obstruct justice, and prevent investigation are brazen and without parallel in their scope and magnitude.

Trump and his family might be able to avoid legal consequences from any breaches of federal law while in office for two reasons. First, there might be a strong reluctance by the current president, Joe Biden, to pursue justice against a former political opponent. In this country, we have a well-established tradition of not prosecuting former presidents for political malfeasance or corruption based on violation of federal law. While the decision to investigate a former president would rest with the incoming attorney general, Joe Biden might recommend not pursuing it. Second, Trump could avail himself of the presidential pardon power to absolve his family, friends, and political allies from legal jeopardy. Whether he could pardon himself remains untested in federal courts because no former president has ever pardoned himself for a federal crime.

LEGAL JEOPARDY AFTER LEAVING
OFFICE FOR STATE CRIMES

In the *Wall Street Journal*, an article titled "Trump Family Business Faces Post-Election Reckoning," dated November 15, 2020, by Brian Spegele and Caitlin Ostroff, the authors discuss some of the financial and legal challenges Donald Trump and the Trump Organization could be facing after he leaves office. As mentioned above, most prosecutors have been reluctant to charge presidents with crimes while they are in the office of the presidency. Beyond elections every four years, the only realistic remedy to deal with a lawless behavior or dereliction of duty by a president is impeachment.

Once out of office, however, the story changes. Two New York investigations will continue after he leaves office. The Trump Organization will also need to avert a cash crunch caused by looming debt maturing on the firm's real estate holdings. Donald Trump made personal guarantees on some of this debt, which adds even further intrigue into efforts to stabilize his financial position. Trump executives, including some of his children, say they plan to focus on brand-building efforts globally after he has leaves office. Those efforts could face steep challenges. In China, where there is deep distrust after his damaging trade war, relations are so strained that this potential market for the Trump Organization could be closed for years to come. In Europe, some of Trump's trademarks have been eliminated by legal challenges. The Trump Organization already has put up for sale several properties including its Washington hotel and two skyscrapers in New York and San Francisco where the Trump Organization are part owners. The *Wall Street Journal* previously reported that the Trump Organization is considering selling its Seven Springs Estate outside New York City.

Any of these sales could help the Trump family avoid the potential cash crunch of having $400 million debt due in the next few years. Many lenders have expressed concern about doing business with Donald Trump in the future. The pandemic has hurt business at Trump hotels and resorts, and the benefits of being president and brazenly violating the emoluments clause of the US Constitution will decline. Republican spending at Trump properties has topped $23 million since 2015 compared with less than $200,000 in the five years prior, according to data from the Federal Elections Commission reported by the Center for Responsive Politics.

The financial challenges discussed here are only the tip of the iceberg for the Trump family and the Trump Organization. Trump has been dealing with IRS audits of his finances for years. Manhattan District Attorney Cyrus Vance, a Democrat, has been pursuing Trump's financial records, and he says criminal tax fraud and falsification of business records could result.

Another investigation by New York State's attorney general, Letitia James, also a Democrat, is examining whether Trump inflated the reporting of asset values to obtain loans and get other economic and tax benefits. Jeffery Engel, a presidential historian at Southern Methodist University in Dallas commented on how unusual this situation is among US presidents because much of the scrutiny stems from actions before he became president. He said the following, "The fact that Trump thought he could run for president with clear irregularities in his financial background and not be discovered, that's the most surprising part to me. It reinforces that he did not fully appreciate what it meant to be president."

Finally, there is the defamation claim case filed by writer E. Jean Carroll. In the mid-1990s, she claimed Donald Trump entered a changing room in a New York department store and raped her. A lawsuit filed by her claimed defamation after he said she was lying, and she was only motivated by money. After Trump's appearance on a *Hollywood Access* episode in 2005, in which, on film, Trump bragged about grabbing women by the genitals without their consent, can Trump supporters really say with a straight face that they think Donald Trump was telling the truth, and Ms. Carroll was lying.

Judge Lewis Kaplan ruled that Donald Trump must remain a defendant in the lawsuit, and he rejected the Justice Department's last-second effort to have the US government replace Trump in the lawsuit. The DOJ argued the president was acting as a government employee when he said Carroll was lying and motivated by money. The judge said Trump was not a government employee within the meaning of the statute, and that even if he were a government employee, this matter with Ms. Carroll would not have been within the scope of his employment. The DOJ's move to substitute the US government for Donald Trump came shortly after rulings by the state judge that required Trump to submit to a deposition as well as a DNA test to see if his genetic material was on the dress Ms. Carroll wore during the alleged attack.

Cyrus Vance is also investigating the Trump Organization regarding how it accounted for hush money payments to two women who said they had sex with Donald Trump. The potential for charges of felony campaign finance violations remains.[43]

While some people might be surprised that Donald Trump did not work out an arrangement to pardon his family additional friends and allies of all actual or potential federal crimes including obstruction of justice (ten instances listed in the Mueller Report), others are not surprised because such pardons would have amounted to de facto admissions of guilt that would have damaged his political brand. Unfortunately for him and his family, he cannot pardon himself of state crimes. This whole stubborn, selfish bid to stay in power might also be a way to buy himself and his family more time to deal with his morass of legal jeopardy.

Let us begin our review of Trump's assault on our legal system with events surrounding his impeachment.

President Trump's Impeachable Conduct: In an article in the *Center for American Progress*, titled "Trump's Impeachable Conduct Strikes at the Heart of the Rule of Law: Part 1," dated September 27, 2019, the author, Maggie Jo Buchanan, discusses the events surrounding Donald Trump's phone call with Ukrainian President Volodymyr Zelensky in 2019. Both the written summary of the phone call and the whistleblower complaint clearly demonstrate that Trump's words and actions were in direct violation of American law.

Before speaking with President Zelensky, President Trump blocked hundreds of millions of dollars earmarked for Ukraine for security assistance. Trump claimed, falsely, that he did this in response to Ukrainian corruption. A Pentagon letter contradicted this claim by certifying that Ukraine had made the institutional reforms required to receive this aid package.

During this call with Zelensky, Trump stated that the United States "does a lot for Ukraine," but that such help is not "reciprocal necessarily." Trump then asked for a "favor"—for Ukraine to investigate conspiracy theories that could benefit Trump politically. Specifically, he asked Zelensky to investigate Hunter Biden, the son of one of his potential political rivals, Joe Biden. Trump wrapped up the phone call by telling Zelensky that he would have his personal lawyer, Rudy Giuliani, and the US attorney general, William Barr, follow up about the investigation. At the time, Ukraine was involved in a conflict with Russia over disputed territory, and it needed this military assistance aid package desperately. It was made abundantly clear in the phone call that US support for releasing these funds was tied to a 'willingness to play ball on issues that had been publicly aired.'

While impeachment does not require a specific violation of a federal or state statute, conduct that Trump clearly engaged in, bribery or extortion, by a public official is both unlawful and grounds for impeachment.

Below are some examples.

➤ The US Constitution explicitly includes bribery as a reason to impeach a president: "The President, Vice President and all civil officers of the United States, shall be removed from Office on impeachment for, and Conviction of, Treason, Bribery, or other high Crimes and Misdemeanors."

➤ The statute governing bribery by public officials, 18 US Code 201, repeatedly states that bribery can occur "directly or indirectly."

➤ The Hobbs Act, 18 US Code 1951, defines "extortion" by a public official as "the obtaining of property from another, with his consent ... under color of official right." Supreme Court Justice, Anthony Kennedy, concurring in the majority opinion on the Hobbs Act in Evans v. United States, elaborates specifically on how quid pro quo agreements may be identified. The official and the payor need not state the *quid pro quo* in express terms, for otherwise the law's effect could be frustrated by knowing winks and nods. The inducement from the official is criminal if it is expressed or it is implied from his words or actions, so long as he intends it to be so, and the payor so interprets it.

➤ Trump's home state is no different: New York has enacted strong prohibitions against extortion by public officials. Under the state's penal code, extortion can occur when a public official "instills in the victim a fear" that if something of value is not delivered, the public official will: use or abuse his position as a public servant by engaging in conduct within or related to his official duties, or by failing or refusing to perform an official duty, in such manner as to affect some person adversely.[44]

At all levels of federal and state law, the communication in this phone call was clearly recognizable as corrupt and unlawful. If Trump had been any other citizen of the United States, he would have been held accountable. He was impeached by the US House of Representatives, but he was not removed from office by the US Senate. Under Republican control, the Senate failed to act honorably or fairly. They refused to hear testimony from additional witnesses present during the phone call such as John Bolton, the national security adviser. They behaved more like family and allies of a crime boss, and as such, they were derelict in their duty to the American people.

Before I delve into more specifics about Trump's failures to respect the rule of law and his obligations under his terms of employment specified in the US Constitution and other federal statutes, I would like to review an op-ed in *Bloomberg News*, titled "A Presidential Primer on the Rule of Law" by Jonathan Bernstein, dated May 29, 2020. In this opinion column, Bernstein refers to an article by Jill Colvin, where she gives examples of powers that Donald Trump claims to have, but he does not:

Threatening to shut down Twitter for flagging false content. Claiming he can "override" governors who dare to keep churches closed to congregants. Asserting the "absolute authority" to force states to reopen, even when local leaders say it's too soon.[45]

He also gives a good example of a power that Donald Trump had as president, but he chose to ignore or fully utilize. In reacting to the pandemic, Trump could have used the Defense Production Act to more fully and more quickly produce products and equipment needed by health-care workers like masks and protective suits and products and equipment needed to treat their patients like ventilators.

This unwillingness to fully use the powers of the presidency and this willingness to grab for powers that are outside the powers of the presidency are both a threat to our democracy. This careless disregard for boundaries is the essence of lawlessness and authoritarianism. It's not that Trump necessarily breaks laws (although he surely does that), but that he appears oblivious to the whole idea of the rule of law—the idea that there are rules that apply to everyone, including the president.

Another way of looking at it is that Trump doesn't seem to understand that he's been hired to do a job, and that he has more than 300 million bosses. As with any job, it comes with written rules, and an employee—that's what he is—must thoroughly master the terms of employment if he or she hopes to perform well. Instead, Trump seems to believe he's won some sort of honor, and it entitles him to things. That's simply not the reality of the presidency. Sure, there are perks (as there are with many jobs), but more than anything, it's employment.[46]

The worst part of failing to recognize and uphold the rule of law is the fundamental abuse of power that begins to take over everything. Government employees, including presidents, have a fundamental obligation to make sure laws are faithfully executed. This is central to preserving, protecting, and defending the Constitution of the United States. Without this, the presidency devolves into a criminal dictatorship.

In practice, this concept of the rule of law can sometimes become confusing and complicated. Often, there can different interpretations of what the law means in various contexts. Presidents do at times try to push the limits of their power. Most do, however, seek a rational and legal justification for their actions, often going through the judicial system to get approvals.

Trump's entire approach to governance ignores many boundaries and lines and ignores much tradition and precedent. He has made no effort in his actions or his communications to provide American citizens with a sense of comfort that he has any real respect for the rule of law.

In the article "Trump continues to claim broad powers he doesn't have," by Jill Colvin in the AP News, we will look further into Trump's executive overreach. In attempting to deal with the coronavirus epidemic, Trump has claimed extraordinary and sweeping powers that most legal scholars dispute. He has repeatedly refused to provide the legal basis for these attempted power grabs.

To be clear, the president does have a wide array of power to respond to public health crises and other national emergencies. It is just that so many powers he has asserted for himself are just not there.

First, he asserted that he could force governors to reopen their economies before they felt ready and safe to do so. Trump claimed, "When somebody is president of the United States, the authority is total." Trump soon dropped this threat, saying instead that he would leave such decisions to the states. Shortly after dropping his claim, he reversed himself and started pressuring governors to allow churches and other places of worship to hold in-person services, even where stay-at-home orders and other limits on large gatherings remained in effect. When asked about this, he responded, "I can absolutely do it if I want to. We have many different ways where I can override them, and if I have to, I'll do that." Without citing any specific statute, a White House spokesman, Judd Deere, said in a statement that "every decision the president has made throughout this pandemic has been to protect the health and safety of the American people."

Matthew Dallek, a historian at George Washington University Graduate School of Political Management who specializes in the use and limits of presidential power, stated very clearly and directly that Trump "certainly does not have the power under any reasonable reading of the Constitution or federalism to order places of worship to open." Dallek went on to say that just because Trump does not have that power does not mean that Trump would not attempt to use the asserted power (like signing executive orders).

Dallek also suggested that Trump could try to leverage other government departments or regulatory agencies like the Justice Department and the IRS to push for investigations or regulatory crackdowns on cities, states, or companies that refuse to do his bidding. Trump also has demonstrated that he is willing to fire watchdogs and auditors, including his recent purging of inspector generals, if they fail to fall in line with Trump's whims and edicts.

Even if he does not follow through with his threats, Trump's statements can still have real consequences. For instance, it could cause governors to reprioritize various policies and procedures to avoid Trump's wrath or to delay decisions until more regulatory and legal certainty developed. Trump's butting into areas over which he had no legal authority caused unnecessary friction throughout the entire pandemic response. Trump attempted to wield his outrageous, erroneous legal interpretations as a weapon to beat these municipal and state officials into submission.

Trump's crusade against Twitter after it put a fact check alert on two of Trump's tweets (claiming mail-in voting is fraudulent) is another example of his bullying approach to dealing with social media platforms that fail to do his bidding or call him out on untruths and misrepresentations.

Trump has also "signed an executive order, challenging liability protections that have served as a
bedrock for unfettered speech on the internet. But
the order—which directs executive branch agencies
to ask independent rule-making agencies, including
the Federal Communications Commission (FCC)
and the Federal Trade Commission (FTC) to study
whether they can place new regulations on social media companies—appeared to be more about politics
than substance."[47]

Most experts doubt that much can be done to regulate social media companies without an act of Congress. The result of Trump's
executive order will likely be much less dramatic than the tweet
warning he sent out to social media platforms that said he had the
power to "strongly regulate" or "close them down." A former federal
judge, Michael McConnell, who now directs Stanford University Law
School's Constitutional Law Center, said this about the president,
"He is probably just venting."[48]

Jameel Jaffer, executive director of the Knight First Amendment
Institute at Columbia University, who won the case that prevented
Trump from banning his critics from his Twitter feed, said there was
no First Amendment issue with Twitter adding a label to the president's false and misleading tweets. He went on to say that "the only
first amendment issue was the president's threat to punish Twitter in
some way for fact-checking his statements."[49]

A Yale University law professor and first amendment expert, Jack
Balkin, said Trump's tweets were perhaps more of an attempt (using
a basketball analogy) to "work the refs." He went on to say, "He's
threatening and cajoling with the idea that these folks in their corporate board rooms will think twice about what they're doing, so they
won't touch him."[50]

Rutgers University media professor John Pavlik, who studies online misinformation, said Trump was using this as an opportunity
mainly "to fire up his base."[51]

Whatever his ancillary motivations, Trump was clearly trying to bully these social media platforms to refrain from challenging him in any way. I believe this demonstrates his desire to threaten the use of regulatory agencies to gain control over political and media adversaries that, if not illegal per say, certainly skirts the edges of acceptable behavior within the rule of law.

In an op-ed in the *Guardian*, titled "President Trump is at war with the rule of law. This won't end well," dated October 9, 2019, the author, Rebecca Solnit, discusses how Donald Trump and top officials are involved in large-scale corruption and below them (at subsenior levels), there is dismantling and disarray. She begins by asking a rhetorical question:

> Do Americans still have a government? I do not know. What I do know is that President Trump and the upper echelons of the executive branch are at war with the legislative branch, the rule of law, the constitution, federal civil servants, and the American people. It's a conflict that pulls in many directions, and if the president threatened civil war the other day as something that could happen if he doesn't get his way, we can regard the ordinary state of things as a low-intensity civil war or a slo-mo coup that's been going on from the beginning. Tuesday's White House refusal to cooperate with impeachment inquiry only escalates their defiance and their chaos.
>
> The chaos takes so many forms. Innumerable stories have made it clear that even the president's own aides and cabinet members treat him like a captive bear or a person having a psychotic breakdown—like someone unstable who must be kept from harming himself and others. They have done that by heaping on the flattery, and by warping and limiting the information he receives, and often by doing their best to prevent his directives from being realized.[52]

The *New York Times* recently reported on a March meeting about the border. According to aides, Trump "suggested that they shoot migrants in the legs to slow them down." When he was told that was not allowed, he ordered the border be closed. This caused the president to go into a rage. By the end of the week, he backed away from his threat, but he began to purge aides who he deemed disloyal for trying to stop him from his worst instincts. She describes Trump's behavior pattern below:

> This is the kind of story we've become used to—outrages and viciousness and inanity and all—but it's worth reading another way, as a story about a bear lashing out at whatever's around him and gobbling up the scraps, they feed him while he's still chained to the wall. When we refer to the "president," we really mean whatever ad hoc group of people with proximity is manipulating him, lying to him, or preventing him from knowing or doing something. They sometimes prevent harm or illegality. But this is only half of the administrative "team." The other half consists of those serving his personal agenda, and in this respect the federal government has become a subsidiary of Trump incorporated.[53]

William Barr is supposed to be the nation's attorney general, and his job it is to provide advice and counsel regarding questions of the law when required by the president of the United States. Unfortunately for our nation, he has spent much of his time traveling the world and pushing the president's conspiracy theories and smears of rival candidates. This stunning violation of his role as the chief law enforcement officer of the United States should shock and disgust Americans of all political persuasions.

Mike Pompeo, the secretary of state, took an oath of office to "support and defend the Constitution of the United States against all enemies foreign and domestic." Since taking that oath of office, he has become an unprincipled stooge for the administration. He was in the group that listened to Donald Trump's phone call with Ukrainian President Zelensky where Trump asked him to investigate Joe Biden and his family and to discredit the story of Russian intervention in the 2016 presidential election. The *Guardian* reported that Pompeo dismissed summons from Democratic committee chairmen in the House of Representatives for five current and former State Department officials to testify on the president's attempts to force the Ukrainian government to provide politically damaging information on the activities of the Biden family in that country. There was nothing there as reported by multiple news sources. Pompeo tried to block Gordon Sondland, former ambassador to the European Union, who was implicated in the Ukrainian shakedown, from testifying to Congress, a clear and obvious obstruction of justice.[54]

The phrase "party over country" has been used to describe the Republican Party for years, but under Trump, the more apt description by Rebecca Solnit is:

> But at this point it is more or less puppet over country, because the loyalty to Trump's corrupt, delusional, floundering endeavors to keep himself in power and out of trouble with the law. Trump's own loyalties are to himself, his profits, and his next political campaign—and perhaps to Vladimir Putin, before whom he grovels regularly, and whose agenda he has served even with this undermining of our relationship with Ukraine and the search for evidence to exonerate Russa in the 2016 election.[55]

Another interesting detail was reported in a recent *New York Times* article:

> In Ukraine, where officials are wary of offending President Trump, four meandering cases that involve Mr. Manafort, Trump's former campaign chairman,

have been effectively frozen by Ukraine's chief prosecutor. The cases are just too sensitive for a government deeply reliant on United States financial and military aid, and keenly aware of Trump's distaste for special counsel Robert Mueller's investigation "into possible collusion between Russia and his campaign."[56]

As mentioned previously by Rebecca Solnit, at the top, the issue was corruption, plain and simple. Down below at less senior levels, the problem was dismantling and disarray. This primarily came in the form of firing, sidelining, or transferring federal employees whose work was deemed politically inconvenient. In 2017, Joel Clement, formerly head of policy analysis at the Interior Department, wrote about being taken away from his work on the impact of climate change on Native Alaskans and reassigned to "an unrelated job in the accounting office that collected royalty checks from fossil fuel companies." The author was aware of numerous situations like this, where employees doing valuable work were told to move across the country to keep their jobs. The point here is that the Trump administration targeted these employees, putting an unfair and troubling burden on them, rendering them ineffectual, and in some cases, driving them out of their career positions. This was not only bad for morale within the civil servant work force; it affected supervision, oversight, and overall productivity.[57]

Another glaring example was the Federal Election Commission (FEC), which normally has six members and requires four members to have a quorum. Under Trump it had three members. Without the quorum, FEC could not investigate complaints, issue opinions, or fine violators. By hobbling, and in some cases, disabling the regulatory agencies, the Trump administration has corrupted the rule of law to benefit billionaires and misogynistic White supremacists, leading to a system in which the rich and powerful gain power and shed accountability.[58]

As dispirited as the writer of this article was about what has happened to the rule of law under this president, she suggested that we should not lose hope. Even though Trump has polluted the three branches of government, she is convinced the people who believe in a civil society will assert themselves and check this reckless president. This article was written before the presidential election, when passivity and disengagement put the country under the thumb of Donald Trump for four miserable years, but political engagement demonstrated by high turnout in the presidential election put Trump in his place, as a lame-duck loser. His whining, his fixation on himself, his bragging about running again in four years, and his petty squabbles with anyone who didn't kiss his ring are all there for the world to see. He displays his narcissism on a minute-by-minute basis with his constant tweeting. Now, he is fighting with some former allies in the pro-Trump media like Fox News because they had the audacity to project Joe Biden the winner in Arizona on election night. The reckless, dangerous, but infantile fool got what he loved to dole out on his reality TV show. He was fired!

Let's look a little further at the relationship between Donald Trump and US Attorney General William Barr. In her article in the *New Yorker*, "Trump, Barr, and The Rule of Law," dated May 5, 2019, Margaret Talbot accuses US Attorney General William Barr of always putting Trump's interests ahead of the American people's interests. Barr, when answering questions about his handling of the Mueller report, mischaracterized Robert Mueller's objections to Barr's spin about the report. Mueller was so upset with Barr that he wrote a letter to Barr stating that he was concerned that the attorney general's summary "did not fully capture the context, nature, and substance" of his team's work. Barr described the letter from Mueller as "snitty" and probably written by "staff people," thereby dismissing objections that Mueller clearly wanted in the historical record. Barr then went on to say that he would not come back and testify in the House, as he was scheduled to do. House Speaker Nancy Pelosi said that Barr had misrepresented Mueller's letter, and that the attorney general had lied to Congress, which she said was a "crime."

Barr is apparently a strong believer in the "unitary executive" theory, which is an expansive interpretation of the powers of the presidency now popular among the conservative legal community. "Barr seems to think that keeping his job requires him to treat anything that does not serve Trump's interests, including the US Constitution, as an urgent threat." Margaret Talbot goes on to accuse the attorney general of "projecting Trump's own venal motives onto his critics and opponents; denying and stonewalling."[59]

As a businessman, Trump had a well-deserved reputation for being litigious. When he was running for president in 2016, *USA Today* reported that he had been involved in about thirty-five hundred lawsuits and was a plaintiff in about two thousand of them.[60] After he became president, Trump continued his litigious ways by loading up lawsuits and attempting to thwart investigations hoping to run out the clock before the 2020 election. He sued the chairman of the House Oversight and Reform Committee, Representative Elijah Cummings, who had requested some of Trump's financial records from an accounting firm. Next, Trump and three of his children sued Deutsche Bank and Capital One to prevent them from releasing information about his financial arrangements, which were subpoenaed by Democrats. Trump also went to court to try to block a lawsuit by two hundred members of Congress alleging that Trump's business dealings violated the emoluments clause of the Constitution. The emoluments clause is also known as the Title of Nobility Clause, Article 1 Section 9 of the US Constitution. It prohibits any person holding a government office from accepting any present, emolument, office, or title from any "King, Prince, or foreign State" without congressional consent.

Trump and his treasury secretary, Steve Mnuchin, have also declined to provide the president's tax returns for the House Ways and Means Committee, which requested them from the IRS in early April 2019. Since Richard Nixon, it had been the practice of all presidents to release their tax returns. Another cabinet secretary, Commerce Secretary Wilbur Ross, denied a request from the Appropriations Committee to testify about his department's budget. President Trump has denied nearly all requests for information and testimony from members of his administration to appear before the Senate, including White House counsel Don McGahn.

The administration's efforts to deny and stymie congressional oversight is wrong. It makes a mockery of the idea of coequal branches of government within our federal system. By refusing to cooperate in any investigations and by failure to provide information related to legitimate requests of Congress, the Trump administration is operating like a crime syndicate.

Trump's attempt to dismiss the emoluments lawsuit by members of Congress was dismissed by a District Court and an Appeals Court. The emoluments clause of the Constitution was put into the Constitution to prevent federal officials from accepting financial benefits from foreign governments without congressional approval. Trump has contended that any profits he has received (from trademarks granted by the Chinese government to Saudi-funded lobbyists staying in Trump hotels do not count because he did not come by these profits as a direct result of duties performed in office. The courts that have reviewed this argument concluded that it is not only "inconsistent with text, structure, historical interpretation, adoption and purpose of this clause to the Constitution, and finally the practice of the Executive branch over the course of many years."[61]

Democrats may be leading the investigations, but their requests for information and testimony are firmly grounded in historical practice and an understanding of the separation of powers between the branches of government. The Democrats are looking into matters of current and future importance including how the White House has handled security clearances and obstruction of justice. Their purpose is to ensure accountability and to prove the need to curb future abuses with potential legislation. The Supreme Court has upheld repeatedly the right of Congress to issue subpoenas. A 1927 Supreme Court decision upheld "the power of inquiry, with enforcing process" has long been "a necessary and appropriate attribute of the power to legislate." Without the power to subpoena records and testimony, how can Congress obtain enough information and background to do its job?[62]

Attempts to get information from the Trump administration were denounced by the president as "harassment." His lack of understanding on how a federal system works, combined with his need to hide and to obfuscate keep him in a permanent state of mortal political combat. He projects his own behavior and distrust on others. He communicates his distrust of everyone and everything to his base of voters, turning them into a pathetic, perpetually angry mob, incapable of logical reasoning anymore. Whatever Donald says, they believe.

I pray that most Americans do not become like this, or I see our prospects as the leading beacon of democracy in the world in serious trouble. In March 2019, the *Washington Post* reported that federal courts had ruled against the administration sixty-three times, "an extraordinary record of legal defeat" that Trump blamed on Obama-appointed judges even though 25 percent were Republican appointees.[63]

In spring 2019, the former FBI director, James Comey, wrote an op-ed in the *New York Times*, in which he commented about William Barr's behavior as US attorney general. He said that "accomplished people lacking inner strength can't resist the compromises necessary to survive Mr. Trump and that adds up to something they will never recover from."[64]

In an article for *CNN Politics*, titled "Trump's unbroken pattern of disdain for the rule of law," dated February 22, 2020, the author, Joan Biskupic, discusses how from the very beginning of his presidency, Donald Trump has shown nothing but contempt for American legal norms and standards as well as the people who carry them out. He publicly mocked federal judges, ridiculed the criminal justice system as a "laughingstock," and used his first presidential pardon on Sheriff Joe Arpaio, who was convicted of criminal contempt.

Initially, Trump critics speculated that his outrageous remarks and actions might backfire on him and hurt the administration's legal positions in court. They also thought that public opinion would cause him to rethink his words and actions and that maybe the dignity of the office of the presidency might change his style and behavior. While under water in polling of job approval and polling of personal approval for his entire presidency, his level of support was sufficiently high among his base of support and most Republicans to prevent him from recalibrating his behavior. His disregard of the rule of law and his disrespect of judges and other people involved in safeguarding our judicial system would continue unabated. He would publicly encourage prosecutors to reward his friends and punish his enemies. He would proclaim people guilty or not guilty before trials, or he would say whether defendants were deserving of the death penalty or complete exoneration. He would place himself as the ultimate arbiter, the one-man band of high justice, the hanging judge. He would view himself as the law itself, very much like a fascist dictator in Europe during the 1930s and World War II or a dictator in a banana republic in Central America or South America.

After his first impeachment acquittal by the Senate on a nearly straight party-line vote, Trump became even more ruthless and emboldened. He almost immediately began removing people from office who had testified in the impeachment hearings in the House of Representatives against his attempt to bribe and extort a foreign official (president of Ukraine) to investigate a family member of a political rival. To Donald Trump, justice is not a fair and impartial system, but a tool to be used to benefit his interests.

Trump publicly criticized the case against his friend and campaign strategist Roger Stone and raised the possibility of a "bad jury." He launched broadside attacks on FBI officials, calling them "scum." What makes Donald Trump so different from other past presidents is the way he fundamentally and viciously attacks nearly all aspects of the rule of law. Because the president heads the executive branch of our federal government, he is seen by most Americans as the most influential person in our national government. The power vested in the presidency provides the current officeholder great opportunity to influence those officeholders below in rank and supporters as well. This power to influence so many is dangerous when it is wielded by someone who supports autocratic values and is not respectful of democratic values and the rule of law. Trump has declared control over the Department of Justice and US Attorney General William Barr by saying, "I am actually, I guess, the chief law enforcement officer."

Trump pardoned friends and associates who breached the public trust in the most egregious ways. The former Illinois governor, Rod Blagojevich, who tried to sell an appointment to a US Senate seat, and Bernard Kerik, a former New York City police commissioner who was convicted of tax fraud and lying to public officials, were both pardoned by Trump.

Trump has also pardoned Roger Stone, who was convicted of lying under oath to Congress and for threatening a witness related to Stone's 2016 campaign work for Trump. This case was one of several that came about from the investigation by special counsel Robert Mueller into Russian interference in the 2016 presidential election. Federal prosecutors originally asked Judge Amy Berman Jackson to sentence Stone to seven to nine years in prison. After Donald Trump inserted himself into the case by declaring the Stone case as "horrible and very unfair" on Twitter, Attorney General Barr agreed that even seven years was too harsh. The original prosecutors in the case resigned, and the Department of Justice (DOJ) recommended a sentence for "far less," without a specific number of years.[65]

Judge Jackson ended up sentencing Stone to forty months in prison. Literally, within hours of the announced sentence, Donald Trump claimed the jury forewoman was politically biased and that Stone had a "good chance of exoneration," but he would wait to decide on clemency. Later, Stone asked for a new trial, but it was unnecessary because Trump, as stated in the paragraph above, pardoned him in 2020.[66]

In an article for *CNN Politics*, titled "Trump intensifies assault on rule of law as he fights for reelection," dated September 9, 2020, the author, Stephen Collinson, discusses how Donald Trump put the rule of law in even greater jeopardy as part of his reelection campaign.

Trump openly called on his supporters in North Carolina to act as poll watchers, to watch out for "thieving, stealing, and robbing" that he warned would happen on Election Day without any evidence to support his claims. He made this awful and ridiculous claim at a packed rally in Winston-Salem where many of his zombie-like supporters flaunted the state's mask mandate. This occurred when the death count from the coronavirus in the United States had reached about 190,000 people. Trump, as usual, placed his political fortunes ahead of the rule of law and common sense.[67]

Of course, we cannot forget his appeals to his voters in North Carolina to potentially break the law by trying to vote twice to test the security of mail-in voting, which again, he claimed was rife with fraud, despite evidence to the contrary. Trump's comments throughout the campaign raised the specter of chaos and voter intimidation at the polls if his supporters took his advice to gather at polling stations. They were part of a long effort by the president to shatter the legitimacy of the election, if he lost, and to prepare the groundwork for a long legal siege over the outcome, if it were close. Never in our history has a president made such a ruthless attempt to disrupt the peaceful transfer of power and to portray our sacred right to vote in a democratic election as unfair and corrupt.

The latest developments concerning attempts to avoid the transfer of power after his defeat by Joe Biden are discussed quite fully in the chapter about Trump's refusal to accede to the results of the 2020 election. While Democrats, including former president Barack Obama, and his wife, Michelle Obama, used the Democratic convention to warn about Trump's efforts to tear at the fabric of our democracy over the course of the Trump presidency, even they could not have dreamed of the lengths he would go to stay in power. The court challenges without evidence, the political threats to Republican and Democratic governors and secretaries of state, the delay to the start of the transition process and briefings, and the constant poisoning of the minds of his voters with incessant, unfounded claims of voter fraud all contributed to the fraying confidence in our democratic institutions.

Fortunately, the 2020 election result was the best antidote to this lawless, disturbing presidency. Hopefully, Congress will eventually pass real reforms making this type of rogue presidency, if not impossible, at least more difficult, in the future.

In an article in *LAWFARE*, titled "Repairing the Rule of Law: An Agenda for Post-Trump Reform," dated September 7, 2020, the authors, Paul Rosenzweig and Vishnu Kannan, discuss the potential end of this period of legal darkness and the way forward. Although written before the election, the authors began to speculate about what could be done in a post-Trump world to restore the rule of law.

> Of Trump's many excesses, his assault on legal norms has to rank high in terms of damage to fundamental values that form the fabric of America. His attacks on the free press, the independent judiciary, and the independence of the Department of Justice have all created significant damage. His abuse of executive discretionary authority has made a mockery of the concept of checks and balances. His gaming of the judicial system has revealed weaknesses in our legal process. His attempts to place himself (and his family and his business interests) above the law called into question the foundational national conceptions of equal justice. In short, President Trump has led a wrecking crew (aided and abetted by William Barr and Mitch McConnell) that has severely damaged American legal norms of behavior.[68]

Lawmakers and voters can either accept this decline in the American legal system, or they can move forward with reforms to strengthen the system. Next, I will take the opportunity to list and briefly discuss some suggestions by these writers.

REFORM OF THE FEDERAL VACANCIES REFORM ACT TO PREVENT PERPETUAL "ACTING" APPOINTMENTS

The Federal Vacancies Reform Act of 1988 was passed to give presidents authority to temporarily fill vacancies in high-level federal government positions. The Trump administration has exploited this authority to avoid the normal Senate confirmation process. First, the authors suggest that no individual should be appointed temporarily to head any agency if his or her senatorial confirmation is for a position in a different agency. Second, the law should deny salary funding to any appointee after a fixed time.[69]

MANDATORY DISCLOSURE OF PRESIDENTIAL CANDIDATE TAX RETURNS AND STRENGTHENING OF PRESIDENTIAL FINANCIAL DISCLOSER

To mitigate concerns about conflict of interest between the president's official duties and his personal financial interests, it has been the long-standing custom for presidents to release their tax returns. President Trump has refused to release any of his tax returns and has fought in court whenever he has faced demands to release tax returns or other financial records. He has also refused to give up control over financial stakes in his various businesses, thus creating massive conflicts of interest. Because presidents are not required to divest themselves of financial interests the way other public officials are required to do, the main way to avoid conflicts of interest is through disclosure. To remedy potential conflicts of interest between a president's official duties in office and his or her business interests, Congress should pass a law requiring disclosure of tax returns and other mandatory financial disclosure forms.[70]

REDEFINING "EMERGENCY" AUTHORITY TO LIMIT SUCH DECLARATION GENERALLY

The president has again and again invoked federal emergency powers to push through a controversial political agenda. He declared a national emergency at our southern border, which enabled him to get funds for the construction of a southern border wall, a priority that Congress refused to fund. He also used emergency powers to criminalize cooperation with the International Criminal Court's investigation of US activity in Afghanistan, effectively stonewalling the entire investigation. The rules for invoking emergency powers were established under the 1976 National Emergencies Act (NEA). Once declared, the emergency declaration lasts for one year unless renewed by the president. Congress retains the right to terminate the emergency every six months.

Current law ensures that it is quite difficult to overturn an emergency declaration. Few of us citizens are ever injured in a way that permits a lawsuit. Congress lacks legal standing to challenge the emergency declaration. The authors of this article would like NEA to allow emergency declarations to be challenged in court and to provide that emergency declarations automatically expire in one year unless Congress extends them. They also suggest that Congress review the 123 statutory emergency power situations and remove those that are no longer necessary or are subject to abuse.[71]

CLEARER PROHIBITIONS ON REPROGRAMMING FUNDS

To bypass Congress' refusal to appropriate funds for the building of his southern border wall, the Trump administration used a national emergency declaration to reprogram funds from the Department of Defense to support the border wall project. To prevent this type of budget reappropriation, Congress needs to specifically prohibit this type of end run around Congress.[72]

ENHANCED INSPECTORS GENERAL PROTECTION

Inspectors general are the most important level of accountability. They are responsible for the oversight and financial and operational auditing of the operations of various federal agencies. Without their oversight, the executive branch has much more discretion and ability to do whatever it pleases with funds appropriated by Congress. Since April 2020, President Trump has fired inspectors general from State, Defense, Transportation, and Health and Human Services as well as from the Intelligence community. Although the official reasons for removal were varied, the replacements were all considered more loyal to the administration than to their mission of oversight and review. The Inspector General Act of 1978 was revised by the Inspector General Reform Act of 2008. The latter act allowed presidents to fire or remove inspectors general if they gave notice to Congress thirty days in advance.

The current law, in the opinion of these authors, is inadequate and does nothing to deter potential presidential misconduct. A good example that they pointed out was the dismissal of Intelligence Community Inspector General Michael Atkinson. Trump's dismissal simply read that he no longer had the "fullest confidence" in Atkinson. Trump readily admitted his real rationale the very next day when he attacked Atkinson for passing the Ukraine whistleblower complaint to Congress. This whistleblower complaint touched off the first House impeachment investigation into the president. The authors of this article stress the importance of providing greater protections for the inspectors general so that they can do their job of auditing and oversight. Reform might include giving inspectors general the right to contest their removals and give them greater formal independence from the executive branch by following the structure of the independent counsel act.[73]

STATUTORY PROTECTION FOR SPECIAL COUNSELS TO ALLOW CHALLENGE TO REMOVAL

Following Robert Mueller's appointment as special counsel to investigate Russian interference in the 2016 election, many legal experts were concerned that President Trump would fire Mueller to prevent him from investigating and exposing Trump's personal and campaign ties with Russia. The concerns were obviously justified when Trump fired the director of the FBI, James Comey, when he refused to pledge his undying loyalty to Trump rather than the rule of law and the independence of the nation's highly professional and highly trained chief criminal investigation organization. Special counsels, under the latest statute, are subject to the authority of the US attorney general. They can be fired for "misconduct, dereliction of duty, incapacity, conflict of interest, or for other good cause, including violation of departmental policies." Trump repeatedly threatened to remove Mueller, but he was dissuaded by close advisers who threatened to resign if he proceeded with firing Mueller. The Senate Judiciary Committee advanced a bipartisan bill that would allow special counsels to appeal their firings to a panel of judges. This bill was never brought before the full Senate for a vote. The authors of this article strongly recommend its future adoption into law.[74]

OVERTURN FRANKLIN V. MASSACHUSETTS

In this decision, the US Supreme Court held that the president was not an "agency" for the purposes of the Administrative Procedure Act. All agencies in the executive branch, however, are subject to its stringent rules. The implications of this act give presidents a great deal of leeway in their actions when they are acting under statutory authority (not constitutional authority). The result of this Supreme Court decision is that presidents are nearly immune from traditional aspects of administrative review. They face no requirements of providing notice and comment, nor are they subject to judicial review for arbitrary or capricious actions while carrying out administrative aspects of statutory and administrative law. The scope of the president's statutory authority includes many actions in the areas of trade, immigration, and public land use. Writer Kathryn Kovacs provides these examples:[75]

Recent purely statutory actions, for which no decision-making record was created include (to name but a few) President Trump's decisions to withdraw from the Trans-Pacific Partnership Agreement, block all property of the government of Venezuela, incentivize domestic production of rare earth metals, impose a 25% duty on imported steel, regulate the acquisition and use of technology from foreign adversaries, sequester agency appropriations across-the-board, cap the admission of refugees for 2020 to 18,000 people, bar the immigration of people who do not have health insurance, and redirect billions of dollars appropriated for military construction to building a wall between the United States and Mexico.[76]

I believe some of the above ideas are good, but others are certainly not. It would be a sensible thing to include the president's actions under statutory and administrative law to be subject to the same rules as the administrative agencies under the executive branch. This would constrain an overreaching president from running roughshod over the rules and procedure embodied in the Administrative Procedure Act.

DEFINE EMOLUMENTS VIOLATIONS AND CREATE A RIGHT OF ACTION

From the day he stepped into the job, President Trump has faced legal challenges for violations of the foreign and domestic clauses of the Constitution. The clauses prevent government officials including the president from accepting payments or benefits from a foreign state or the federal government, unless authorized by Congress. There are several lawsuits that challenge the president's decision to not divest his business assets upon taking office. Mostly these lawsuits have been unsuccessful because of a lack of standing or a cause of action. The authors suggest that Congress could pass a law creating the right of action for injured parties such as Congress itself, businesses who compete with the president's businesses, or those who are injured by actions the president takes in response to receiving such gifts. This proposed law could also define liquidated damages.[77]

AUTOMATIC HATCH ACT PENALTIES

The Hatch Act generally prohibits federal employees from engaging in "political activity" on federal property, "while on duty," "when wearing a uniform or official insignia identifying the office or position of the employee," or when using government property, such as vehicles, computers, printers, copiers, and telephones. Several Trump administration officials have been accused of violating the Hatch Act. Kellyanne Conway, former campaign manager and political adviser, has been accused of serially violating the Hatch Act, and the Office of the Special Counsel recommended her firing. More recently, the president's renomination convention, with events and speakers, on the White House grounds, appeared to have widespread violations of the Hatch Act by many people. The authors point out that the Hatch Act is not self-enforcing, and no outside organization has the standing to enforce its provisions. The act could and should be amended to automatically terminate the employment of anyone found by the Office of the Special Counsel (the body charged with review of Hatch Act violations) to have violated the act's provisions. It could be amended to provide for criminal penalties, as well.[78]

MINIMUM QUALIFICATIONS FOR WHITE HOUSE STAFF

In numerous cases, the Trump administration has mocked and marginalized expertise at the highest levels of the federal government. One example was appointing his son-in-law, Jared Kushner, a real estate developer, to broker peace in the Middle East, to solve the opioid crisis, and to manage the country's response to the coronavirus. A second example was hiring a college senior from George Washington University to a top position in the Presidential Personnel Office. A third example was having a radiologist, Dr. Scott Atlas, instead of an epidemiologist, as an adviser and spokesman on the coronavirus. The problem was the law governing the hiring of White House staff does not have any minimum qualification requirements for these positions. Again, the authors suggest that Congress pass a law requiring minimum qualifications for these White House positions.[79]

EXPEDITING JUDICIAL REVIEW OF CONGRESSIONAL DEMANDS FOR RECORDS IN RELATION TO OVERSIGHT AND IMPEACHMENT

The Supreme Court has made it clear in past decisions that congressional subpoenas in support of oversight of executive authority are valid and are subject to judicial review. During the recent impeachment hearings, the Trump administration refused to comply with subpoenas for Ukraine-related documents. The House of Representatives responded to this by including an article of obstruction of Congress in its impeachment charges. They did not challenge the administration in court, however, because it would have taken too long. Likewise, a subpoena for testimony of a key presidential adviser has been pending for two years. The lack of a timely process for reviewing conflicts between Congress and the president has had the effect of giving the president immunity from congressional review. Congress certainly could pass a mandate on expedited judicial consideration including time limits that would require relatively quick decisions by the courts.[80]

MANDATORY FEDERAL AGENT IDENTIFICATION

On several occasions, most recently in Portland, Oregon, federal officers were deployed where they did not identify themselves. Generally federal law does not require federal officers to identify themselves or the agencies that they work for. Except for federal officers working under cover, Congress could easily pass a law requiring federal officers to have a badge or wear a uniform of the agency they represent.[81]

ENHANCED WHISTLEBLOWER PROTECTION TO PREVENT RETALIATION IN THE INTELLIGENCE COMMUNITY

The intelligence community as a category of regulation and oversight by Congress is often a special case because of the sensitive national security implications of its work. Even though there have been statutes enacted to protect whistleblowers and ban retaliation, it continues. The authors suggest that Congress could strengthen the protections by creating a private right of action for whistleblowers that includes a right to seek damages.[82]

PERMIT THE INTELLIGENCE COMMUNITY INSPECTOR GENERAL TO REPORT DIRECTLY TO CONGRESS WITHOUT GOING THROUGH THE GENERAL COUNSEL OF THE OFFICE OF THE DIRECTOR OF NATIONAL INTELLIGENCE

In August 2019, on the advice of the Justice Department, the director of National Intelligence, Joseph Maguire, withheld a whistleblower complaint from Congress, despite the intelligence community inspector general deeming the complaint an "urgent concern." In response, House Intelligence Committee Chairman Adam Schiff subpoenaed the director and demanded his testimony. To avoid this type of conflict, delay, and withholding of key information, Congress could amend the statutes to make it abundantly clear that the intelligence community inspector general reports directly to Congress, not the director of National Intelligence.[83]

PARDON REFORM

As for now, the president's pardon power is nearly absolute. Unfortunately, President Trump's use of the pardon power stymied testimony and obstructed investigations of himself and others in his administration. The idea that a president might pardon his own criminal partners (as in the Roger Stone case) is the reason why founding father George Mason opposed the pardon power altogether. The authors suggest that Congress consider a Constitutional amendment that makes pardons illegal for individuals personally known to the president and makes misuse of the pardon power judicially reviewable.[84]

DISQUALIFICATION OF FAMILY FOR POTUS

Americans fought the Revolutionary War to throw off the chains of being governed by a king. Still, there has been a tendency to accept family dynasties in the history of our political governance (Bush family, Clinton family, Kennedy family, and Roosevelt family). The authors suggest Congress consider a Constitutional amendment along the following lines:[85]

> For a period of twelve years following a person's service as President of the United States, whether elected or acting and for however many days, no person shall be a candidate for, or serve as, President who is the present or former spouse, parent, child, cousin, or in-law of such person, in each case whether by marriage or otherwise. But this Article shall not apply to individuals related to any person holding the office of President, or acting as President, when this Article was proposed by Congress.[86]

In their op-ed in the *Washington Post*, "Six post-Trump reforms to help protect the rule of law," dated October 15, 2020, Bob Bauer and Jack Goldsmith, law professors respectively at New York University Law School and Harvard University Law School, proposed six major reforms. President Trump's four-year unrelenting effort to utilize the Department of Justice to protect himself and further his political ends has fortunately suffered some remarkable failures. For instance, his frequent demands that the department indict people he considers political enemies has gone nowhere. President Trump's attempts to fire Special Counsel Robert Mueller and to stop publication of his report, were squelched by others in the administration.

> Norms and laws worked much better in these instances than many feared they might. But Trump's incessant norm-breaking and possible law-breaking still damaged the appearance and reality of even-handed justice. The White House and Justice Department notably failed on several occasions to adhere to relevant norms of independence. Some deviations were significant. And a future president could follow Trump's playbook with much greater competence.[87]

After Trump leaves office, the authors stress the need to fix the damage he caused to the rule of law and to protect it against future abuse. They lay out six proposed reforms.

1. The next administration will face the issue of whether and how to investigate, and if warranted, how to prosecute Trump for crimes committed while in office. If the decision is to go forward with investigations, it must go forward in a transparent way supervised by the next US attorney general but investigated by a special counsel.
2. A significant challenge to investigating possible presidential crimes is the lack of clarity in current statutes on how obstruction of justice applies to the president. To put real checks on future presidential behavior, Congress needs to amend these laws that pertain to corrupt interference in the administration of the law to protect the president himself, his family, or to affect an election.

3. Congress should reform the pardon power that Trump has clearly abused and threatens to continue abusing. Congress should amend the bribery statute to make it a crime to bestow a pardon to try to influence testimony to an investigation. Congress should also ban self-pardons.

4. The special counsel regulations that governed Robert Mueller's investigation need reform. A special counsel is supposed to be a quasi-independent investigator who examines potential wrongdoing by senior government officials including presidents. Mueller's investigation demonstrated problems with current regulations including limits on the special counsel's authority to collect and then provide Congress and the public with facts and testimony about alleged wrongdoing by a president. The regulations should ensure that special counsels can report these facts publicly even if they are fired or the US attorney general rejects their prosecution recommendations. The authors of this op-ed also recommended that the special counsel should only be able to be fired for cause.

5. The Justice Department needs to amend its internal rules and regulations to clarify that obstruction-of-justice statutes apply to improperly partisan law enforcement actions by department officials. It should also make clear that any actions that fall short of obstruction of justice should still be treated as violations of department norms.

6. The Justice Department should reform its rules on investigations involving a president or senior officials in his or her administration. The authors believe these investigations should be conducted by an inspector general rather than a criminal prosecutor. Any criminal wrongdoing uncovered should be pursued by a special counsel rather than a criminal prosecutor, who is more under the control and influence of the attorney general. In addition, the authors believe Justice Department regulations should specifically ban the attorney general from prejudging ongoing investigations against

uncharged individuals, a norm that current Attorney General William Barr has often recklessly defied.[88]

None of these reforms presented by Bob Bauer and Jack Goldsmith can stop a determined president from publicly commenting on ongoing investigations that debase the rule of law, but together, these proposed reforms could deter a president and attorney general from trying to obstruct the legal process, even a president as malevolent and determined as President Trump.

In his op-ed in the New York Times, "Can America Restore the Rule of Law Without Prosecuting Trump," dated November 17, 2020, Jonathon Mahler, presents the country with a difficult but vital question to answer. Given that Donald Trump's potential criminal liability is a vital key to understanding his presidency, should he be held accountable for any provable crimes committed during the four years he has been in office?

President-Elect Joe Biden is going to face many huge challenges immediately upon assuming the presidency on January 20, 2021, including mitigating the ongoing damage from the coronavirus pandemic, repairing our institutions and faith in government, and repairing our relations with allies around the world. The most challenging issue that he will wrestle with is what to do about his predecessor's flagrant and relentless subversion of the rule of law. While there has been controversy in legal circles about whether a president can be prosecuted while in office, there is no controversy about whether he can be prosecuted after leaving office. No ex-president has ever been indicted before, but no president has ever left office exposed to so much criminal liability as President Trump.

As a lame-duck, defeated president, Trump remains under investigation for state crimes in New York, as mentioned previously in this chapter. Those investigations revolve around his actions as a private citizen and businessman. The central issue for the Biden administration is what to do about criminal acts potentially committed by Trump while a candidate and then later, president. These would most likely be federal crimes, only prosecutable by the federal government.

As president, Trump brashly called for the imprisonment of political opponents, shattering a long-standing norm against doing such a thing. This is ground upon which past presidents have tread lightly and carefully by going out of their way to avoid using the power of their office to seek retribution from their predecessors. George H. W. Bush pardoned six Reagan White House officials who were involved in the Iran contra affair, warning of "a profoundly troubling development in the political and legal climate of our country: the criminalization of policy differences."[89] By granting this pardon, he was sparing members of his own political party. President Obama created an even more relevant precedent for president-elect Joe Biden, by choosing not to prosecute members of the George W. Bush administration who had authorized the unlawful torture of detainees during our "war on terror." During his nomination hearings before becoming US attorney general, Eric Holder, also used the same phrase: "criminalization of policy differences."

The writer of this referenced article in the months leading up to the 2020 election had heard from many legal scholars who expressed the view that it was unlikely Trump would be prosecuted for federal crimes. They mostly believed that Trump's day of reckoning would be Election Day. Now that the election has come and gone, Trump, most of his political party, and many millions of Americans have refused to accept the results of this election. Accountability for this travesty of a presidency seems far away.[90]

The political and legal stakes of an indictment would be extremely high. Because the commander-in-chief's powers under the Constitution are broad, it might be so difficult to secure convictions, and the damage would be extremely high from a failed prosecution of a former president. An acquittal could also affect future efforts at holding a former president accountable and might even embolden future abuse of authority. Putting Trump on trial would be like putting seventy-four million people who voted for him on trial. Joe Biden is going to be focused on trying to rebuild trust in our institutions like the Department of Justice. Prosecuting Trump could complicate efforts to restore independence and integrity to the justice system and would further inflame his pathetic partisans. The idea of sending a former president like Donald Trump to prison does seem less than totally realistic, even if deserved.

Looking back on our history, Americans generally are willing to move on even from egregious conduct. The problem here is somewhat different, however, because Trump's disregard for the law has been constant and pervasive throughout his four years in office. Every president tries to leverage the power of the office to push through their initiatives and to leave a lasting imprint on the nation's future. The author of this article stresses that Trump's attempts at using his power to leave his mark were radically different in both the degree and kind of things he was willing to do. President Reagan and President George W. Bush were both willing to stretch the limits of their authority in pursuit of national security. Trump, on the other hand, stretched the limits of his authority not just to enrich himself and his family, but to block investigations into his personal and official conduct to maintain his hold on power.[91]

Trump's conduct while in office was the result of his disturbing personality and total lack of character. His deeply flawed behavior was also enabled by the accumulation of lawmaking, legal theorizing, and historical precedent that has given the president near total freedom from accountability. Applicable tools of law enforcement to prevent presidential excesses and outright criminal behaviors have over time been neutered and made nearly useless. Below, the author of this article, Jonathon Mahler, lists some of the instances that have effectively demonstrated the futility of reigning in Donald Trump from his dark impulses.

> Under the special counsel regulations, the independent prosecutor who was charged with investigating the Trump campaign's links to Russia effectively served at the pleasure of the Trump administration. The federal prosecutors who indicted Michael Cohen for an illegal campaign-finance scheme were bound to respect a decades-old legal opinion from the Justice

Department asserting the president who, according to Cohen, directed him to carry out the scheme, was immune from prosecution. There was nothing, and no one, to stop Trump from ordering numerous officials not to cooperate with his impeachment inquiry. Not that this mattered; Trump's acquittal by the GOP controlled Senate was a foregone conclusion before the hearings even opened. One after another; Trump's close associates faced charges for actions committed on his behalf, even as he walked through still more open doors, confident that as long as he remained in office, he was untouchable.[92]

Trump's behavior regarding the rule of law was never like any previous president's behavior. While it was at times tied to furthering a political agenda, it went well beyond that. Trump's efforts at subverting our legal norms and standards were an obsessive part of his character and makeup. Looked at in this way, Trump's actions and behaviors as president were merely reflections of his actions and behaviors while a businessman in New York and while a candidate running for office. One potentially illegal act led him to commit the next potentially illegal act. His tax filings, if not downright illegal, were shady while only a businessman. From there, his reported efforts to pay off two women, one a porn star, to keep quiet about their sexual romps are being investigated as unreported and hence, possibly illegal campaign contributions. While president, there have been so many instances of potential public corruption and abuses of power, ad nauseum, that it has been difficult to keep up with all of them. Finally, there have been the gross abuses of power to remain in office after the voters fired him in the 2020 election.

As mentioned earlier by Jonathon Mahler, the stakes of prosecuting Donald Trump might be high, but the costs of not prosecuting him are also high. Not prosecuting Trump for his potential violations sends a very loud, clear message, one that transcends not only his presidency, but also the entire country's commitment to the rule of law. Because the entire Trump presidency has been about him and his wants and desires, this malignant narcissist has put himself above the law. Anne Milgram, the former attorney general for New Jersey, told Mahler: "If he isn't held accountable for possible crimes, then he literally was above the law."[93]

Let us again look at each of the areas where Trump has trampled on legal norms and practices.

POSSIBLE FINANCIAL CRIMES

Below is a bullet point list of examples from the Mahler article.

➤ Trump was constantly litigating business disputes, answering many lawsuits with counterlawsuits and wearing down his adversaries with endless rounds of delays, motions, and appeals.

➤ Compelling his employees to sign sweeping nondisclosure agreements.

➤ At the risk of defaulting on a $640 million loan to Deutsche Bank, Trump sued the bank for $3 billion claiming the institution helped cause the global financial meltdown that had made him temporarily insolvent.

➤ Unhappy with a property tax valuation placed on one of his golf courses that he had paid $47.5 million to purchase and renovate, Trump sued the town of Ossining, New York, claiming the property was worth only $1.4 million.

➤ Trump over the years realized that the American system of justice provided the opportunity to solve many problems if you were willing to spend considerable money on lawyers and double down on your claims and assertions. After Trump's financial problems in the early 2000s made it extremely difficult for him to borrow money from established, reputable financial institutions, he began to seek partnerships with private individuals like Russian oligarch Aras Algarov, who Senate investigators linked to organized crime.

➤ Trump's real estate training program was essentially a pyramid scheme, encouraging consumers to purchase high-price seminars for allegedly proprietary investment advice that came from third-party marketing companies.

➤ Trump used money raised by his nonprofit foundation to settle lawsuits against his for-profit businesses.

➤ Trump's lawyer, Michael Cohen, alleged that Trump deliberately inflated the value of his assets to secure bank loans and cheaper insurance rates and deflated the value of these assets to lower his tax burden.

➤ Trump's tax strategy may have stretched the limits of tax avoidance; he has so far refused to disclose these returns to the public.

➤ Trump may have grossly overstated the value of several properties to obtain large tax deductions known as conservation easements.

➤ He wrote off expenses associated with his family compound in Westchester, New York, claiming it was an investment property.

➤ He wrote off $70,000 worth of haircuts as a business expense while appearing on *The Apprentice*.

➤ He paid his daughter, Ivanka, more than $740,000 in consulting fees while she was an employee of the Trump organization.[94]

Most state financial crimes have a five-year statute of limitations, so much of what he might have done will not be chargeable. Anything done after 2015 might still be chargeable. Cyrus Vance's inquiry appears to be related to a wide range of potential white-collar crimes, some of which have been mentioned and speculated upon. Given Trump's history of working with foreign partners with a need and desire to conceal certain sources of income, other potential charges might include money laundering. If investigators prove a pattern of illegal activity, he potentially could be indicted under New York's racketeering statute.

Prosecuting Trump under state law would pose a great challenge because there are stronger rules of evidence than in federal courts. Trump could also face federal prosecution for tax fraud. Currently he is in a drawn-out audit by the IRS. In criminal tax-fraud cases, the prosecutors are required to prove intent to defraud, which is a high standard to meet. The number of entities (partnerships, limited liability companies, and shell companies) and the volume of transactions and deductions could make it difficult for a jury to follow a criminal tax fraud case. Most tax lawyers that Jonathon Mahler talked with about this article suggested that the results of these IRS audits were much more likely to give rise to large civil penalties, but not criminal charges.[95]

ELECTION LAW VIOLATIONS

When Donald Trump announced his presidential candidacy, he entered onto a new stage with a set of new laws governing his conduct as a candidate and offering new types of potential liability. Since fund-raising, the lifeblood of any political campaign, was going to be more difficult for a long-shot antiestablishment figure like Donald Trump, Trump sought financing through some unconventional, and potentially illegal, ways. Shortly before the first Republican caucuses, he used his foundation to host a televised fund-raiser for military veterans and then redirected portions of the funds raised to his campaign. New York State attorney Eric Schneiderman investigated, and Trump's foundation was eventually fined $2 million for misappropriation of funds and shut down under court supervision.

When potentially damaging revelations threatened to submerge his campaign involving sexual relationships with two women, Stormy Daniels and Karen McDougal, Trump's attorney, Michael Cohen, arranged for six-figure hush money payments.

Trump's campaign eagerly welcomed Russia's efforts to interfere in the election. The campaign chairman and chief political consultant, Paul Manafort, shared internal polling data with a Russian intelligence agent, while another political adviser, Roger Stone (known as the king of dirty tricks), right after the release of the *Access Hollywood* tape in which Trump joked about sexually assaulting women, helped facilitate the publishing on WikiLeaks a large group of Democratic emails stolen by Russian hackers.

Many of Trump's campaign associates, including Michael Cohen, Paul Manafort, and Roger Stone, have since faced federal charges and been convicted and sentenced to prison. Once out of office, Trump could potentially be investigated and charged for his conduct during the campaign. While Robert Mueller's investigation did not find sufficient evidence to prove Trump's participation in his campaign's involvement with Russia, a fifth and final volume of the Senate Intelligence Committee's bipartisan report on Russian interference in the 2016 election made it clear that Mueller's report was not exhaustive. The Senate report detailed numerous instances of engagement between the Trump campaign and Russian actors. Jonathon Mahler, after talking with several prosecutors, believed that the Mueller investigation closed the possibility of a criminal inquiry into Trump's conduct with the Russians. "People can disagree about how it was done or how it went, but that doesn't mean it wasn't a thorough process," Milgram said. 'It doesn't feel to me like someone would go digging there to see if there was more. That could feel vindictive because Mueller already made the call."[96]

An election law case against Trump might be a more inviting case for a Biden Justice Department to review and consider charges. When Michael Cohen testified in federal court that Trump directed him to arrange for hush-money payments, Trump was part of the investigation but was protected by the Justice Department policy against indicting a sitting president. Instead, he was named an unindicted coconspirator referred to as "Individual 1" in the prosecutor's filings.

Campaign finance experts agree that Trump could be indicted for these hush-money payments to Stormy Daniels and Karen McDougal, as these payments were clearly meant to prevent disclosure of information that could have damaged Trump's campaign. These payments violated campaign finance laws including accepting contributions of more than $2,700 and the failure to report contributions to the Federal Election Commission (FEC). Because the amounts exceeded $25,000, they would be considered felonies, each punishable by a sentence of from one to five years. Cohen provided congressional investigators with copies of the canceled checks from Trump and the Trump Organization. Reimbursements for the payments made to Daniels were classified for accounting purposes as legal fees.[97]

OBSTRUCTION OF JUSTICE

In his article, Jonathon Mahler sets the stage very well for the next topic—obstruction of justice.

> The presidency offered Trump both new opportunities and a new degree of protection. He would have all the formal and informal powers of the office at his disposal, but he would also have full immunity from criminal prosecution, thanks to a legal opinion from the Justice department's Office of Legal Counsel in 1973 stating that a sitting president should not be indicted. It was just a memo, not an actual ruling, but it had been honored by federal prosecutors for close to 50 years. The power of the office would not only allow Trump to enrich himself and his family but to frustrate any investigations into his actions as president, or for that matter, into his prior conduct.

> Nearly all of Trump's modern predecessors separated themselves from their financial interests before entering office to eliminate the possibility of any conflicts.

Trump announced that he would do the opposite, consolidating his businesses in a family trust. His two eldest sons would run the Trump Organization, and he would become the trust's sole beneficiary, allowing his family to take full advantage of the office's financial potential.[98]

Almost immediately after the 2016 election results, money began flowing into the inaugural committee, which raised $107 million. The laws governing contributions to the inaugural committees are much less onerous than the laws governing campaign finance. Despite this fact, Trump's inaugural committee appears to have broken these laws. First, it might have violated its nonprofit status by paying more than $1 million to rent space at Trump's new Washington hotel, at rates well above market rates or the hotel's internal pricing guidelines and spending $300,000 to rent a room in the hotel for a private after-hours party for Trump's children. The inaugural committee's disclosure report to the Federal Elections Commission contained some outright false entries concerning contributors and amounts, and it has already caused federal prosecutions.[99]

Just a few months into the Trump presidency, the FBI began an investigation into his campaign's links to Russia. Trump tried to stop this investigation. His first attorney general, Jeff Sessions, recused himself from the inquiry because he had been involved with the campaign. Trump strongly asked him to change his mind and unrecuse himself. Trump also pressured FBI Director James Comey to announce that Trump was not a target of the investigation and to back off on investigating Michael Flynn (Trump's national security adviser), who had pleaded guilty to lying to investigators about a meeting with Russian ambassador Sergei Kislyak. Trump eventually fired Comey, which led to the appointment of a special prosecutor, Robert Mueller. Trump soon tried to stop Mueller, asking his White House counsel, Don McGahn, to fire him. When the story of Trump's order became public, Trump told McGahn to publicly deny it, and to create a false record to document it.

As Mueller's investigation continued and started to charge people tightly affiliated with Trump's campaign, Trump began publicly floating the idea of pardons, for instance for Paul Manafort, his campaign manager at the time, who was convicted of eight felonies and pleaded guilty to two others. He also tried to intimidate and discredit another potential witness, Michael Cohen, his personal lawyer. Initially, Trump said he wouldn't "flip," and then later when he did, called him a "liar."[100]

Mueller's original scope was to investigate the Trump campaign's Russia connections, but it only took a short while for him to begin a parallel investigation into possible obstruction of justice. Mueller proceeded with the investigation as though he did not have the authority to indict a sitting president, but he did detail ten potentially obstructive acts. In Mahler's conversations with dozens of prosecutors and legal experts, there was consensus that Robert Mueller presented more than enough evidence to seek a grand jury indictment against Trump for obstruction of justice. In the spring of 2019, when Mueller's report was released, more than seven hundred former federal prosecutors from Republican and Democratic administrations signed an open letter stating that if those same acts had been committed by anyone but the president, they would have resulted in multiple felony charges. When political figures and senior advisers are prosecuted, it is often for obstruction. Examples include Scooter Libby, an adviser to Vice President Dick Cheney, who was never charged with leaking the name of a covert CIA operative to the media, but he was convicted of lying to a grand jury investigating the leak. Similarly, Roger Stone was not prosecuted for his efforts to get Trump elected; he was prosecuted for lying under oath, withholding documents, and threatening an associate if he cooperated in the investigation into the campaign's ties with Russia. Of course, as expected, Trump commuted his sentence.[101]

Obstructing justice is the means by which many powerful people attempt to place themselves above the law. An obstructive act requires "corrupt intent," which is sometimes difficult to prove to a unanimous jury.

PUBLIC CORRUPTION

After temporarily replacing Jeff Sessions as US attorney general with Matthew Whitaker, he eventually replaced him with William Barr. As part of a conservative group of legal thinkers, Barr years before developed and promoted a new theory of presidential power known as "the unitary executive." His argument was essentially that Article II of the Constitution not only gave the president complete and total control over foreign policy and covert operations, but that it also protected the president from investigation and possible charges by independent prosecutors. When chosen by Trump to be the US attorney general, Barr was given the chance to defend his very expansive view of presidential and executive branch authority. Even before he was sworn in as US attorney general, Barr wrote an unsolicited memo that characterized Mueller's investigation as a "fatally misconceived" assault on the powers of the presidency. Barr said the president's authority on law enforcement matters was complete and total, even concerning the president's own conduct. Once in the position, as mentioned previously, Barr drafted a misleading letter of summary of Mueller's findings and then refused to provide Congress an unredacted version of the Mueller report, citing executive privilege.[102]

I have found this unitary executive theory to be worthless and corrupting on its face. What Barr is suggesting and promoting is the idea that there are no boundaries or limits on the actions of a president regarding law enforcement. This sounds to me like the ramblings of someone happy to applaud and participate in any unconscionable behavior, all in the name of unchecked executive authority. Under this idiotic theory, presidents could behave like fascist dictators, carry out venomous policies on its citizens, and either cover up or boldly flaunt their lawlessness and broken public trust. Such a theory should be considered nonsensical; if carried to its logical extreme, it would end oversight and provide no way of stopping a corrupt president from becoming a dictatorial monster right before our eyes. I do not think our Founding Fathers supported the idea of the chief executive of the United States becoming our version of Hitler, Mussolini, or Caligula.

While the framers of the Constitution undoubtedly wanted to provide the president with nearly unquestioned authority on national security matters, they did not in my opinion want to give him or her a blank check. By following Barr's "unitary executive theory" in Trump's impeachment hearing, Trump was able to get away with directing various agencies to refuse to comply with congressional subpoenas for documents and to refuse to testify. This puts the president above the law and facilitates easy unchallengeable breaches of the public trust.

PARTISAN COERCION

Under William Barr, the Justice Department seemed willing to do anything the president wanted. It began a counterinvestigation into the FBI's investigation into the Trump campaign's ties to Russia. It tried to block the distribution of John Bolton's book because of its very unflattering look into the national security activities of Donald Trump. It tried to intervene in a defamation lawsuit brought by a writer and columnist, Jean Carroll, who accused Trump of rape in the late 1990s, long before he was president.

Trump, as mentioned previously, continued his march against accountability and transparency by firing five inspectors general, by commuting Roger Stone's prison sentence, by nominating Chad Wolfe as acting director of Homeland Security, in order to avoid the Senate confirmation process, and by disregarding a federal judge's order to restore the Obama-era DACA program that enabled hundreds of thousands of immigrants, who had spent their childhood and early adulthood in the United States, to remain in the only country they had ever lived.[103]

As Trump was exercising his power, unfettered by Congress or his own Justice Department, there were potential threats awaiting him if he lost the election of 2020. Not only were the investigations by the Manhattan DA and the State of New York's attorney general in progress; a watchdog group was accusing Trump's reelection campaign of funneling $170 million in funds to unidentified recipients controlled by the campaign's recently demoted campaign manager, Brad Pascale, and other officials. Soon to be out of office after his election defeat, Trump was going to be facing financial problems outlined previously in this chapter.[104]

In the final weeks and months in office, Trump moved into more questionable activities of potential criminality by directing the full weight of the executive branch toward his reelection efforts. He used the White House as a stage replacing the Republican Convention and a naturalization ceremony as part of the show. Days after being released from the hospital after contracting COVID-19, Trump held a campaign rally on the south lawn of the White House. "Still behind in the polls, the president became even more desperate, lashing out at some of his strongest allies for not using their power aggressively enough. He called out his attorney general, William Barr, for failing to arrest his political rivals, including Joe Biden and his son, Hunter Biden. He tried to get his secretary of state, Mike Pompeo, to make public Hillary Clinton's emails from more than four years ago. At least nine of Trump's high-level officials have been investigated for Hatch Act violations. One of them, Kellyanne Conway, violated the act on more than sixty occasions, prompting the Office of Special Counsel to recommend that Trump remove her from her position as a senior White House official. Her response showed her contempt for the rule of law: "Blah, blah, blah. Let me know when the jail sentence starts."[105]

The Hatch Act has criminal provisions from which the president is not exempt. The prohibition against using one's official authority to influence an election is the core of this statutory law. Trump's flagrant violations of the Hatch Act at the Republican Convention on White House grounds were commented on frequently by the media before and after the convention. Neither Trump nor his senior staffers seemed worried. His own chief of staff, Mark Meadows, commented, "No one outside the Beltway really cares."[106]

In the final analysis, the debate about what to do about Donald

Trump and his eroding impact on the rule of law is less about him and his complete lack of honor and character and more about the structural problems his presidency exposed for all to see. Trump may have used the executive branch as a tool for personal financial gain and to manipulate the legal system to avoid consequences for his actions, but it was the structure of the country's legal system and the lack of integrity by him, most Republican leaders and officeholders, and a large majority of his voters that enabled this to happen. Once out of office, he might still not face legal consequences.

In a previously referenced article by Bob Bauer and Jack Goldsmith, the one subject they could not agree on was what to do with Trump. Bob Bauer advocated for a complete, fair, and transparent investigation while Jack Goldsmith urged more caution, preferring instead to focus on reforms.[107]

In writing this book, I must say that I lean toward a full investigation. Unlike previous presidents, who may have done some questionable things subject to policy differences and narrowly focused actions, President Trump launched a full-blown attack on legal standards and American values. For this reason, I hope he is held legally accountable for those misdeeds that can be proven in court. Even if he never serves a day in jail, I hope that if a guilty judgment is rendered in court that it requires him to publicly apologize to the American people and to spell out clearly the exact nature and scope of his many questionable actions and misdeeds.

We do know there was some concern on his part as the idea of White House pardons for himself, his family, and other senior officials were floated before leaving the White House. The idea of the self-pardon has never been tested before in court. Another disgraceful possibility would have been his resignation before January 20, 2021 so that President Mike Pence could have pardoned him. As mentioned previously, neither of these scenarios came to fruition because they would have been perceived as a full-blown declaration of guilt by Donald Trump.

Our nation may desire healing at some point, but the matter of justice cannot be overlooked in a cowardly quest to please Trump's

Republican army. History will ultimately judge how America responded to this venal attack on our institutions and standards of decency. Joe Biden is going to be presented with an opportunity to reform our institutions, repair the damage of the last four years, and to recapture our values.

The question that every American needs to answer for themselves is this: What do we do about a president who has so brazenly corrupted our legal system and who has torched our standards under the rule of law? A secondary but related question is this: Is electoral defeat enough? My answer to the secondary question is *"no."* Stephen Vladeck, a constitutional law professor at the University of Texas, had an interesting take on this question: Breaking the law is not political difference."[108]

If this man is not held accountable, we are giving permission in the future for this type of behavior to continue. We cannot allow this to stand! We simply cannot! While I do not need to see him in an orange jumpsuit in prison, I do at the least need to see him admit his wrongs and ask for forgiveness for his four-year affront to the dignity of our legal system and rule of law. This public apology would be incredibly humiliating for Donald Trump, but he might need to do it if he wants to avoid real potential criminal penalties. It also would be a wake-up call and a slap in the face to his many enablers, rationalizers, and supporters that have been so unwilling to face the ugly truth about this man. They really cannot deny the reality of his malfeasance, corruption, dereliction of duty, abuse of power, and solicitation of insurrection when he talked about blanket pardons for himself and his family. Even more so, they cannot continue this cultlike charade in their own minds, particularly if a court or series of courts make him express regret, make him ask for forgiveness, and make him enumerate in full detail his many potential offenses.

Jonathon Mahler sums this up quite well with the last sentence in his article: "It might also require recognizing that to really move on from Trump, healing may have to come from something fundamentally different from what it has in the past, and that without accountability, it may in fact be impossible."[109]

In the *Washington Post* article, "Former US Attorneys—all Republicans—back Biden, saying Trump threatens 'the rule of law'," by Tom Hamburger and Devlin Barrett, dated October 27, 2020, the writers report that twenty former Republican US attorneys accused President Trump of threatening the rule of law, and they pledged their support in the then upcoming election to Joe Biden. These former senior federal prosecutors said in an open public letter that Trump treated the Department of Justice as his personal law firm, by pressuring attorneys there to protect his allies and attack his political enemies. This is the latest of several groups of Republicans who could no longer hold their noses and vote for Trump.[110]

In a Reuters article by Tim Reid, titled "Republican former U.S. attorneys endorse Biden, call Trump threat to rule of law," dated October 27, 2020, the writer also reported on the defection of twenty former Republican US attorneys. Other groups were Republican Voters Against Trump, Former Republican National Security Officials for Biden, and forty-three Alumni for Biden. Trump on Twitter last year referred to "Never Trump Republicans" as "human scum." Fortunately for our country, enough "human scum" defected from Trump to guarantee his defeat and free us from this lawless, indecent, and inhuman presidential reign of terror. If this ugly political movement, under this ugly character and personality, tries to resurrect itself in 2024, it will be met by Democrats, independents, and Never Trump Republicans on the battlefield of ideas, character, and competence. This writer sincerely believes Donald Trump in a rematch would be even easier to beat, particularly if he has to plea pardon himself and his family for various potential federal and state crimes, both felonies and misdemeanors.[111] Now that he was impeached a second time over soliciting insurrection at the Capitol, his chances of ever running again for federal office are slim to none.

CHAPTER 4

RACISM AND WHITE SUPREMACY

FROM THE BMJ *Newsroom, dated October 27, 2020, "Fatal police shootings of unarmed Black people in US more than 3 times as high as in Whites," the fatal police shootings of Black people as a percentage of total Black people in the United States is more than three times as high as the fatal police shootings of White people as a percentage of total White people in the United States as reported in the Journal of Epidemiology & Community Health.[112] These numbers have remained stubbornly similar over the past five years. We are sadly familiar with the names of the 2020 victims:[113]*

Casey Goodson

Angelo Crooms

Sincere Pierce

Marcellis Stinnette

Johathan Price

Dijon Kizzee

Rayshard Brooks

Carlos Carson

David McAtee

Tony Mcdade

George Floyd (died from a choke hold)

Dreasjon Reed

Michael Ramos

Daniel Prude

Breonna Taylor

Manuel Ellis

William Green

Not on the above list is Ahmaud Arbery, an unarmed Black man (age twenty-five) who, while out for a jog, was confronted and killed by Travis McMichael and his father, Gregory. This racially motivated hate crime was not perpetrated by an on-duty police officer; hence the victim was not included on the above list of police killings. Only under pressure from the community, when a local attorney provided a copy of a video taken of the confrontation and the shooting, did the wheels of justice begin to roll in this case. The fact that these two men were not arrested until seventy-four days after the killing sparked outrage and sadness throughout the community of Brunswick, Georgia. One of the killers was a former law enforcement officer of Glynn County. With this as background, this chapter will examine the creeping racism and attachment to White supremacy that has infected the GOP during the Trump takeover of the Republican Party and the Trump presidency.

In the September issue of the *Atlantic,* the article "Is This the Beginning of the End of American Racism?" by Ibram Kendi explores whether Donald Trump has revealed the depths of our country's prejudice, and whether he has inadvertently forced us to face our day of reckoning, whether he became the tipping point that brought us out of our state of denial and into a state of acceptance that racism needs to end now and forever. Like so many of the controversies and needless fights during the Trump presidency, a morning tweet on July 24, 2019, ignited a political and racial war of words on a scale that we have not seen in some time.

> So interesting to see Progressive Democrat Congresswomen, who originally came from countries whose governments are a complete and total catastrophe, the worst, most corrupt and inept anywhere in the world (if they even have a functioning government at all), now loudly and viciously telling the people of the United States, the greatest and most powerful Nation on earth, how our government is to be run. Why don't they go back and help fix the totally broken and crime infested places from which they came? Then come back and show us how it is done. These places need your help badly, you can't leave fast enough.[114]

Trump was referring to four freshmen members of Congress: Ilhan Omar of Minnesota, a Somalian American; Ayanna Pressley of Massachusetts, an African American; Rashida Tlaib of Michigan, a Palestinian American; and Alexandria Ocasio-Cortez of New York, a Puerto Rican American.

On the South Lawn of the White House, President Trump was asked by the media if he was bothered by the fact that more and more people were calling him a racist. He, of course, denied being a racist, and then launched an attack on Reverend Al Sharpton, calling him a racist. He said that he had done more for the African American community and that they were so thankful. The writer of this article felt that this was a hugely significant moment in the history of race relations in our country. He believed that Trump awakened Americans to the fact that our racial history up to the present was not something to be proud of; in fact, it was demonstrated by the president's own words to be "arrogant, mean, and ugly." He also believed that Trump's words made the act of denying our racial reality impossible. Those nasty, cutting words to four US congresswomen, citizens of the United States, were so insulting, so misogynistic, and so beneath the dignity of the office of the presidency.[115]

In Ibram Kendi's view, we are amid an anti-racist revolution. I agree with him completely. The spring and summer of 2020 witnessed demonstrations for racial justice in cities large and small and in wealthy suburbs throughout the United States. Veteran activist protesters were joined by new people—Black, Brown, and White—who never protested before in their lives, in a joint show of solidarity, grief, and righteous anger for the pain and injustice the families of these victims were forced to endure. The protests were aimed at pushing state and local policymakers to hold violent police officers, those with records of brutality complaints, accountable. They also were pushing to ban choke holds and no-knock warrants. They also wanted to shift more funding from pure law enforcement to social services (like mental health services) to prevent the killing of people who were impaired from mental illness like schizophrenia or drug abuse. Finally, they wanted to end the practice of sending in highly armed, amped-up police officers to respond to incidents in which the suspect is neither armed nor dangerous. Beyond advocating for policy changes in the policing practices in their cities, these people were asking—no, demanding—for an end to racism in America. The overwhelming majority of the people in these protests were nonviolent, were carrying signs, and were listening to the speeches of local leaders and clergy.[116]

Most of the violence and looting was perpetrated by people living outside the community like the Boogaloo Boys, the Proud Boys, other White supremacists, and anarchists. The FBI was involved in the investigations and arrest of some of these anarchists and far-right White supremacists. Kyle Rittenhouse, a seventeen-year-old who shot and killed two people and wounded a third person, was arrested and ordered to stand trial for felony murder in Kenosha, Wisconsin. Actor Ricky Schroeder and Mike Lindell, CEO of My Pillow Inc., helped raise the $2 million bail for this young killer. Rittenhouse, a minor who should have never been allowed to have a gun, drove from northern Illinois to Kenosha, Wisconsin, to become judge, jury, and executioner. This wicked little creep attended a Trump rally less than a week before he showed up to kill two people and wound a third person. Donald Trump, rather than try to bring calm to a nation in pain and to seek racial reconciliation, was the match that lit the fuse.

One more comment is worth making concerning Mike Lindell. My wife and I have used his patented pillows in the past with no complaints. Never again will we purchase from this man's company! Contributing and soliciting funds for the bail of a vigilante was not only disgusting and disturbing; it makes me wonder what kind of person he is on the inside.

In the grip of a nation watching its Black citizens being murdered or crippled by senseless police brutality, he makes common cause with a murderer, and by proxy, with the police officer who shot Jacob Blake seven times, leaving him crippled for life. What has become of the hearts and minds of Donald Trump supporters? This soulless descent into darkness is mind-numbing to people who want America again to be the beacon of hope, fairness, and justice for all Americans of all races and religions. This ugly march of hate must stop. I pray daily that more people of goodwill stand up and oppose this descent into chaos and rage. People like Lindell and Schroeder need to be called out loudly and frequently. This vicious, divisive political tribal warfare is destroying our country and making our people hate one another. If we do not look deeply inside ourselves and turn away from this "us vs. them" mentality, we will soon see a country that is no longer worthy of itself. More and more Americans will withdraw into their tribes, losing friendships and family. Trump supporters, please stop fanning the flames! Please open your hearts and open your minds! You are believing the rantings of a losing demagogue and the false propaganda of a polluted, self-serving ultra-right-wing media, whose only goal is to profit off your gullibility.

President Trump attempted to portray these righteous demonstrations as the work of thugs, looters, and criminals. Fortunately, most people watching this unfold on television did not see it that way. According to a Monmouth University poll, 57 percent of people sampled said police officers were more likely to use excessive force against Black suspects than against White suspects. This poll represents a large magnitude change compared to 33 percent in a poll taken in 2014 after a grand jury refused to indict a New York police officer in the killing of Eric Garner. By early June, about three in four Americans were saying "racial and ethnic discrimination" was a big problem in the United States, up from about one in two Americans expressing this belief in 2015, the year Donald Trump launched his presidential campaign.[117]

It would be easy to see these shifts as a direct result of the horrid events Americans were forced to witness on television in 2020. The disproportionate effect on people of color from the COVID-19 pandemic was jarring and painful. Then, we saw the video of the police officer in Minneapolis kill George Floyd by kneeling on his neck while Floyd begged for mercy. Of course, then we heard and saw on the news the horrific killing of Breonna Taylor, shot to death in her own home during a no-knock raid by Louisville police looking for drugs, which they never found. Despite these triggering events, the fundamental views on race in America were already under way before these latest examples of police violence surfaced. Kendi posits that what is happening to Americans' attitudes is the result of an extended process that parallels the political career of Donald Trump.

In the immediate days leading up to Trump's attack on these four congresswomen, referred to as the "Squad," the four, especially Omar, had been disagreeing with House Speaker Nancy Pelosi over a $4.6 million border-aid package that they felt did not go far enough to restrain Trump's immigration and naturalization policies. Pelosi, despite the disagreement she was having with the "Squad," stood up and defended them by saying: "When @realDonaldTrump tells four American congresswomen to go back to their countries, he affirms his plan to Make America Great Again has always been about making America White again."[118]

White people telling people of color to go back to their countries is a cruel racial slur because their country is the United States of America. They are every bit as American as Donald Trump. Ocasio-Cortez was born in New York. Tlaib was born in Detroit. Pressley lives in the Boston area. Omar's family emigrated to the United States when she was a small child. Most Americans are the descendants of immigrants. My mother's ancestors (Swedish, Norwegian, and Finnish background) immigrated to the United States (Michigan) in the late nineteenth century. My father's great-grandparents (British, Irish, and Scottish background) also immigrated about the same time to the United States (Wisconsin).

As Democrats expressed outrage at the words of President Trump, most Republicans went silent and refused to condemn the president. A few, including Mike Turner of Ohio and Will Hurd of Texas, called the president's tweet racist. Trump, emboldened by the silence of nearly all the officials and legislators within his party, doubled down on his attacks. He tweeted the following in all caps, "IF YOU ARE NOT HAPPY HERE, YOU CAN LEAVE." Then the president added: 'If Democrats want to unite around the foul language and racist hatred spewed from the mouths and actions of these very unpopular and unrepresentative Congresswomen, it will be interesting to see how it plays out." Democrats had had enough, and they introduced a resolution to strongly condemn the president's racist tweets. The next morning, Trump tweeted this in response: "Those tweets were NOT racist. I don't have a racist bone in my body!"[119]

For better or for worse, most Americans see their country reflected in the behavior and the words of their president. For Trump and many of his supporters, America is and must remain White. Trump began his campaign for president on June 16, 2015, with attacks on people of color including his birtherism attack on President Obama. On

Mexicans, he remarked, "They're bringing drugs. They're bringing crime. They're rapists." On President Obama, he said, "He's been a negative force. We need somebody that can take the brand of the United States and make it great again."[120]

Trump presented himself as that somebody; he presented himself as the great White hope. In his mind, America would not be great again until he erased Obama's image from the minds of Americans. He wanted to erase Obama's accomplishments and legacy by repealing the Affordable Care Act and ending the Deferred Action for Childhood Arrivals (DACA) policy. He wanted to build a wall to keep out immigrants, and he would ban Muslims from entering the country. For many Americans, the Obama presidency was a living example of the United States living up to its standards of liberty and equality of opportunity. By climbing to the pinnacle of political success and becoming president, Obama was pushing the nation closer to the ideal of a postracial America.

Kendi was not as optimistic about the immediate future. He told friends and family that he thought Trump had a good chance at winning. He also believed the progress toward a postracial society of the Obama years would be followed by a move in the opposite direction under Donald Trump. In Trump's victory speech on the 2016 election night, he vowed to be president for all Americans.

Within days of being sworn in, Trump broke that promise. He issued executive orders calling for the construction of a wall along our southern border and the deportation of individuals who "pose a risk to public safety or national security." He entered his first of three Muslim bans. By the end of spring, Attorney General Jeff Sessions had directed all federal prosecutors to seek the harshest prison sentences, wherever possible. He also laid the groundwork for the suspension of all consent decrees that provided federal oversight of law enforcement agencies that had demonstrated a history and pattern of racism in their enforcement practices.[121]

Led by Steve Bannon and Stephen Miller, the Trump administration began working on ways to restrict immigration by people of color. Trump said the following at a private White House meeting in June of

2017: Haitians "all have AIDS," and Nigerians would never "go back to their huts" once they came to the United States.[122]

Then came the White supremacist march and rally in Charlottesville, Virginia. On August 11, 2017, about 250 White supremacists marched on the University of Virginia's campus, carrying torches. The eerie event evoked memories from history books—the nightriders of the Ku Klux Klan. Demonstrating against the city of Charlottesville's plan to remove statutes honoring Confederates, the White supremacists chanted "blood and soil," "Jews will not replace us," and "White lives matter."[123]

Clashes erupted that evening and the next day with antiracist counter protesters. White supremacist James Alex Field drove his Dodge Challenger into a crowd of counter protesters, killing Heather Meyer and injuring nineteen others. Trump said the following about the protest the next day: "We condemn in the strongest possible terms this egregious display of hatred, bigotry, and violence on many sides, on many sides." Then he added, "There are some very fine people on both sides." Linking White supremacists with fine people was too much for me and many other people. It crystallized in my mind what was in the heart of Donald Trump.[124]

On September 5, 2017, Trump began his long and unsuccessful attempt to eliminate the DACA program, which deferred deportations on about eight hundred thousand undocumented immigrants who had arrived in the United States as children. The Trump administration also began rescinding the Temporary Protected Status of thousands of refugees from wars and natural disasters years ago in Sudan, Nigeria, Haiti, El Salvador, Nepal, and Honduras. Near the end of his first year in office, Trump mused "Why are we having all these people from shithole countries come here?"[125]

After all these racist comments, Trump continued to deny that he was racist. Many Trump supporters continue to place blame on Black people for racial inequities in housing, income, and crime. Blacks are told to be more like Whites and that their lower achievements rest with their inferior behavior. After four years of Trump and four more years of police brutality toward Black and Brown people, this charade by Trump supporters is no longer supportable. It has become more and more ludicrous to blame Blacks for their station in life and to urge them to behave more like Whites. In the Trump years, the real problem is obvious. It is not, for the most part, Black people's behavior; it is White people's behavior.

The United States has often been a land of contradictions, a land of lofty ideals but also a land of missed opportunities. Ibram Kendi describes this conflict between ideals and realities:

> The United States has often been called a land of contradictions, and to be sure, its failings sit alongside some notable achievements—a New Deal for many Americans in the 1930s, the defeat of fascism abroad in the 1940s. But on racial matters, the US could just as accurately be described as a land in denial. It has been a massacring nation that said it cherished life, a slaveholding nation that said it valued liberty, a hierarchical nation that declared it valued equality, a disenfranchising nation that branded itself a democracy, a segregated nation that styled itself separate but equal, an excluding nation that boasted of opportunity for all. A nation is what it does, not what it originally claimed it would be. Often, a nation is precisely what it denies itself to be.[126]

There was a time in our history, just before and during the Civil War, when most Americans realized that they could no longer deny the evil of slavery in the South. They were willing to fight and die to end this subhuman practice. Like the awakening occurring in the hearts and minds of many Americans in the years leading up to the Civil War, the awakening to the evils of racism is now occurring because of the wake-up call Americans received watching and hearing the words and deeds of the Trump administration over the last four years.

With the vote in the House of Representatives condemning

Donald Trump's tweets about the four congresswomen as racist, only four Republicans joined the Democrats. Of the entire Republican caucus, 187 or 98 percent refused to condemn the president.[127] This placed the Republican Party squarely on the side of racism, like the Democratic party in the South before and during the Civil War. This wretched state of denial by the political party that I supported most of my adult life was simply too much for me to handle. I have become an independent, who will no longer support the GOP until this disgusting attachment to Donald Trump and his brand of racial politics is uprooted and discarded from our public discourse. Whether this happens in the GOP in my lifetime or not, I am not sure. For most of the rest of the country, this attachment to racism is receding.

Unfortunately, for the Trumpists and the Republican Party, this racist stench remains. The day after being rebuked by the House of Representatives, Donald Trump held the first rally of his reelection campaign in North Carolina. As he was verbally punching Omar, the crowd started chanting, "Send her back, send her back, send her back!" Trump stopped speaking for many seconds, basking in the racial slur and the comfort of his mob. Soon thereafter, Republicans were in damage-control mode and began disavowing the chant. Trump at first went along with the disavowal and disavowed the chant, but one day later, he disavowed the disavowal, calling the chanters "incredible patriots" and denying their racism, as well as his own. By the end of July, for the first time, most registered voters said the president was a racist.[128]

Ibram Kendi reached the conclusion that Donald Trump's denial of his own racism would never stop. He would continue to claim that he loves people of color. He would continue to call anyone that calls him out on his racism, racist. Trump hoped that his thinly disguised racism would help suppress the vote and lead to his reelection. Trump's behavior has pushed most Americans to a point where they can no longer rationalize the racial sins of America. The question that remains for most Americans is what they will do about it.

Kendi suggested there were two paths forward. The first would be the defeat of Donald Trump in the election by Joe Biden. In fact, this is what happened. Under this path, the nation believes it is headed again in the right direction. On this path, Americans consider racism to be a significant problem, but they deny the true inertia of the problem and the need for drastic action. On this path, monuments to racism would be dismantled, but Americans would fail to reshape the country with comprehensive antiracist policies. With Trump gone from office, many Americans would not feel the need to be as actively antiracist anymore. This path, while it would rid America from overt racism, would not get to the core of the problem.[129]

The second path forward, posits Kendi, is that Americans finally realize that they are at a point of no return. "No returning to the old habit of denial. No returning to cynicism. No returning to normal, the normal in which racist policies, defended by racist ideas, lead to racial inequities."[130]

On this second path forward, Trump's state of perpetual denial of racism will permanently change the way Americans view themselves. Under this path forward, the one-term Trump presidency will provide a real and lasting reckoning. The protests we witnessed this spring and summer will transform state legislatures, C-suites, and university-admissions offices. This is the great hope moving forward. On this path, Kendi suggests that Americans will demand equitable results, not just speeches that make themselves feel good. On this path forward, he hopes the American people will give their policy makers an ultimatum: use your power to radically reduce inequity and injustice or expect to be voted out in the next election.

In closing this deeply thoughtful and uplifting article, Abram Kendi says:

> The abolition of slavery seemed as impossible in the 1850s as equality seems today. But just as the abolitionists of the 1850s demanded the immediate eradication of slavery, immediate equality must be the demand today. Abolish police violence. Abolish mass incarceration. Abolish the racial wealth gap and the gap in school funding. Abolish barriers to citizenship.

Abolish voter suppression. Abolish healthcare disparities. Not in 20 years. Not in 10 years. Now.[131]

Incidentally, in this truly thought-provoking and soul-searching
article, the author, Ibram Kendi, revealed that he was recently diagnosed with colon cancer. My prayers are with this man and his
family. About two weeks before the 2020 election, I had been going
through a three-month illness with horrible fatigue, nonstop migraine
headaches, weight loss, and the wonder if I would ever get better.
Fortunately, our family physician and his nurse practitioner took the
time and listened carefully, ran many tests, and sent me to a rheuma-
tologist who diagnosed an autoimmune disease (giant cell arteritis).
He sent me the same day to an ophthalmologist who the same day sent
me to the emergency room at Piedmont Hospital in Newton, Georgia,
for a 1,000 mg infusion of prednisone, which likely saved my vision
and almost immediately caused me to feel like I was finally on the road
to recovery. My gratitude to these four medical professionals and the
rest of their caring and friendly staff cannot be put into words, but I
will try. Thank you from the bottom of my heart. Without your caring
and knowledge, I would not have been able to write this book and get
back to life. Again, it is my sincerest hope that all turns out well for
Ibram Kendi as well.

In an NPR online interview, titled, "Americans Say President
Trump Has Worsened Race Relations Since George Floyd's Death,"
dated June 5, 2020, the Domenico Montanaro reveals that two-thirds
of Americans say President Trump has increased racial tensions after the death of George Floyd, according to a new NPR/PBS News
Hour/Marist poll. In the same poll, Trump's job approval numbers
continued to remain upside down, 41 percent approval and 55 percent
disapproval. Of the those disapproving of the president's job performance, 47 percent disapproved strongly.[132]

This poll in early June showed Joe Biden making gains among
the following groups in a head-to-head matchup with Donald Trump:
independents, Whites, women, and people living in suburbs. The
poll also revealed that Donald Trump was viewed as responsible

for increasing racial tensions by about 90 percent of Democrats and African Americans, about 75 percent of independents, and 63 percent of Whites. Even among Republicans, about 60 percent said Trump was responsible for increasing racial tensions, or they were not sure. Between Trump and Biden, 52 percent of the people polled thought Biden would do a better job on race relations compared to 34 percent for Trump.[133]

Throughout the protests, Donald Trump attempted to portray the protesters as angry, violent, and radical. Interestingly, the polling showed most Americans disagreed with his characterizations. Overall, 62 percent of the people polled by Marist viewed the actions of the demonstrators around the country as legitimate and justified as opposed to unlawful. This was true for Democrats and independents; however, 59 percent of Republicans viewed the protests as unlawful. In this interview, Montanaro stressed that these numbers represented a sea change in the attitudes of Americans since the civil rights movement of the 1960s.[134]

Polling on the attitude of people toward the police showed that most people still felt their local police treated Blacks and Whites equally, but that the percentage had declined by 8 percent compared to 2014 when Marist last asked these questions. However, within the Black community, there was a huge racial divide with about 50 percent saying they have little or no confidence that the police treat everyone equally regardless of race.[135]

In a transcript of a *Washington Post* podcast, "Trump and race: How the president's rhetoric and policies divide us," dated October 27, 2020, Allison Michaels lays out a compelling case that Donald Trump was and still is a man who uses race to divide Americans. She opens the conversation by pointing out the long and ugly racial history of our country. Although founded under the idea that all men are created equal, the United States has not lived up to those words for much of its history. Some presidents, like Woodrow Wilson, used the power of the office of the presidency to enforce segregation, while others like Dwight Eisenhower and John F. Kennedy used executive power to fight against it. Others have used the bully pulpit to calm racial tension during times of crisis or to unite the nation under one creed. She cited several examples:

> George W. Bush: "The enemy of America is not our many Muslim friends. It is not our many Arab friends."

> Jimmy Carter: "I say to you, quite frankly, that the time for racial discrimination is over."

> Barack Obama: "For native born Americans, it means reminding ourselves that the stereotypes about immigrants today were said almost word for word about the Irish and Italians and Poles, who it was said were going to destroy the fundamental character of America. And, as it turned out, America wasn't weakened by the presence of these newcomers. These newcomers embraced this nation's creed, and this nation was strengthened."[136]

By contrast, of course, we have President Trump, who relishes in exploiting racial prejudice for political gain. He cannot seem to stop himself from using racial dog whistles when communicating with his tribe of followers, nor can he seem to denounce White supremacists without eventually backtracking and showering them with praise.

The United States political system has been on a path of increased partisanship for at least the past twenty-five years, but this partisanship has ratcheted up dramatically in the last four years under Donald Trump's leadership. In this transcript of her podcast, Allison Michaels highlights the rising tensions in our country surrounding race where Trump's rhetoric, policies, and relationship with local law enforcement have combined to leave us more divided than the country has been, perhaps, since the Civil War. In this podcast, she interviews Philip Rucker, Washington bureau chief for the *Washington Post*. Rucker mentions how not only does Trump sometimes make outright racist comments, but he also amplifies and supports racism from many of his supporters, for instance, not calling them out when they are waving Confederate flags or when they are using hateful, racist language at his rallies. Rucker believes Trump gins up the racial animas deliberately because he believes it helps him politically by energizing, mobilizing, and galvanizing his aggrieved White supporters who see and are upset about the demographic changes taking place in America. Many of these supporters want to see America as it was when they were growing up—White-dominated.[137]

Trump's racial record, along with his father, Fred Trump, is quite blemished. Both have been defendants in numerous lawsuits including evidence of racial discrimination in housing and rental policies. In addition, there was the advertisement Trump paid for about the Central Park Five, an inflammatory full-page ad in several New York newspapers calling for the reinstatement of the death penalty after five Black and Latino teens were accused of raping a woman in Central Park in 1989. Thirteen years later, those teens were exonerated, but Donald Trump refused to apologize for the ad or admit he was wrong. When Trump decided to run for president, most Americans were unfamiliar with his history regarding race relations. The Republican Party focused their message in 2016 on the economy, taxes, and government spending. Trump focused on these too, but he also included messages that free trade policies were destroying manufacturing and unfettered immigration was destroying our culture.

> Working class Americans are left to pay the price for mass illegal immigration, reduced jobs, lower wages, overburdened schools, hospitals that are so crowded, you can't get in, increased crime, and a depleted social safety net.[138]

Trump's approach in describing immigrants was unusual. Per Philip Rucker, he was much more extreme than any previous presidential candidates. He not only suggested they were harming the economy, but he also equated them with bringing crime and violence into the country and used quite hateful language to describe them.

> When Mexico sends it people, they're not sending their best. They're sending people that have lots of problems. They're bringing drugs. They're bringing crime. They're rapists. And some, I assume, are good people.[139]

Another guest on the podcast, Dr. Rashawn Ray, a fellow at the Brookings Institute, whose research focuses on racial and social inequality and police-civilian relations, when asked about whether Trump's rhetoric in 2016 was a liability, said it was not, and that research showed it contributed to his victory. He believed his comments were not dog whistles aimed at a small, targeted base of White supremacists but instead were simply loud calls aimed at his entire base of supporters. Allison Michaels pointed out that at the time, 2016, many Republicans thought that when he became president, he might dial down his heated race-related rhetoric, but instead he became emboldened and tuned it up. "Interestingly and not unexpectedly, hate crimes increased by over 200 percent in the locations where Trump used his bully pulpit," Michaels said.[140]

Dr. Ray brought up how Trump continuously framed COVID-19 as the "Chinese virus." He was trying to play to the stereotypes about immigrants from Asia, and particularly China. He also pointed out that much of Trump's language and political messaging to people living in suburbs was tied to race. The Trump quote below is the one he used to try to attract suburban voters, particularly college-educated women, where late campaign polling and exit-polling revealed that he was hemorrhaging support.

> If you have a predominantly white, stable, middle-class community with low crime, if we don't change policies and if you don't reelect me, you're going to see your neighborhood fall to high crime. It's going to fall

to low-income people. And the racial composition of
your neighborhood is going to change.[141]

A particularly egregious time (mentioned previously) when
Trump's racism spilled into the open was in the aftermath of the
deadly White supremacist rally in Charlottesville, Virginia, in 2017.
After neo-Nazis marched with flaming torches through the streets
of Charlottesville, the president said that he thought there were good
people on both sides of the debate. Really! Really! Are you kidding
me! No wonder he became a loser one-term president.

A second particularly egregious moment (also previously mentioned but worth emphasizing) was when the president suggested
that four congresswomen, all obviously US citizens, should go back
to the countries from which they originated. The problem for Trump
was this: they were citizens from the United States by birthright or
naturalization of citizenship.

A third incident (also previously mentioned but worth emphasizing) was after the killing of George Floyd by Minneapolis policeman
Derek Chauvin. The president, after that tragic event, did everything
in his power to pit Black Americans against White Americans by the
way he talked about the Black Lives Matter movement, the protests in
the streets, and the law-and-order efforts. He specifically referred to
the protesters as dogs who needed to be dealt with harshly and firmly
by the police when an overwhelming majority of the protesters were
nonviolent. Some past presidents have uttered dog whistle language
to describe African Americans such as the pejorative phrase "welfare
queens." Trump went far beyond dog whistles in communicating his
overt racism to his base. Apparently, according to Dr. Ray, Trump
viewed any type of publicity as good, even when it was clearly foul
and racist in content and context.

Next, Dr. Ray addressed Allison Michaels's question about
whether this hostile and inflammatory rhetoric translated itself into actual policy. A good example he mentioned was a Trump memo to government agency heads instructing them to not engage in implicit-bias
training. He also tried to define certain civil rights organizations as

radical and dangerous. The irony is that the Department of Homeland Security has pushed back strongly against this by stating:

> Well, when we actually look at the evidence, the groups that we should frame as terrorist groups and the biggest threat to our democracy and our security are actually right-wing extremist groups, particularly white-nationalist and white-supremacist groups.[142]

Dr. Ray also discussed the implications of Trump's actions to reduce the ability of the CDC and other government agencies to attack the disproportionate impact of the COVID-19 virus on communities of color. This racial animus also was demonstrated by Trump's heavy-handed approach toward protesters by clearing them out across from the White House so that he could attend a photo op outside a nearby church, and by his deployment of reserve troops in several cities like Portland and Seattle despite protests from their mayors. He did not deploy active-duty troops, though he did deploy law enforcement officers to Portland and Seattle as well as several other cities in response to the protests.[143]

When asked by the moderator, Allison Michaels, whether there was any truth to Trump's claim that he had done more for Black people than any other president, Dr. Ray said Trump would respond that the Black unemployment rate was among the lowest ever under his presidency. However, he said that that was before the pandemic hit, and that being employed does not necessarily mean that your job enables you to maintain a decent standard of living for you and your family. Nor does it mean that it will cover your rent or health insurance. Many of the jobs held by members of the Black and Latino community were front-line jobs with heavier exposure to COVID-19. Examples were public transportation, retail grocery, and meatpacking.[144]

The second thing Dr. Ray mentioned that Donald Trump would point to would be criminal justice reform, the First Step Act. This bipartisan legislation passed in 2018 aimed to reduce the rate of incarceration of Black people and the mandatory minimum sentences.

Trump took credit for signing this legislation, but the person who pushed this through the Senate was New Jersey Senator Corey Booker, a Democrat.[145]

Allison Michaels next asked Dr. Ray if he thought this moment in history (right before the 2020 election) seemed different. She asked if he thought there was more racial awareness, and if he thought the country was ripe for real change? Dr. Ray answered that the events of 2020 have been so frequent and so stunning that he believes the past year will forever change America. I must say that I strongly agree with him. Watching various news reports and videos of the police shooting Jacob Blake in Kenosha, Wisconsin and choking George Floyd in Minneapolis were so jarring and emotional that I think my perspective changed in a profound way. In the past, I felt there were instances of police brutality in the United States, but I never thought it was that widespread. These two events and many others this past year crystalized in my mind the pervasiveness of this racial divide. I felt the frustration and the anger that most people of color were no doubt feeling, not in a calculated logical way, but in a sad, strong emotional way. Polling on the issue of the Black Lives Matter protests and overall race relations in the United States supported this time as a seminal moment in history. More Americans were in support of the protesters than in support of President Trump's law and order rhetoric. The year 2020 forced Americans, both White and Black, to face up to racial disparities that have existed since the birth of our nation. The widespread unrest and the increased demand for real action are a testament to the impact of the police brutality observed with our own eyes and the president's heated, racially charged words heard with our own ears.[146]

In closing this podcast interview, Allison Michael asked Dr. Ray if he thought Trump would moderate his language in the closing days of the campaign. Dr. Ray expressed his opinion that it was unlikely. He said:

> I suspect not, in part because I don't think very much about Trump at all changes. He's a 74-year-old man.

He's stubborn, to some degree, like a lot of 74-year-old men. And he is who he is. He's Donald J. Trump. And I think what he believes is largely what he says. And I don't see him changing his beliefs even if he wins a second term. In fact, I think if he wins a second term, he will interpret that as validation for his beliefs, for the things that he has said, and a sign that, you know, if he behaves this way and makes these sorts of comments about race, not only will he not be held accountable for it, or punished for it, but he will, in fact, be rewarded for it by the American people.[147]

I think it is quite clear that Dr. Ray was spot-on in his opinion. Not only did Donald Trump not change his rhetoric, but he also doubled down on it, and suffered defeat after one term in office.

Let us now look back in time to one year after his 2016 election victory. About 60 percent of Americans said his election led to worse race relations, and only 8 percent said that it had improved race relations. For former president Obama one year after his election, only 13 percent of Americans said his election had led to worse race relations.[148]

One year after Trump's election, 40 percent of Whites said race relations were generally good, while only 28 percent of Blacks and only 3 percent of Hispanics said the same. One year after Trump's election, 44 percent of the public thought not enough attention was being paid to racial issues. Polling after George Floyd's death, referenced earlier in this chapter, revealed that Trump's standing on the issue of race relations had regressed by the late spring and summer of 2020.[149]

In the *Los Angeles Times*, an article, "Trump and Biden couldn't be more different on the complicated issue of race," dated August 17, 2020, the author, Tyrone Beason, highlights many examples of Donald Trump's reckless remarks and tweets about race. Besides the numerous examples already cited, he makes a great point about how Trump seems so unaware of basic facts about life in America for Black Americans. For instance, Blacks have a much higher rate of being killed in interactions with the police, or that despite historically low unemployment prepandemic, the wealth gap between Black households and White households remains as wide as it was thirty years ago. According to Beason, Trump has been "defensive, obtuse, and vulgar" when discussing racial inequities, White supremacist violence, and his own stereotyping of Black people, Latinos, Muslims, Asians, and immigrants from Central America as threats to public health and safety.[150]

At a rally in Duluth, Minnesota, Trump said that Joe Biden would turn the state into a "refugee camp" and that Minnesota would be "overrun and destroyed." He has in the past referred to some majority Black countries as "shithole countries," and that the United States "should prefer immigrants from places like Norway." He even suggested that Kamala Harris, born in Oakland, California, might not be eligible to serve as vice president. Trump was literally playing the same false card he played against President Obama.[151]

In fairness to Trump, he did sign the Tax Cuts and Jobs Act into law in 2017 creating enterprise zones in census tracts where the poverty rate was about twice as high as the rest of the country. He also signed a bipartisan bill that renewed annual funding for Black colleges and universities.

Despite these positive acts, the president launched his campaign promising to build a wall along the US-Mexico border. His no-tolerance immigration policies led to the separation of over six hundred children from their parents, who were seeking protection as asylum seekers at the US border. The parents were deported to their original countries while the children were kept in the United States, still separated from their parents. This policy cannot be viewed by anyone with a semblance of decency as anything other than child abuse.

Joe Biden, who, thankfully, won the presidential election despite Trump's efforts to subvert the election results, could not be any more different than our lame-duck president on issues of race and immigration. Joe Biden is a man who has a strong vision of unity and hope, but he is not a Pollyanna. During a speech in Philadelphia in early June, he said the following:

> The battle for the soul of this nation has been a constant push and pull for more than 240 years, a tug of war between the American ideal that we're all created equal and the harsh reality that racism has long torn us apart.[152]

As a candidate, Biden promised not to ever exploit the nation's racial wounds for political gain like his Republican opponent, Donald Trump. Black voters, especially those over age fifty, backed Biden by very wide margins. He had a long-standing relationship with the Black community through his support for civil rights legislation and his service as vice president under Barack Obama.

His past included some controversial positions on race. In the 1970s as a young senator, he allied with segregationists to fight against court-ordered busing in Boston. He also was criticized over his support for the 1994 crime bill that had been blamed for mass incarceration of young Black men. In the past, he has occasionally made clumsy statements that appeared tone-deaf or insensitive. Despite the occasional verbal fumble and the distant support of two policies that were not in the best interests of the Black community, he has been a reliable ally of the civil rights movement.

Although he has not been a supporter of reparations for the descendants of enslaved Africans, he has recently proposed some detailed plans to close the wealth gap between Black and White Americans as well as to fight inequities in the criminal justice system, housing, education, and elsewhere in the economy. He has also promised to appoint the first Black woman to the US Supreme Court. He plans to expand home ownership among people of color by creating a new tax credit of $15,000 to help low-income and middle-income families buy their first home. Biden also wants to create a $30 billion Small Business Opportunity Fund to expand public-private partnerships in communities of color. He promised to eliminate state and local regulations, including discriminatory zoning ordinances that make it harder for people of color to buy or rent a home. He plans to direct more than $50 billion in venture capital funds to small businesses owned by Black entrepreneurs and other people of color. He plans to require the Federal Reserve to track data on racial disparities in the economy and to report those figures regularly.[153]

In the area of criminal justice reform, he is committed to more accountability and transparency for police officers who use deadly force and to provide better training for all police officers. He promised to eliminate mandatory minimum sentences for nonviolent crimes, to reform the cash bail system, and the practice of incarcerating people for drug use alone.

Joe Biden promised to create a path to citizenship for the nation's eleven million immigrants in the country illegally as well as longtime refugees from countries devastated by natural disasters and civil unrest who are shielded under Temporary Protected Status. He would offer free tuition for Latino, Black, and Native American students whose families make less than $125,000 a year at public colleges and universities, historically Black colleges and universities (HBCUs) and at other private educational institutions that serve people of color. Also, his platform calls for forgiveness of federal student loan debt related to undergraduate tuition from HBCUs and minority-serving institutions for debt holders earning $125,000 or less annually.[154]

Joe Biden also promised to direct the Justice Department to prioritize the prosecution of hate crimes, which surged during the Trump presidency.

On NPR in a report transcript titled "From Debate Stage, Trump Declines to Denounce White Supremacy," dated September 30, 2020, the author, Sarah McCammon, discusses how President Trump declines criticizing and denouncing White supremacy. During an exchange on the debate stage, moderator Chris Wallace repeatedly asked Donald Trump if he would condemn White supremacists. Trump replied by blaming violence on left wing groups and eventually by saying, "Proud Boys, stand back and stand by." As mentioned before, the federal government has judged White supremacist terrorism among the most serious threats facing the nation. In recent testimony to the House Homeland Security Committee, FBI Director Christopher Wray said that most domestic terrorism threats and violence come from "racially motivated violent extremism," mostly from people who subscribe to White supremacist ideologies.[155]

Contradicting Trump's assertions, Wray described antifa as an ideology or movement rather than an organized group. He did say the FBI was investigating some cases involving people who self-identified with antifa. He also said protest-related violence did not appear to be well organized or connected to one group. While protests at times turned violent, most of the protests were peaceful.[156]

Trump had a history of refusing to denounce racism and White nationalism and then awkwardly partially reversing himself. During the 2016 campaign, he was forced to issue a clarification after initially refusing to condemn former Ku Klux Klan leader, David Duke.[157]

In the summer of 2020, the Senate Armed Services Committee voted to strip military bases of Confederate names, monuments, and symbols within three years. Trump opposed this vociferously on Twitter, trying to spur other Republicans to resist this effort to remove Confederate names and statues. Unfortunately for the president, many members of his own party expressed an openness to the idea of removing Confederate names, monuments, statues, and symbols as protests against police brutality and racism spread around the country.

A Defense Department panel set up in response to the Senate Armed Services Committee vote supporting removal of Confederate names on military bases and statues also included a ban on the use of military force against peaceful protesters around the country and against the use of the National Guard against protesters in Washington, DC.

Below is a list of US military bases named after Confederate generals.

Fort Lee—Robert E. Lee

Fort Bragg—Braxton Bragg

Fort Pickett—George Pickett

Fort AP Hill—Ambrose Powell Hill Jr.

Camp Beauregard—P. T. Beauregard

Fort Benning—Henry Benning

Fort Gordon—John Brown Gordon

Fort Hood—John Bell Hood

I do not believe in erasing history and destroying all Confederate statues around the country. I do believe, however, the most suitable places to locate these statues are in Civil War museums and in national battlefields run by the National Park System. These are places people can affirmatively choose to visit. I do not think they should be located on the grounds of public offices, city streets, or public parks because these are locations most people cannot avoid. Black citizens are almost forced to see these as daily reminders of the people who fought to keep their ancestors enslaved. As a White person, I might not fully understand the pain and anger they feel regarding these statues, but I can appreciate the affront to their ancestors these statues represent. Celebrating those responsible for conducting a civil war to maintain people in bondage is not something worth celebrating. A particularly offensive example is the bust of Nathan Bedford Forrest, a Confederate cavalry general, on the grounds of the Tennessee Capital building in Nashville, Tennessee. To visit or do business at the state capital, African Americans should not be expected to walk by a bust of a man responsible for the massacre of surrendering Black Union troops at Fort Pillow and the first grand wizard (1867–69) of the Ku Klux Klan in Tennessee.

In the *Guardian*, an article titled "Trump's refusal to condemn white supremacy fits pattern of extremist rhetoric," dated September 30, 2020, by Adam Gabbatt, describes Trump's willingness to use inflammatory rhetoric to motivate his voting base. In addition to his unwillingness to confront White nationalists and White suprema-cists, Trump leans heavily on extremist rhetoric to stoke unfounded fears of voter fraud. As discussed previously, he planted this seed in the minds of his voters before the election and continues to water the crop of lies to this day. His goal is to destroy the legitimacy of democracy and the victory by Joe Biden. He encouraged his people to occupy polling stations, and he encouraged right-wing militias to protest while armed at state capitals.

During one of the debates, Donald Trump was asked if he was willing to condemn White supremacist and militia groups, and in-stead of answering the question directly, he deflected the question and equated the violence at various protests with left-wing groups. After initially indicating that he did not know who the Proud Boys were or what they stood for, he then asked the Proud Boys, a White supremacist group, "to stand down, but stand by."[158]

This pattern of encouraging his supporters to behave like his personal vanguard of shock troops is like nothing we have ever seen before. He wanted his people at polling stations to intimidate po-tential Black and Brown voters. He wanted his people at rallies to shout, "Lock her up," referring to the governor of Michigan, Gretchen Whimer, even after a plot to kidnap and murder her had been uncov-ered by the FBI. He defended Kyle Rittenhouse, a militia member who attended MAGA rallies and then murdered two people in Kenosha, Wisconsin, and wounded a third person. He encouraged people to de-scend on locations where votes were being counted. Election workers at one of these locations in Arizona had to be escorted to their cars by the police late in the evening because of fear that a snarling, hostile pro-Trump crowd might attack them.

The author of this article summarizes Trump's symbiotic rela-tionship with White nationalists and White supremacists with the closing quote from Rashad Robinson, president of Color of Change, a nonprofit civil rights group:

> Donald Trump needs white nationalists at the ready
> because he needs violence to win the election. He

wants white nationalists to invade polling places across the country and prevent voters from voting, to invade our streets and attack people who are protesting, and to prevent ballots from being counted.

He made clear that his campaign is not about winning votes. It's about holding on to power—no matter the cost.[159]

Donald Trump's attachment to White supremacists and his dependence on protracting racial division within the United States is, to him, like oxygen he needs to breath. He has left an ugly legacy, a historical footprint that is going to be impossible for him and his political party to eradicate. He left the incoming president a political climate marred by deep distrust, anger, and hyperpartisan division. Far from a patriot, Donald Trump is a traitor willing to sacrifice racial harmony to maintain his throne of power.

Let us look again at the implications of the death of George Floyd on American public opinion. In a previously cited article, "Trump's Indifference Amounts to Negligent Homicide," the following emotional paragraph is well worth quoting.

"This past summer, viewers around the world saw eight minutes and 46 seconds on video that few of them will ever forget. That's how long a Minneapolis police officer kept his knee on the neck of the prone George Floyd. The officer's face was impassive, barely showing interest, as his victim pleaded, and struggled, and choked, and died. The officer's affect was like that of a fisherman, watching his catch flop helplessly toward death as it ran out of breath on the pier. Legally, the courts have yet to determine what those eight minutes and 46 seconds meant; the officer has pleaded not guilty to second-degree manslaughter and second-degree murder. But the video had such power because people around the world understood what they were seeing. One man was in control of another. One man calmly watched as another died. In the layman's sense of the term, these were images of manslaughter, of homicide."[160]

Fortunately, Derek Chauvin was convicted on all counts of the murder of George Floyd. Three other Minneapolis police officers will stand trial for not stopping Chauvin's deadly actions or rendering aid to the victim.

CHAPTER 5

IMMIGRATION, XENOPHOBIA, AND THE WALL

ON THE OXFAM website, in an article titled "Politics of Poverty, 5 ways President Trump's xenophobic agenda has accelerated during the COVID-19 pandemic," dated April 30, 2020, the author, Noah Gottschalk, discusses how President Trump has used the coronavirus public health crisis to deny asylum seekers their rights and to make generational changes to immigration policy. From the very beginning of his administration, Donald Trump has launched multiple blistering attacks on America's fundamental values of welcome, inclusion, and tolerance. Rather than de-emphasizing these attacks during the coronavirus crisis, the administration has redoubled its efforts. The author, Noah Gottschalk, lists and discusses five of the most damaging attacks by the Trump administration that need to be urgently opposed by Congress and the American people.

PUSHING A NEW IMMIGRATION BAN THAT SCAPEGOATS IMMIGRANTS

President Trump's new executive order restricting immigration is probably his most flagrant attempt to use COVID-19 as justification to implement his toxic and radical xenophobic agenda. Although the ban was initially presented as a temporary response to the economic impact of the coronavirus pandemic, it quickly became apparent that it was a fundamental focus of the administration's long-term strategy to dramatically restrict immigration to the United States.

The Trump administration has a long record of undermining workers' rights from efforts to eliminate protections for child labor and overtime. Recently, it reduced reporting requirements around COVID and failed to provide clear guidance and enforcement during the pandemic. Instead, the administration prioritized trying to force meat processing facilities to remain open over the health and safety of their workers. Immigrants are on the front line of the meat-packing industry, risking their health to keep this important industry running during the pandemic. This executive order should not be a distraction to the Trump administration's horrible record on labor rights or its appalling failures responding to the pandemic.[161]

DENYING ASYLUM SEEKERS THEIR LEGAL RIGHTS AT THE US-MEXICO BORDER

President Trump's relentless focus on the US-Mexico border continued throughout his presidency. His shrill claims that the wall is needed more than ever pales in comparison to the fact that the United States has the most coronavirus cases and deaths in the world. Mexico and Central American countries are at greater risk of new infections from the United States than the other way around.

Rather than working to stop the spread of the virus from the United States, the administration is strengthening its efforts to keep people with a low likelihood of spreading the virus out of the United States, including people fleeing violence and persecution in their countries of origin. Turning people away who are seeking safety in the United States violates the international legal principle of refoulement, which mandates that countries cannot return people to a country or territory where they might face persecution, imprisonment, or death. There are no exceptions to this lifesaving obligation to not force people back into potential great harm. As Oxfam has argued to the administration, proper testing, quarantining, and other protective measures can be used and implemented to fulfill dual obligations—to protect the health and safety of the American people and to protect people fleeing violence and persecution in their home countries.[162]

EXCLUDING UNDOCUMENTED IMMIGRANTS AND THEIR FAMILIES FROM CORONAVIRUS RELIEF

An estimated eleven million undocumented people live in cities and towns spread across America. They work in critical industries on the front lines in agriculture and construction. They pay into systems like Social Security, unemployment insurance, and Medicaid despite the inability to collect any of these benefits. Millions have borne and raised children who are now productive US citizens. Congress' exclusion of undocumented people and their families has left these people less able to afford food, clothing, housing, and health care. International law requires nation states to respect the health of all people within their borders, regardless of migratory or other legal status. The website Oxfam, the source of this referenced article, is working diligently to ensure that the next stimulus package passed by Congress does not make the same mistake of ignoring these people, and in the interim is pushing state governments to provide whatever relief they can.[163]

CONTINUING IMMIGRATION ENFORCEMENT AND UNSAFE DETENTION

The Trump administration continues to undermine the well-being of immigrant communities throughout the country by harassing immigration raids and arrests. These actions instill and spread fear among the people in these communities, keeping them mainly in their homes and deterring them from seeking necessary medical care when needed.

Raids and arrests separate mothers and fathers from their children, forcing them into our country's huge and nontransparent immigration detention system. The COVID-19 epidemic has revealed the ugly, pervasive inhumanity of the US immigration detention system. Imprisoning vulnerable people, violating their human dignity, and putting at risk the health of both the detained migrants and the detention center workers and staff is not something our nation should be proud of. It reminds me of the callous and careless contempt our country has often shown toward our indigenous people on American Indian reservations. These immigration detention centers are especially vulnerable to the spread of COVID-19 because of well-documented substandard conditions, overcrowding, and poor and limited access to health care. This system is costly and unnecessary compared to better alternatives with a proven track record of success.

Oxfam is supporting legislation sponsored by New Jersey Senator Corey Booker and Representative Pramila Jayapai, that would restrict immigration enforcement activities to apprehending dangerous criminals, not families looking for a better life. One of the goals of this legislation is to ensure the release of people from detention starting with the people most vulnerable to the coronavirus.[164]

CONTINUING DEPORTATIONS

As global air traffic has slowed markedly since the beginning of the coronavirus pandemic, the Trump administration is continuing its deportation flights, sending people who may have been exposed to the virus while in detention to countries not well prepared to receive them and to medically treat them. This is particularly a problem in Central America. "The medical infrastructure in Guatemala is insufficient to respond to a public health crisis of this magnitude (20% of the country's cases are deported people from the US). In Honduras, an estimated 1.5 million residents do not have access to medicine or hospitals because of the lack of medicine and hospitals." The Trump administration, according to Oxfam, should immediately stop these deportations under the Asylum Cooperative Agreement to Guatemala, Honduras, and El Salvador to prevent further spread of the coronavirus.

Oxfam and its financial supporters are fighting hard on behalf of these undocumented people who have been marginalized for too long by this country. They hope that members of Congress will hear from their constituents, who are unwilling to accept this xenophobic agenda any longer. We have been asked by our Lord and Savior, Jesus Christ, to love our neighbors as ourselves. We need to live out our faith. America is at our best when we show our love, not when we react with fear.[165]

In *Politico*, an article titled "Behind Trump's final push to limit immigration," dated November 30, 2020, the author, Anita Kumar, criticizes the Trump administration's efforts since Election Day to change visa processing and citizenship testing to facilitate a large-scale reduction in immigration. These changes include making it easier to deny visas to immigrants, lengthening the citizenship test, and appointing new hard-line members to an immigration policy board.

Some of the president's aides have even urged the president to take on birthright citizenship. The author cites two people familiar with the discussions who believed this would not be legal given that birthright citizenship is enshrined in the Constitution. A third person familiar with the discussions said this attempt at negating birthright citizenship has been dismissed.

These moves appear to be an attempt to make his administration's legacy on immigration permanent. It started with his sweeping ban on travel from Muslim countries, then his separation of children from their parents at the US-Mexico border, and finally his extreme reductions on refugees and temporary foreign workers. Now his focus has been to limit the incoming president, Joe Biden, from reversing these policies. Ali Noorani, executive director of the National Immigration Forum, an immigration advocacy group, said: "The Trump administration has been widely effective in terms of grinding our immigration system to a halt."[166]

Presidents often push through last-minute changes before they leave office, but Trump's actions seem to have an increased urgency perhaps because they thought they would have a second term to accomplish their immigration wish list. The president continues to claim the election was stolen and still refuses to acknowledge Joe Biden as the new president. Trump's team has mobilized quickly to enact changes in the waning days of his presidency such as troop withdrawals and repeal of various environmental regulations. The final push on immigration has been overseen by Stephen Miller, the senior aide who has guided Trump's immigration policies for the last four years.

Trump failed to fulfill some of his immigration promises. The most significant was his attempt to end the Obama-era program Deferred Action for Childhood Arrivals (DACA). Despite having lost in the courts before on this issue and overwhelming support for continuing this program, Trump terminated the DACA program. Fortunately, the US Supreme Court overturned their action, citing that it violated the Administrative Procedure Act. Trump made immigration the centerpiece of his campaign in 2016 and in the midterms in 2018. In 2020 he talked less about this issue because the country was in the throes of the COVID-19 pandemic.

Joe Biden has vowed to undo Trump's immigration policies and to work with Congress to put together a comprehensive immigration deal. This will not be an easy piece of legislation to craft and then pass. In the past several decades, Congress has tried to pass comprehensive immigration reform. In some ways this issue reminds me of attempts to reform Social Security. The saying was, "Don't touch the third rail of Social Security." Both parties have been very dug in on their positions. Attempts at building a bipartisan coalition have so far failed. Any new laws or executive actions will face much legal scrutiny.

Everything pushed by Trump during the remaining weeks of his lame-duck presidency complicated Biden's efforts to reverse the Trump initiatives. Some of the Trump efforts relate to ongoing initiatives and other efforts are new, proposed since the election. Efforts to enact new regulations at that late date in a president's term were impeded by federal law mandating waiting periods for any major regulatory changes.[167]

Some changes, however, can be enacted quickly. On November 13, 2020, for instance, the citizenship test that used to be one hundred questions will now be 128 questions with more questions on history and politics. Four days later, the administration said it would give federal immigration officials more discretion in approving immigration applications through updates in the US Citizenship and Immigration Services Policy Manual. The update will provide officers with an expanded list of positive and negative factors that they can use to either accept or reject applicants. Trump administration officials have said the new language would make decisions fair and consistent. Immigration advocates dispute this, saying the new factors, such as strength of family ties, history of employment, and community standing would lead to longer processing times and more denials.[168]

The same day, the administration published a proposed rule that would limit work permits for immigrants awaiting deportation but not in custody. The administration was also trying to push through more restrictions on the H-1B high-skilled worker visa program, which it says US employers were abusing by replacing American workers with cheaper foreign labor. The update would reduce the types of jobs foreign workers can apply for, while also requiring employers to pay foreign workers more. It also wants to abandon the normal random lottery process for these visas, instead, replacing it with a prioritization program for employers offering the highest-paid positions.[169]

Most US business groups have opposed these changes, but Trump's hardline base supports them. Other groups are pushing the Trump administration to go further in the closing days of his presidency. Chris Chmielenski, deputy director at NumbersUSA, which supports immigration restrictions, said he hopes the administration will limit a program that provides work permits to international students, something the Trump administration previously considered, but never moved forward. Without question, there was considerable pressure within the administration and outside the administration to push hard right up until the last day in office.

In *USA Today*, an article titled "Biden might need years to reverse Trump's immigration policies on DACA, asylum, family separation, ICE raids, private detention and more," dated November 13, 2020, by Alan Gomez and Daniel Gonzalez, discusses what can be done to reverse Trump immigration policies and how difficult it will be to do so. Untangling Trump's policies will be difficult because so many are overlapping. Joe Biden needs to avoid overwhelming the entire system and to avoid encouraging another new wave of migrants. The authors of this referenced article look at twelve of these policy moves and evaluate the difficulty and the likelihood of success reversing them.

ELIMINATING THE TRAVEL BAN

On September 4, 2017, by executive order, Donald Trump signed his travel ban, which implemented a complete and total shutdown of Muslims from entering the United States from eight countries (mostly Muslim, along with North Korea and Venezuela) and which halted the refugee program. This was his third attempt at implementing a travel ban; the first two attempts were blocked by federal judges because they were "steeped in animus and directed at a single religious group." This version was initially blocked by a federal judge, but it was ultimately upheld by the US Supreme Court and still is in force.

The Trump administration maintained that the ban was needed to overhaul the process by which foreigners were vetted to ensure that terrorists were not entering the country through legal channels. Opponents believe it undermines who we are as a nation, one that welcomes immigrants as a strength of the nation.

Joe Biden can change this policy by simply issuing a new executive order rescinding the ban and order the Department of Justice to stop defending the Trump travel ban in federal court.[170]

HALTING WALL CONSTRUCTION

On January 25, 2017, by executive order, Trump ordered the federal government to "plan, design, and construct a physical wall along the southern border." Building a wall on the US-Mexico border and making Mexico pay for it was Trump's top campaign promise. Mexico's president steadfastly refused to pay anything for constructing this wall. Congress also refused to fund the $13.2 billion initial estimate to complete the wall. By July, the Trump administration had secured $15 billion for border construction, of which $4.4 billion came from Congress. The remaining (about 60 percent) came from diverting funds from Pentagon accounts for military projects. In February 2019, Trump declared a national emergency over the border crisis to justify taking this money from the military accounts to fund the barrier construction on the southern border.

When Trump took office in 2017, there were 653 miles of border barriers in place, which was about a third of the length of the total border. Of the 653 miles of existing barriers, 350 miles was fencing to prevent pedestrians from crossing the border, and about 300 miles was designed to prevent vehicles from crossing the border.

Since then, the Trump administration has completed about four hundred miles of new fencing as of the end of October 2020 with plans to have completed another fifty miles by the end of the year. Most of the fencing is eighteen- to thirty-foot high "bollard" fencing (long steel slats filled with cement). Most of the fencing is replacement of existing fencing. Very little is actually new fencing.

Joe Biden promised not to tear down any of the construction already completed, but he also promised not to authorize additional barriers. Some additional border fencing will probably get built after

Biden takes office because contracts have already been signed and construction is in process.[171]

REVIVING REFUGEE SYSTEM

On October 28, 2020, Trump signed a presidential determination putting a cap on refugee admissions at fifteen thousand in 2021. One of Trump's first acts as president was to suspend the entire refugee program and indefinitely block all Syrians from entering the United States under the guise of national security. The program was restarted in October 2017, but it was halted again in March 2020 because of the public health concerns over the coronavirus pandemic. The power to set limits on the number of refugees entering the United States each year resides with the president. "The cap has fallen from 110,000 in the final year of Barack Obama's presidency to 50,000 in the first year of Trump's presidency to 15,000 announced by Trump in October of 2020." The reductions in refugee admissions has led to layoffs and office closures at the nine humanitarian organizations that help relocate and assimilate refugees. If Biden raises the cap, it will take time for these organizations to restaff.

Before Donald Trump became president, the cap was normally set each fall. Trump broke with this precedent in March 2017. As a result, Biden could immediately raise the cap upon assuming the duties of the president in January 2021.[172]

PROTECTING DACA

On September 5, 2017, a memo was signed by Elaine Duke, Homeland Security secretary, terminating the Deferred Action for Childhood Arrivals (DACA) program. After supporting this program while running for president in 2016, Trump reversed himself in September

2017, announcing he was going to end it. Nearly 650,000 undocumented immigrants participated in this program, which protected them from deportation and allowed them to legally work in the United States. The Trump administration said it would end the program and issued an ultimatum to Congress to pass a law granting permanent protection to the Dreamers (children of undocumented immigrants born in the United States). Congress and the administration could not reach a deal, and the Dreamers were rescued at the last minute by a federal judge who ruled that the Trump administration used a flawed process to terminate DACA. The case went all the way up to the US Supreme Court, where by a 5-4 decision, the DACA program was upheld. The court ordered the administration to start accepting applications again. This was a huge victory for the Dreamers, who relied on this program to be able to work, to go to school, and to live without the fear of being deported. Most of these people have lived their entire lives in the United States. This was their home.

Biden can mostly fix this by issuing a new memorandum rescinding Donald Trump's 2017 memorandum. During Trump's two-year fight with Congress over this issue, some Dreamers were denied the ability to apply for the protections granted by this program. He will need to grant these protections in a new memorandum. He will also be urged to expand the number of people eligible for DACA and to put DACA recipients on a path to citizenship.[173]

RESTORING THE ASYLUM SYSTEM

On June 11, 2018, a decision signed by then Attorney General Jeff Sessions limited who could apply for asylum in the United States. Asylum is granted to people who fear persecution in their home countries based on their race, religion, nationality, membership in a specific social group, or their political opinion. For years that has included victims of domestic abuse and gang violence. The Trump administration has been trying to eliminate these last two categories of asylum seekers, which has hurt women and members of the LGBTQ community. The Trump administration has been trying to limit or halt asylum requests along the southern border with federal judges striking down several of them. Nevertheless, Trump and his staff keep trying to redefine and limit those who can apply for asylum.

In 2018, Jeff Sessions intervened in an asylum case of a Salvadorean woman who had been repeatedly abused by her husband and had been unable to receive help from the Salvadorean government. Sessions issued an order that claimed only victims of repression by a foreign government, not victims of private crimes, were qualified for asylum. Immigration attorneys have challenged the Sessions directive, and courts have responded with conflicting rulings, depending on the judge drawn for the case. The Trump administration is trying to make the Sessions directive a permanent new regulation in the closing weeks of his term in office. In the meantime, this cruel practice has resulted in many people being denied protection and being returned to dangerous conditions including potential death.

Joe Biden could quickly resolve this by rescinding the Sessions directive. If, however, the regulation implementing the Sessions directive becomes final before Biden takes office, it would take additional months to propose a new rule and get it finalized because new administrative rules must go through a prolonged process of public comments, reviews, and final publication.[174]

ALLOWING MORE IMMIGRANTS TO REQUEST ASYLUM

Customs and Border Protection policy restricts the number of people who can request asylum each day at US ports of entry. In the last year of the Obama administration, customs and border agents began a policy of limiting the number of asylum requests at ports of entry in southern California. The Trump administration continued this metering policy in 2017 and then expanded it to include all ports of entry along our southern border after groups, mostly Central American migrants, began traveling through Mexico in what was then referred to as migrant caravans. The number of asylum seekers allowed each day is limited based on the available space at US holding facilities. The number varies from port to port, but generally is less than fifty per day per port. Those not allowed into the United States are placed on wait lists and turned back to Mexico. At times, the number of asylum seekers has exceeded one thousand per day at some ports of entry. Some of these asylum seekers have waited weeks to months before being granted entry to the United States. This policy was intended to address health and safety concerns from overcrowding at ports of entry and holding stations.

Under US immigration law, people who arrive at the border without legal authorization have the right to seek asylum protections in the United states if they can demonstrate a credible fear of persecution or torture if they are returned to their home country. Critics of the current metering system say it incentivizes illegal border crossings between ports of entry and thus puts migrant asylum seekers and their families in danger from human coyotes, American border vigilantes, and overzealous border patrol agents.

Joe Biden has said he will end the metering policy and return to this simple policy. Each asylum seeker, according to Biden, will be allowed to "make their case instead of sitting in squalor on the other side of the river." To amend or end Trump's policy, Biden would only need to send a memo to Customs and Border Protection (CBD) directors at each port of entry.[175]

ENDING "REMAIN IN MEXICO" PLAN

On January 25, 2019, a memo signed by then director of Homeland Security Kirsten Nielsen ordered asylum seekers to return to Mexico while their cases are being deliberated. In late 2018, the number of Central American migrants (including children) reaching our southern border increased significantly. Fear of political persecution and gang (primarily drug smuggling) violence were the motivating factors causing families to uproot from their native countries and trek northward through Mexico to the United States. To help stem the flow of migrants, the United States tried to broker a deal with Mexico to house these asylum seekers.

When those talks faltered, Kirsten Nielsen signed the Migrant Protection Protocols, better known as the "Remain in Mexico" plan discussed in the previous subsection. The result of this policy was not good. At times, the makeshift border encampments numbered more than sixty thousand migrants, straining local Mexican resources, and causing unsafe living conditions. Migrants complained of robberies, kidnappings, and very unsanitary living conditions. Nielsen and other Trump officials defended the plan by claiming that most migrants previously released into the United States while awaiting decisions on their asylum requests had not showed up for their immigration court appearances. Immigration advocates refuted those claims. "According to a report from the Transactional Records Access Clearinghouse (TRAC), from September 2018 to May 2019, more than 80% of asylum seekers attended all of their court hearings."

The process to rescind this policy simply would require a Homeland Security official to issue a new memorandum rescinding Nielsen's 2019 memorandum. A new system to facilitate, track, and integrate the asylum seekers into the United States during the adjudication processing of their cases would be required to successfully implement it.[176]

REOPENING THE SOUTHERN BORDER

On March 20, 2020, an order was signed by the director of the Centers for Disease Control and Prevention, Robert Redfield, suspending entry of people from countries where communicable disease exists. After limiting international travel from China near the beginning of the coronavirus outbreak, the Trump administration sealed off the northern border with Canada and the southern border with Mexico in March. To seal the border, immigration enforcement agents relied on a law (Title 42) that gave authority to the director of the Centers for Disease Control and Prevention to halt admissions to the United States if their home countries were suffering from a communicable disease. "Through September of 2020, Custom and Border Protection agents have forced nearly 200,000 migrants to return to Mexico including adults, unaccompanied minors, family units, in some cases within a matter of hours."

The order needs to be renewed every thirty days, which means Joe Biden's appointed CDC director could let the last Trump order sunset or issue new guidance limiting the use of Title 42.[177]

PULLING BACK ICE AGENTS

On January 25, 2017, Trump signed an executive order that allowed immigration agents to target all undocumented immigrants for potential arrest. Under former president Obama, Immigration and Custom Enforcement (ICE) agents were ordered to focus on undocumented immigrants with criminal records and to avoid collateral arrests (undocumented immigrants whose path they crossed each day). Trump's order allowed ICE agents to arrest any undocumented immigrant they encountered even if they only had immigration violations, not malicious criminal violations, on their records. Trump also resorted to the practice of large-scale work-site raids, also used by President George W. Bush but largely avoided by President Barack Obama. "The largest raid under Trump involved seven poultry plants in Mississippi in August of 2019 that netted 680 arrests, including two women who were on break breastfeeding their babies when they were arrested."

Joe Biden can easily change this policy with a simple executive order that focuses enforcement priority on undocumented immigrants with criminal records.[178]

ENDING PRIVATE IMMIGRATION DETENTION CENTERS

On January 25, 2017, President Trump signed an executive order that ordered Homeland Security to "allocate all legally available resources" to add more immigration detention centers. The federal government had a history of using private prisons to operate immigration detention centers. "Trump, however, expanded this practice to detain a record number of migrants and enable record profits for private prison companies. The stock prices of two private prison companies, GEO Group and CoreCivic, the two largest prison companies doubled in days after Trump's election. Over the four years of the Trump administration, ICE has signed contracts to open 19 new immigration detention centers run by private companies. Critics have asked ICE to cut their relationship with private prison companies citing widespread reports of abuse against detainees and substandard care." Joe Biden has vowed to halt this practice, arguing that "'no business should profit from the suffering of desperate people fleeing violence.' But that could be one of the most difficult immigration policies to change due to contractual obligations and the government's reliance on the industry." During the past year, ICE has begun signing long-term contracts with private prison companies, thus strengthening the relationship between the federal government and private prisons, and neutering future presidential administrations from doing much about it. "USA Today analysts found that in 2019 more than 75% of detainees were detained in privately-run facilities. ICE only runs five detention centers, relying on state and local jails for the rest. John Sandweg, who ran ICE under the Obama administration, stated that the numbers show it nearly impossible to cut off the private prison companies because ICE would have nowhere to put tens of thousands of detainees now housed there."

Those contracts cannot be turned off. Joe Biden would need to rethink the entire process of immigration detention and perhaps rely more on supervised release programs. Biden could sign an executive order rescinding Trump's detention expanding initiative and banning new private prison contracts. Unfortunately, terminating existing contracts would take much longer. Congressional approval that limits the number of migrants detained might also be needed.[179]

SPEEDING UP FAMILY REUNIFICATIONS

On April 6, 2018, a memo signed by Jeff Sessions ordered a "zero-tolerance" policy by ordering the criminal prosecution of all illegal border crossers. This mean heartless and, yes, I'll say it, vicious policy is a legacy I wouldn't want to carry to my grave. He, under Donald Trump's direction, was criminalizing the behavior of poor families seeking a better and a safer life for their families. What has happened to the Republican Party? From the party of Lincoln, which directed the freeing of African Americans from slavery and bondage through the brutal but necessary Civil War to the steadfast refusal of Ronald Reagan to accept the subjugation of countries by the evil Soviet Union, who stood in West Berlin, and said "tear down this wall," we have devolved into a country that for the last four years has scapegoated, bullied, and separated mothers and fathers at the US border from their children. Fortunately, Trump received so much bipartisan international blowback for this family separation policy in 2018 that he signed an executive order rescinding the original order and halting this unconscionable affront to our values and decency.

In fairness, Trump did not originate the policy of separating migrant families. Under President Obama, separations occurred infrequently where a parent was recognized as a criminal or a threat to the child. This happens to US citizens in our country when a parent is deemed unfit to raise a child because of criminal activity, dangerous drug addiction, and refusal to seek or maintain treatment. What is so radically different under Trump's blanket family separation policy is that it applied to all undocumented immigrants crossing the border. More than two years after Trump finally banned the policy, under withering pressure from nearly everyone around the world and most people in the United States (even the US evangelical community), more than six hundred parents were deported and have yet to be reunited with their children. The Trump administration reluctantly estimated in court documents that it could take another two years to fully implement a system to track these children and perhaps have a chance to reunite them with their parents. Joe Biden has said that he will do everything humanly possible to stop future unlawful, immoral separations of families and to do everything humanly possible to reunite the already separated families.

Since Trump has already reversed himself on his disgusting family separation policy, Biden does not need to rescind the policy per se. Lee Gelernt, an ACLU attorney who has been involved in multiple lawsuits trying to bring justice for these families, suggested four actions Biden could do to right the wrong of this moral outrage. First, he could grant legal status to each of these deeply aggrieved families; second, he could allow the deported parents to return to the United States immediately; third, he could establish a fund to help separated families deal with the mental trauma they endured; and fourth, he could put child welfare advocates and professionals, not immigration enforcement agents (thugs), in charge of future decisions regarding family separations.[180]

REVERSING "PUBLIC CHARGE" RULE

On October 10, 2018, the US Citizenship and Immigration Services filed a public charge rule change notice in the Federal Register to make immigrants who receive public assistance ineligible to receive green cards. This rule change would have allowed immigration officials to consider the use of food stamps, Medicaid, public housing vouchers, and other forms of public assistance to deny green cards to immigrants. The overall thrust of this rule change was to dramatically reduce legal immigration. The justification the Trump officials gave was that this would ensure that legal permanent residents would be able to support themselves and not be a public burden dependent on government assistance. Critics called it a wealth test that would cripple efforts by poor working-class immigrants trying to make a better life for their families but still needing a bridge of social services to accomplish that.

The US Supreme Court ruled that this rule could be implemented (except in Illinois) due to other court rulings. The new rule would take effect on February 24, 2020, as the pandemic had begun to hit the United States. The new rule increased fears that immigrant families would avoid seeking medical care because it could put in jeopardy getting green cards in the future. The Trump administration later amended the rule, making an exception for COVID-19-related illness.

In November, a federal judge struck down the public charge rule saying the Trump administration violated the Administrative Procedure Act, but an appeals court judge stayed the lower court decision, pending an appeal.

Biden's Homeland Security secretary could try to replace the Trump public charge rule with one that is more favorable to immigrants. The bureaucratic rule-making process could take another six months before any new rule is finalized. A new public rule could still face legal challenge.[181] President Biden has since ordered a full-scale review of the public charge rule.

In the op-ed "Trump's racism and xenophobia haven't caught on," in the *Washington Post*, by Jennifer Rubin, dated September 13, 2020, the author points out that Trump's history of racism was known to the public before he ever ran for president. She points out that polling indicates his views, while popular with his base of voters, are not popular with most Americans. She speculates: "Perhaps his repugnant personality makes whatever views he espouses suspect; alternatively, confronted with a cruel bigot, maybe the country recoiled."[182]

For all his explicit race-baiting and for all his attempts to play the White grievance card, most of the public has been supportive of Black Lives Matter. Most also support Black athletes' efforts to raise public awareness on the topic of racial injustice and police brutality. Most also recognize the sad reality of systemic racism in our society. "A recent Pew Research poll found the following: Overall, 44% of

Americans now say that it is a lot more difficult to be a Black person in the US than it is to be a White person, while 32% say it is a little more difficult and 23% say it is no more difficult." The share that says it is a lot more difficult has increased by 9 percentage points since the summer of 2016. The increase is almost entirely from White Democrats. Apparently, they have been moved to take a good hard look at racial injustice. Apparently, White Republicans are perfectly happy owning their racism, or at least, are indifferent to it.[183]

After the George Floyd killing in May 2020 in Minneapolis, an outpouring of righteous indignation and empathy swept the nation as evidenced by the multiracial and multigenerational protests that occurred in so many cities and even in so many small towns. Now that Donald Trump has been kicked to the curb and fired, the hope remains that Joe Biden will be able to convince Congress to pass legislation and funding that will result in real, not cosmetic, changes to strengthen voting rights, to improve police-community relations, and to provide better educational opportunities for Black and Brown Americans.

From the day Donald Trump rode down his golden escalator at Trump Tower in 2015 to announce his presidential run, his rhetoric and policy actions have demeaned and dehumanized immigrants. He tried to tie immigrants with crime, and he tried to characterize them as job thieves. On both counts, he was and still is factually wrong. His divisive rhetoric stirred up fear and loathing in his base of supporters. His grievance-driven approach to politics worked to divide, not unite, Americans. Except among his hard-core supporters, an increasing share of registered voters in the United States, both Trump voters and Biden voters, said in the Pew Research poll that newcomers into the country strengthen the country, not the other way around. In this 2020 survey, 60 percent say the newcomers strengthen the United States, while only 37 percent say it threatens our customs and values. Four years ago, 50 percent said immigrants were more of a threat, and only 46 percent said immigrants strengthened the country.[184]

Despite Trump's Muslim travel ban, Islamophobia is also down according to this poll. Four years ago, 54 percent of registered voters said Islam was more likely than other religions to encourage violence among its followers. "In 2020 in the same Pew Research poll, 45% of registered voters said Islam was more likely to encourage violence among its followers, and 51% said it is not more likely to encourage violence among its adherents."[185] Jennifer Rubin speculates that much of this shift in opinion could be the result of a larger perceived threat from White supremacist violence than Islamic terrorist violence.

Trump's anti-immigrant initiatives including the border wall, DACA repeal efforts, and attempts to punish sanctuary cities have mostly failed. Trump's morally detestable child separation policy at our southern border turned into such a political nightmare for the Republican Party that it had to be reversed, but not before horrific damage was done. The stain from this repugnant policy will not be cleansed from the Republican Party for years, or maybe never.

The evangelical community within the Republican coalition bear the most responsibility. Where was their courage when evil knocked on their door? Too many let their desire for tax cuts and Supreme Court appointments overwhelm their fundamental decency. Too many became far worse than their perceived political enemies. Many became hypocrites and selfish fools. Too many let a depraved narcissist lead them around by the nose without a word of dissent uttered. Fortunately, many evangelicals and the rest of the Trump coalition were a minority of the voting public in the last election. Enough Republicans abandoned the ugly Trumpist movement to swing the election to Joe Biden. The bottom line is this: Trump's xenophobia and racism did not leave a permanent stain on the country. It only left a stain on the Republican Party and a huge swath of the evangelical community.

Jennifer Rubin closes this op-ed with: "Real progress in addressing racial injustice and comprehensive immigration reform is possible next year—provided Trump and his Republican allies lose and lose badly. If nothing else, Trump has reminded us just how ugly the face of blood-and-soil nationalism can be."[186]

In *BBC News*, an article titled "Trump wall: How much has he actually built," by Lucy Rodgers and Dominic Bailey, dated October 31,

2020, the authors discuss the construction progress and the impact of the wall on achieving Trump's immigration reduction goals. Building his big, beautiful wall on the US-Mexico border was his signature promise of the 2016 campaign. This concrete barrier was going to stop the flow of illegal immigrants and drugs across our border.

LENGTH OF NEW WALL BUILT

Before he took office, there were 654 miles of barrier along the southern border. It was comprised of 354 miles of barricades to stop pedestrians and 300 miles to stop vehicles. Now, according to US Customs and Border Protection in its October 6, 2020 report, the southern border has 669 miles of primary barrier and 65 miles of secondary barrier which is usually positioned behind the primary barrier as a further obstacle. In areas where no barricades existed before, the Trump administration has built 15 miles of new primary barrier. About 350 miles of replacement barrier and some new secondary barrier has been built. More is planned, with 378 miles of new and replacement barrier under construction or in the preconstruction phase. Donald Trump, as is typical for him, does not make a clear distinction between new barrier and replacement barrier, instead just cavalierly referring to all of it as new wall. He justifies this by saying the replacement barriers require complete demolition of the old structure and rebuilding of old worthless barriers. New wall that has been built and finished is far less than the 2016 campaign pledge to build a wall along the entire 2,000 mile stretch of border. Later he clarified the amount would only be half of the original pledge of 2,000 miles and in February of 2020, he reduced the pledge to substantially more than 500 miles. The truth is that he is substantially short of his target, even if one includes all the replacement and secondary barrier to the new barrier. Joe Biden has said he will not tear down any of this wall, but he will not expand it either.[187]

MOST OF THE WALL IS NOT WALL AT ALL

In addition to scaling back his original length of the wall, Donald Trump has also changed his view of what constitutes a wall. Throughout the 2016 campaign, Trump talked about the wall being made of concrete, but once elected, he referred to it being made of steel, thus allowing border agents to be able to see through it. Most of what has been built so far is steel fencing (eighteen to thirty feet high) with bollards anchored below the surface in concrete. It poses a formidable barrier, but it is not the high, thick masonry structure that is typically referred to as a wall.[188]

HOW IT IS BEING PAID FOR REMAINS CONTROVERSIAL

Despite his pledge to supporters at numerous campaign rallies, that Mexico would pay for the wall, the wall is not being paid for by Mexico. The US government is paying for the wall entirely. About $5 billion has been appropriated by the US Congress, and an additional $10 billion from Department of Defense funds has been diverted to pay for the wall. He rationalized this diversion of funds by declaring our southern border a national emergency. Trump's decision to largely bypass Congress has sparked legal challenges from environmental groups, the American Civil Liberties Union (ACLU) and the states of California and New Mexico. Two lower courts ruled in favor of these groups, concluding the diversion of funds from the DOD was unlawful. The US Supreme Court has ruled that barrier construction could continue pending the appeals process. It plans to hear the full appeal in 2021. The Democrats in the House of Representatives have also started a separate legal action challenging the legality of the wall funding.[189] Those funding challenges will likely be dropped by the Biden administration because they will no longer move forward on wall construction. If they were to move forward, they almost certainly would not use military funds for that purpose.

ILLEGAL CROSSINGS APPEAR TO HAVE FALLEN THIS YEAR

The latest figures suggest that the number of migrants apprehended at the southern border has fallen in 2020 after nearly doubling between 2018 and 2019. How much this drop in apprehensions is the result of new barriers is not clear. Some immigration experts say the drop is more likely from the deterrent effects of a whole series of anti-immigration measures introduced during the Trump presidency. Those migrants fleeing violence and persecution in their home countries found tighter asylum rules, longer wait times, and lower limits on refugees accepted. In addition, the coronavirus allowed the border agents to expel more easily migrants seeking asylum status in the United States. Most immigration experts said the wall did not have nearly the same impact on decreasing immigration as the other host of measures aimed at limiting legal and illegal immigration. Another contributing factor could have been the deteriorating economic conditions in Mexico after the coronavirus hit.[190]

A KEY MIGRANT CAMP IS EMPTYING

Thousands of these refugees attempting to gain asylum status in the United States were forced to stay in temporary border towns just south of the US-Mexico border. With little in the way of infrastructure or resources, these shantytowns offered little protection from violent organized gangs. According to Human Rights Watch, these migrants were constantly under threat from criminal organizations that would kidnap members of families in these temporary border towns on the assumption they had rich relatives in the United States who would be willing to pay for their safe return.

The people in these temporary refugee towns were dealt a cruel blow with Hurricane Hanna, too, forcing them to deal with infestations of rats, snakes, and mosquitoes, and causing many to leave. The combination of famine, plague, hurricane, and the legal restrictions to immigration caused many of the inhabitants to lose hope. Unfortunately, they did not have anywhere to go. They could be arrested and killed if they went back home, but they could not enter the United States. They were stuck in limbo in a state of poverty, danger, and uncertainty.[191]

THE BARRIER IS UNLIKELY TO STOP MOST KINDS OF DRUGS COMING INTO THE UNITED STATES

Trump has asserted that 90 percent of the heroin in the United States comes across the southern border and that a wall would help in the fight against drugs. Strengthening and extending the border barriers is unlikely to do much to reduce illegal drugs like heroin, cocaine, and methamphetamine because most come through established border checkpoints, known as ports of entry. While most of the heroin in the United States does come through Mexico, the Drug Enforcement Agency (DEA) says most is hidden in vehicles mixed with other goods smuggled through legal entry points. Cartels will not be stopped or dissuaded from distributing their products by a border wall. They will use boats to drop drugs on California beaches and dig tunnels to go under the wall.[192]

A *USA Today Network* special report, "The Wall," in 2018 won a Pulitzer Prize for journalism. The byline for this reporting included Anne Ryman, Dennis Wagner, Rob O'Dell, and Kirsten Crow. It had some interesting insights into the challenges of completing the wall, the likelihood of success in achieving its goals, the cost, and the time to complete. More than thirty reporters flew the entire border by helicopter and drove it as well. They conducted interviews with migrants, farmers, families, tribal members, smugglers, border patrol agents, vigilantes, and ranchers. They looked at government maps in detail and fought to obtain property records.

> Texas which had almost no fencing accounts for more
> than half of the border. Public records revealed the

wide-open area would require disrupting or seizing nearly 5,000 parcels of property. In Texas, any new wall would need to be built some distance from the border because the border runs right down the middle of the Rio Grande River. Most Texas land is privately owned. Some of the wall would be on land owned by the federal government such as levees. In 2006, federal officials pursued private land for the current border fences. More than 300 condemnation cases were filed against landowners. Some were settled for as little as $100 for easements. In one case the US paid $5 million for six acres. In 2017, nine years after the original cases were filed, 85 cases were still in litigation. Some property owners died fighting their cases through the legal system. Terence Garrett, chair of the University of Texas Rio Grande Valley, predicted that about 20% of landowners would accept what the government offers for their land and about 80% would not. He predicted years, if not decades, of court cases before this could all be resolved.[193]

The mapping shows that despite years of construction and more than $2 billion spent, much of the border is not fenced. Where fencing exists, it is full of gaps. About 1,350 miles of the border is open with no barriers. These fenced areas are often on harsh deserts, which makes attempts to cross the border dangerous. Much of the border is hundreds of miles from the nearest big city. Building new barriers for unfenced areas will require building roads first.

Sometimes the fencing is close to the river, and sometimes it is more than a mile away. Some chunks of property, therefore, sit on the south side of the current border barriers. To date, there is no cost benefit analysis showing what accomplishments to expect from the wall, or what cost is acceptable.

The reporters working on this story discovered many previously unknown stories and unintended consequences surrounding the building of the wall. The debate over the wall comes at a time (2017–18) when border crossings were declining. "Based on Border Patrol apprehension data, illegal traffic on the border was at its lowest point in four decades and it has been falling consistently since 2000. In some areas it was 10% of its peak levels."[194]

Despite the findings of lower border crossing attempts, the number of migrants found dead in the desert in 2017 was higher. As border security tightened, migrants sought more dangerous areas to cross, driving up the death rate even as border crossing attempts declined.

The actual number of deaths was vastly underreported. *USA Today* found in its investigation of records in four border states and conversations with thirty-five medical examiners, counties, sheriff's offices, and justices of the peace that federal authorities often fail to count border crossers in some areas. "According to these sources, migrant deaths are anywhere from 25% to 300% higher than the Border Patrol's official figures."[195]

Fencing might inhibit some drug trafficking, but it will not stop it. The San Diego area has some of the most secure, fenced border, but it is also where most of the drug smuggling occurs.

Border area ranchers like the idea of more security, but they stressed that without guards, the wall by itself would simply be a speed bump for those determined to cross the border illegally.

Native Americans who live on lands straddling the border are not happy and say they are willing to fight the building of the wall because it would disrupt tribal members from services and sacred pilgrimages.

Family members of victims killed by border bandits or others without legal status support the building of the wall, claiming it might have stopped some of the criminal activities that led to the death of their family members.

Biologists say the jaguar could become extinct without a connection across the border to Mexico. Only five jaguars have been photographed in Arizona since 1996 and none verified as a female. They claim that building the wall would end the connection to the female jaguar population and end any chance of reestablishing the jaguar population in the United States.

Produce growers in Mexico say that any new tariffs on their exports purportedly to pay for the wall will ultimately be paid by consumers. Mexico provides much of America's fresh produce, especially tomatoes, and tariffs would simply raise prices.

A human smuggler told *USA Today* reporters that a wall will not stop people from trying to cross the border, but it will allow him to charge more money to assist them.[196]

In the *Texas Tribune*, an article titled "Records show Trump's border wall is costing taxpayers billions more than initial contracts," dated October 27, 2020, by Perla Trevizo and Jeremy Schwartz, the authors found that change orders modifying original contracts were costing about five times more per mile than it did under previous administrations. Many of the contracts and change orders have been given out without press releases or other public notices.[197]

At a recent rally in Arizona, Trump told the crowd that the wall was almost finished and that they were not paying a cent for it. Trump's stunningly flagrant lies are disgraceful, but just as disgraceful is the gullibility of his supporters who believe these lies. In writing this book, I have said some very harsh things about the intellect and character of Trump supporters. While it is painful to shine a light on them, it is necessary. Without holding them accountable and without at least some of them learning and accepting the truth of their addiction to Donald Trump, how does our country heal from these four years of unadulterated political hell!

Some contractors have been fined for OSHA violations, particularly in excavation. Any serious accidents resulting in severe injury or even death could result in administrative delays, termination of existing contracts, negotiation of new contracts, and potential work stoppages.[198]

President-elect Joe Biden said he would discontinue work on the wall and cancel contracts where possible. Joe Biden will have many things to consider such as the phase of construction, gaps in the wall that could be exploited by border crossers, and termination costs borne by taxpayers. Trump might have boxed Biden in, limiting his options for dealing with the wall and its ballooning costs.

A *Washington Post* article titled "Feuds flare along Trump's border wall as construction ramps up during his final days in office,"
dated December 3, 2020, by Maria Sacchetti, explores some of the
difficulties and conflicts occurring as Trump pushes to build as much
of his border wall as possible before leaving office. Landowners and
local authorities are becoming angered in the final days of the Trump
administration's push to build more wall in the remaining days of his
presidency.

An Arizona rancher complained that detonated explosives blew
car-sized rocks onto his property, and municipal water officials in
El Paso deployed dump trucks recently to block wall builders from
cutting off their only road to a vital canal along the Rio Grande. The
municipal water authority expressed outrage at the wall construction
crews, making it clear they needed twenty-four-hour access to this
road to be able to facilitate repairs to this canal that supplies drinking
water and irrigation water to over eight hundred thousand county
residents. Landowners in Laredo, Texas are urging elected state and
local officials to pressure the incoming Biden administration to keep
their property safe from construction crews working on the wall.[199]

Federal officials claim that Trump has built 415 miles of new barriers, and that they expect to reach 450 miles by the end of the year. As
mentioned previously, most of the new barriers are just replacement
barriers not newly fenced barriers on previously open land. Critics
say the wall is an expensive political and economic boondoggle that
keeps trampling on landowners' rights in the process of building it.
Landowners have also complained that construction crews have damaged wildlife habitats, portions of saguaro cactus forests, and private
property.[200]

In writing this chapter, the question that keeps haunting me is
which is worse, the harsh immigration restrictions on our southern
border, the xenophobia perceived by the Muslim world and our allies
elsewhere, or the lies about the wall, and its economic and environmental costs. The immigration restrictions, particularly the treatment
of migrants seeking refugee status and the separation of families, tug
at my heartstrings and embarrass me as an American. For most of our

history, Americans strived to be a beacon of hope, a welcoming land of opportunity, and a force for good in the world. We can no longer allow a vicious demagogue to corrupt our character and set us apart from one another and from those in need around the world. We need to be welcoming persecuted peoples, not rejecting them. We can no longer talk self-righteously about family values and then separate families by sending parents back to countries where they could face possible arrest, torture, or death, and then leaving their children in immigration detention centers and sometimes eventually foster homes. We must reclaim the moral high ground as a nation.

We also need to stop this xenophobia propagated by the outgoing president. To deal with the many challenges in a dangerous world, especially battling terrorism, we need to maintain a dialogue with Muslim countries. We need to work together with some Muslim countries in intelligence gathering and counterterrorism activities. If we close the door to them and withdraw unto ourselves, we will eventually have few if any friends in the world. Allies in the world make it possible to achieve large goals that cannot be achieved by one country alone.

Finally, we can control our borders and the entry into our country without the political albatross of Donald Trump's beloved wall. Surveillance drones, radar, helicopters, and cameras all can be used to alert mobile border control agents to interdict unlawful incursions into our country. The escalating cost of this wall and the message it sends to the rest of the world are not worthy of praise. We need to end this insular, withdrawn attitude of "America first." Instead, we need to reclaim our role of world leader by setting an example, devoid of fear of newcomers and open to the strength and diversity that they provide.

We also need to be careful to not be fooled into lumping all migrants trying to get into the United States into the same category. Americans, of course, do not want criminals, drug users, or terrorists allowed into the country. Obviously, we want to maintain control over our borders, but we also want to offer hope for the downtrodden, provide safety for the persecuted, give economic opportunity to new migrants, and supply workers to industries in which most Americans are unwilling to work, such as construction and agriculture.

Americans who voted for Donald Trump need to remember that most of their family probably came here as immigrants looking for freedom, hope, and opportunity one or two centuries ago. If we can remember that, and we can remember to love our neighbors as ourselves, we can be the nation that honors God, family, and friends—old and new.

CHAPTER 6

TARIFFS AND TRADE WARS

IN THIS CHAPTER, we will explore the phony claims and empty promises of Donald Trump's trade policy. At a rally in 2016, Donald Trump made one of his biggest promises to the assembled crowd: "If I'm elected, you won't lose one plant, I promise you that." He claimed his proposed trade negotiations would bring back jobs to the industrial Midwest. His "America first" approach has relied heavily on slapping tariffs on trading partners including Europe, Canada, Mexico, and China.

PHONY CLAIMS AND PLANT CLOSINGS

John Cavanagh debunks Trump's policy and claimed results in a *USA Today* op-ed, dated September 17, 2020: "Trump trade wars have led to lost jobs and US factories. We need a worker-centered recovery." Four years later, it is abundantly clear that his trade policies have failed US workers. The trade wars have led to higher costs, lost markets, and increased plant closures. Economic Policy Institute research shows that we lost eighteen hundred factories between 2016 and 2018. Trump's increasingly bellicose trade battle with China with its back-and-forth escalating tariffs caused annual job growth in the manufacturing-heavy state of Ohio to drop from 36,200 in 2016 to 3,700 in 2019 in a report John Cavanagh co-authored. Average weekly earnings also declined for Ohio manufacturing workers during the same period.[201]

In Michigan, Fiat, Ford, and General Motors all closed plants since Trump's brash campaign promises in 2016. Auto companies reduced their capital investments in the state by 29 percent over the first three years of Trump's presidency compared with the previous three years under President Obama.[202]

In this op-ed, John Cavanagh asks the question, Where did these US manufacturers invest? The answer was: China. Trump's war of words and his imposition of high tariffs did nothing to prevent these companies from investing capital into this fast-growing market. In 2019, US firms invested $14 billion in China, more than in 2016. Tesla and General Motors were the leading US capital investors in China (mostly for electrical vehicle production). The two companies' decisions were motivated partly by Chinese consumer subsidies for pollution-reducing technologies. Trump, however, cannot escape his responsibility for encouraging this major offshoring because of the corporate tax cuts he pushed through the Congress in 2017. Up to a certain threshold, US companies no longer owe the IRS anything on offshore profits. Above the threshold, they owe a federal tax rate that is just half of what they would pay on domestic profits. The result could not have been more obvious. The companies took their tax savings and shipped thousands of jobs out of Ohio, Michigan, and other states.[203]

Of course, during the recent campaign, Donald Trump had no apologies to offer for his broken campaign promises of 2016. Instead, he falsely claims to have created new car plants in these states. In a campaign stop in Freeland, Michigan, on September 10, Trump claimed he'd brought back jobs, and that "if Biden wins, China wins." The man was, is, and always has been a shameless liar.[204]

In the past two years, Trump has thrown more gasoline on the fire in his ongoing trade war with China. He has been attacking Chinese firms Huawei (a tech giant) and TikTok (a consumer video app). He has proposed tax breaks for US companies to return jobs to the United States. Basically, he has asked taxpayers to buy back their jobs.[205]

BETTER APPROACHES

Cavanagh, in this op-ed, suggests a better way to address this Trump-created loss of jobs. He suggests a trade policy that lifts worker wages and improves working conditions everywhere, including China. If corporations were to face stiff penalties for violations of labor and human rights, they would be less eager to slash US jobs and exploit workers elsewhere. That would be good news for workers in all countries. Now that we are in a pandemic, the offshoring of production of personal protection equipment has created critical shortages. Keeping more of this production in the United States would be good for workers and good for our overall national security. Cavanagh states unequivocally that to get our country's manufacturing and trade policy back on course, corporations need to contribute their fair share to the national recovery. He proposes strategically targeting public investment in job creation training, health and social services, new infrastructure, and green industries of the future. Trade rules that restrict the ability to deal with this manufacturing and job crisis should be abolished.

Cavanagh also states that Trump's bullying and brute-force use of tariffs has backfired badly.[206]

KRUGMAN ANALYSIS ON TRADE WAR FAILURE

In some notes for a paper, "Why DID Trump's Trade War Fail?", well-known economist Paul Krugman said that for the most part Trump's economic policies have looked like typical Republican economic policies. The major exception has been his trade policy. He states that Trump has been the most protectionist president since the 1930s, and that Trump effectively destroyed the framework that governed trade policy since Franklin Roosevelt signed the Reciprocal Trade Agreements Act (RTAA) in 1934. The RTAA established a system that took away the power of Congress to insert special-interest provisions into tariff legislation. It gave the executive branch the sole power to negotiate trade agreements with other countries, and it gave Congress the right to simply vote up or down on these agreements. The RTAA also provided some relief to industries facing sudden competition from import surges and perceived unfair competition. Without new or revised legislation, tariffs could be imposed for the following reasons: disruptive competition from abroad, foreign subsidies, dumping, or national security.[207]

One of the key ideas behind the RTAA law was that the president would take a broader view than Congress when negotiating trade agreements including diplomatic considerations and the overall state of the world economy and the world trading system. Because the RTAA gave exclusive power to the president to negotiate or change US trade policy, it enabled Trump to launch a significant trade war. My belief is that Trump used populist tariff and trade policy to appeal to a large slice of potential voters, the noncollege educated, to build his new coalition. Most economists believe that the burden of tariffs (which are basically taxes on imports) fall on the consumer and that the net effect of tariffs on US real income is negative. In Paul Krugman's notes, he explores a different question: Why did tariffs not achieve Trump's stated goals of reducing the overall US trade deficit or the US manufacturing trade deficit?

He lists three key reasons:

1. General Equilibrium: Trade balances are determined only by a nation's savings-investment balance. As a result, trade policy should have no effect on trade surpluses or trade deficits.
2. Crosscutting Policies: The 2017 Tax Cut and Jobs Act was predicted to bring about large capital inflows into the United States. This increase in national income and cash flow, by its very nature, should increase the trade deficit. Rich nations

typically run high trade deficits because they have more money to spend on luxury consumer goods from abroad.
3. Structure and Design: The Trump tariffs were designed poorly.[208]

Many economists have mocked Trump for citing trade deficits as evidence that foreign countries are taking advantage of us. This has been a way for Trump to rally a large part of his voter coalition, who are, quite simply, not educated in the field of international finance and trade.

In the December 2020 publication, *International Journal of Accounting and Taxation*, the article "Exploring the Impact of Tariffs on Foreign Direct Investment and Economic Prosperity," the authors Vanessa Fong and Dr. James N. Mohs discuss how foreign direct investment is a major way to enter new markets.

Foreign direct investment (FDI) is normally a major way to enter new markets. It facilitates tax benefits, cheaper labor, and production costs. An increase in global income, the result of lower costs for domestic manufacturers, in turn, results in the host country's ability to afford more consumer imports. As a result, this rise in imports increases local government revenues through tariffs or import duties. If tariffs are modest, it helps local businesses and local government without dissuading foreign investment. Tariffs can have a significant impact on local government, multinational enterprises, and consumers. If tariffs become too high, they can reduce foreign direct investments. Exports become too expensive which reduces the multinational firm's return on investment (ROI). Exporters could cut prices to maintain sales, but this would shrink profits. High tariffs can also expose a country to retaliatory tariffs by its trading partners. This happened when

Trump raised tariffs. China responded in kind, setting off a trade war.

The increase in tariffs would drive up the cost of imports, and while in theory, it could lower competitive price pressure in the host country, it also gives local businesses the opportunity to raise prices for goods and services to extremely high levels and severely limits the available variety of goods and services to be offered and consumed in the local (host) country. Consequently, it severely reduces the purchasing power of most local consumers, making the cost of living incredibly expensive.

Recent history has shown the global trend has been toward lower tariffs. By lowering the costs associated with international trade, this in turn has opened doors for domestic companies to access foreign labor and resources and deliver goods and services into new markets. Despite the benefits of low or no tariffs, many countries have been reluctant to maintain lower tariffs such as the United States under the Trump presidency.

Transfer pricing refers to the agreed upon cost for the transaction for goods and services between related parties, and it is a process that is directly impacted by tariffs. These transfers can be from a subsidiary to a parent (upstream) or from a parent to a subsidiary (downstream) and occur across borders. Countries that impose high tariffs are creating high barriers to trade and are sacrificing the basic objective of transfer pricing: to minimize overall cost. To benefit from transfer pricing, companies need to optimize the impact of two key factors: the agreed upon price and the tax implications (corporate income taxes and tariffs).

High tariffs can deter foreign companies from accessing goods and services from high tariff countries. The bottom-line is quite simple to understand. High tariffs rarely if ever benefit both parties in either a transfer-pricing or an arms-length (non-transfer-pricing) situation. Beyond the purely economic mechanism of tariffs, there is a sense of comradery and shared dependence. The United States and Canada are a great example. Canadian companies provide oil and other natural resources, and the United States provides finished goods and other services. Both countries benefit from low friction trade costs (before Donald Trump's imposition of high tariffs/protectionism). Countries that prosper from international trade design tariffs that benefit all parties. Trade liberalization or total free trade benefits all parties.

History has shown that high tariffs have a direct negative impact on foreign direct investments and transfer pricing. Countries that have chosen to impose low or no tariffs have prospered (United States, European Union, and Hong Kong) while those that have chosen to impose high tariffs have not prospered (Bahamas and many African countries).[209]

Dr. Paul Krugman states that since the United States is a persistent capital importer, rising protectionism should, all other things being equal, reduce our capital imports, and hence, reduce our trade deficit. Therefore, he says, "It is a mistake to extrapolate that trade deficits are a macroeconomic phenomenon to the conclusion that trade policy can't effect deficits."[210]

He also raises another pertinent point—that too many people refer to manufacturing trade as if it were all trade. Yes, while manufacturers are a large part of all trade, service providers are also a significant and viable part of trade. The United States, in fact, exports large quantities of services and agricultural products and, with the rise in fracking, energy. At this point, manufacturing represents about 55 percent of US exports of goods and services.[211]

In other words, Trumpian trade policy could have functioned as a twenty-first century, advanced country version of import-substituting industrialization. It did expand manufacturing in some other countries that adopted it, but not in the United States.

TAX CUT IMPACT

As a result, Krugman suggests that we look in other directions to explain why the Trump trade policy failed to produce any viable expansion of manufacturing. He proposes the idea that the 2017 Tax Cut and Jobs Act was a major reason. Proponents of this large reduction in corporate taxes were adamant that it would lead to a surge in economic growth. They surmised that it would reduce the cost of capital and increase the US capital stock, which would then, in turn, increase GDP and wages. Conservative think tanks like the Tax Foundation and administration economists believed that US capital stock would increase by 30 percent over the course of a decade. What happened is what usually happens when wealthy countries increase their current capital inflows; they increased their imports, and therefore, they increased their manufacturing trade deficit. The bottom line, according to Krugman, is that the corporate tax cut did not work out as advertised. Neither the surge in business investment nor the expected inflow of foreign capital ever materialized in any continuing and meaningful way.[212]

Another interesting conclusion that emerged from his study and notes was that there was a brief plunge in one form of measured capital outflow: reinvested earnings from foreign subsidiaries of US corporations. This was almost exactly matched by a brief surge in US dividends earned abroad. This happened because many multinational companies use internal transfer pricing on intermediate production inputs and rental rates on intellectual property to shift their measured profits around to low-tax jurisdictions like Ireland. As a result, a large percentage of measured direct investment is fictitious. The International Monetary Fund (IMF) estimated this to be about 40 percent.[213]

Small changes in tax strategies can lead to large apparent changes in where earnings, and hence value added, are reported. This is what was behind the "leprechaun economics, the implausible 34 percent growth rate reported by Ireland in 2015."[214] In the first quarter of 2018, "overseas subsidiaries of US multinationals transferred ownership of some of their assets back to their parent companies, causing a surge in dividends and stock buybacks and a large-reported disinvestment."[215]

Krugman addresses the question as to why there was not a real surge in corporate investment. One answer is that most "business investment goes to short-lived assets like equipment and software, each of which is not too sensitive to the cost of capital." Another factor "may have been the trade war itself, which created (business) uncertainty. Businesses were unwilling to invest in projects that were dependent on access to foreign (production) inputs because those inputs would or might be subject to (significant) tariffs."[216] A second answer might be that these companies "were reluctant to invest in import-competing production, because the Trump tariffs might not last."[217] With Trump's recent election loss, this proved to be a fortuitous prediction. Normally, the tax inflows would bring about a strengthening in the value of the dollar. However, this was not what happened.

DESIGN OF THE TRUMP TARIFFS

This brings Professor Krugman to the third explanation—the design of the Trump tariffs. There is some literature on the differing effects of tariffs on final versus intermediate goods. One of the most import-ant insights of the literature was that developing countries might pro-vide a higher effective rate than the headline (final tariff) rate might suggest. If a country puts a 20 percent tariff on imported cars, but imported parts account for 80 percent of the cost, that country is pro-viding 100 percent effective protection to the activity of auto assembly. With Trump's trade war, tariffs were focused mainly on intermediate rather than final goods. In essence, this would have provided incom-plete tariff protection for the entire final assembly of the car. The net effect might have discouraged domestic manufacturing.[218]

A final point made by Professor Krugman was that Trump's tar-iffs and trade war were largely focused on China. Rather than protect-ing US manufacturing, it might have caused a shift to other overseas sources. The overall takeaway from Professor Krugman's research and analysis is that Trump's willingness to shatter previous US trade policy to pursue his protectionist agenda failed in providing much protection to the sectors he was trying to favor. Whether or not you liked Trump's protectionist trade goals, you need to face the fact that the policy was too poorly designed to achieve them.[219]

I tend to agree with most traditional thinking on tariffs and trade wars. Tariffs are taxes, and they create added cost to consumers and more friction in the international trading system. The grade for out-going President Trump on this subject is clearly an F for failure.

DISMANTLING OF THE TTP

Before completing this chapter, I would like to take the opportunity to specifically review our president's statements and actions regarding a previously negotiated trade agreement by the Obama administration: The Trans-Pacific Trade Partnership. Three days after assuming the office of the presidency, Donald Trump fulfilled one of his campaign promises by pulling the United States out of the Trans-Pacific Trade Partnership, a twelve-nation free-trade agreement negotiated during the Obama administration but never submitted to the Senate for ratification. In addition to the United States, other countries' signatories included the countries of Australia, Brunei, Canada, Chile, Japan, Malaysia, Mexico, New Zealand, Peru, Singapore, and Vietnam. When Trump withdrew, the agreement could not enter into force. As a result, the remaining eleven countries negotiated a new deal, which incorporated most of the provisions of the TPP. The expression "don't cut off your nose to spite your face" comes to mind after seeing this implosion of America's diplomatic and economic leadership. This appears to be one of the most blind, strange, and ignorant actions taken by an American president in many years. In an article in *Foreign Policy*, "Trump's Five Mistaken Reasons for Withdrawing from the Trans-Pacific Partnership," by Robert D. Blackwell, on June 22, 2017, the inaccurate reasons are enumerated below.

1. "The number of jobs and amount of wealth and income the United States have given away in so short a time is staggering, likely unprecedented. And the situation is about to get dramatically worse if the Trans-Pacific Partnership is not stopped."[220]

REBUTTAL

Under more realistic assumptions, the US International Trade Commission (USITC) and the Peterson Institute for International Economics (PIIE) estimated TPP would have modestly increased US annual real income by $57.3 billion (0.23%) and $131 billion (0.5%), respectively. "While TPP opponents argue that manufacturers of products the US exports abroad, including passenger vehicles and apparel, would see employment gains, these export-intensive industries pay more than other positions. According to the PIIE models, the movement of workers to more competitive sectors would have increased real wages by 0.5%. Moreover, the PIIE study shows that any TPP job-displacements would have been less than 0.1% of existing "job churn," or temporary unemployment as workers move to other companies. The United States should seek to empower workers to take better jobs with adjustment assistance and training programs. Canceling TPP weakens the overall US economy without addressing the problems many workers face.[221]

2. "The TPP would make it easier for our trading competitors to ship cheap subsidized goods into US markets—while allowing foreign countries to continue putting barriers in front of our exports. The TPP creates a new international commission that makes decisions the American people can't veto."[222]

REBUTTAL

TPP would have accomplished the opposite and altered unfair foreign business climates without changing US policy. The agreement would have eliminated over 11,000 tariffs (TAXES!!!!) on goods the United States exports by 2030, which, according to the PIIE models, would have increased annual US exports by $357 billion by that year. TPP also would have eliminated the ability of foreign government-run businesses (state-owned enterprises) to subsidize products and undercut US firms with cheap goods. Additionally, it would have addressed child labor practices and introduced minimum wages in Vietnam and other member nations, making it easier for US workers to compete. At the same time, TPP would have had minimal effects on existing US practices. Eighty per cent of US imports from TPP countries face no tariffs, and for many that do, such as Japanese autos, tariffs would not have expired for at least 25 years. Far from a bad deal, TPP would have forced member states to reform their markets with few US concessions.

Objections that TTP would enable "corporate attacks on our laws" and undermine US sovereignty are similarly misplaced. These arguments refer to the pact's Investor-State Dispute Settlement (ISDS) System, which is a measure allowing US firms to seek remedies for unfair treatment abroad using panels of independent arbiters instead of potentially ineffective foreign courts. For this reason, the United States pushed against resistance from other nations to include ISDS in TPP. Since it entered trade agreements with ISDS included, the United States has not lost a case. Moreover, TPP's article 9.16 specifically grants member states the right to "ensure that investment activity in its territory is undertaken in a manner sensitive to environmental, health, or other regulatory objectives." In effect, ISDS would curb anti-free market practices that hurt US businesses, not critical laws that protect ordinary citizens.[223]

3. "The TPP is a deal that was designed for China to come, as they always do, through the back door and totally take advantage of everyone."

REBUTTAL

TPP excluded China, granting the United States economic and strategic advantages. PIIE models estimate that China's economy would have been $18 billion smaller had TPP passed. It would also have been difficult for China to join TPP after-the fact; according to Center for Strategic and International Studies (CSIS) researchers, TPP's rules limiting SOEs and protectionism would have forced China to adopt significant free-market reforms before entering. Critics claiming China would have exploited TPP's rules of origin to profit from TPP products ignore that rules for sectors like apparel would have been tougher than current standards and that the United States would have maintained pre-TPP automotive tariffs after the deal's passage. Exclusion from a trade area worth 40% of global GDP would have slowed China's economy.

TPP was also a crucial measure to counter China's use of economic tools for geopolitical purposes. China uses such methods of geoeconomics coercion, including trade restrictions and its SOE's activities abroad, to punish countries opposing its aim of regional hegemony. Without TPP, the United States will be less equipped to protect its allies from Beijing's pressure. Furthermore, US allies in Asia saw TPP as a symbol of the US commitment to the region. Without it, they are more likely to increasingly doubt America's willingness to defend them and therefore be tempted to acquiesce to China's hegemonic agenda. Withdrawing from TPP also helps China's campaign to negotiate its Regional Comprehensive Economic Partnership (RCEP), designed to be rival regional trade deal excluding the United States. It also gives China a greater ability to build infrastructure in Asia as part of its massive and geopolitically based Belt Road initiative. Both will increase China's geoeconomics leverage over its neighbors at America's strategic expense.[224]

4. "The "Trans-Pacific Partnership" is an attack on America's business. It does not stop Japan's currency manipulation. This is a bad deal."[225]

REBUTTAL

TPP included a side agreement obligating members to "avoid manipulating exchange rates—to gain an unfair competitive advantage," and it mandates that each country disclose currency interventions. Without TPP, there is no effective way to regulate these practices. Still, tougher enforcement measures and punishments would have done more to promote Pacific free trade and stop currency manipulation, which PIIE analysts argue has cost millions of US jobs.

Yet despite Trump's complaints, many past offenders, including Japan, have not recently manipulated their currencies. Although the yen is currently weak compared to the dollar, this is because of domestic policies designed to spur Japanese consumption, not from purchases of dollars to boost exports. Moreover, CSIS observes that Japan is a critical partner in any US strategy to compete with China due to its support for American troops and Western institutions. The PIIE model projects that TPP would have increased Japanese annual real income by 2.5% by 2030. A stronger Japan would not only build its security forces and resist Chinese geoeconomic coercion, but it would also help other US allies do the same. Leaving TPP on the falsehood that Japan manipulates currency weakens US allies and benefits China.[226]

5. "It is the policy of my Administration—to begin pursuing, wherever possible, bilateral trade agreements to promote American industry, protect American workers, and raise American wages."[227]

REBUTTAL

Bilateral agreements have significant disadvantages. Unlike unilateral arrangements like TPP, one-on-one deals involve separate rules for trade with each country. In past negotiations, this approach has created a complex "noodle bowl" of regulations, and companies doing business in multiple foreign countries face excessive costs as they attempt to comply with each set of laws. According to a survey from KMPG auditing company, 77% of firms contacted did not use all available trade agreements; 23% named "complexity of rules" as the "biggest challenge" they face to international trade. TPP would have made Pacific trade laws simpler and uniform, giving US businesses and workers more economic opportunities. Bilateral talks also provide fewer incentives for countries to make concessions to the United States. Canada and Mexico accepted fairer agricultural prices and stricter labor laws than they did in NAFTA to join TPP and gain access to Asian markets.

Despite the US decision to leave the agreement, TPP is not yet dead. The other eleven member countries are attempting to negotiate a revised version that does not include the United States. It is not too late for President Trump to change course and join the effort. A revised pact would benefit the US and global economies, strengthen America's Asian allies, and serve as a bulwark against the rise of Chinese power. We urge the self-proclaimed master of the *Art of the Deal* to again reverse himself to America's enduring strategic benefit.[228]

It is now too late for President Trump to reverse himself on TPP because to put it clearly, he neither has the intelligence, nor the insight, to do so. But even more relevant, He *lost* the *election!*

Trump's intellectual laziness and willful ignorance regarding TPP and various other international agreements and previously negotiated treaties hurt our country and helped our adversaries. Is that someone to be proud of? Is that someone worth following? Is that someone worth selling out your honor for? Republicans, your embracing of this sad spectacle in our history, your embracing of this traitor, and your embracing of a dimwitted but dangerous political cult, makes all of you complicit in the most failed four years in modern American history.

CHAPTER 7

THREATENING THE PEACEFUL TRANSFER OF POWER

THE UNWILLINGNESS TO accept the results of our presidential election might be the worst of all things done by the Trump administration. The results of the presidential election of 2020 could not have been any clearer. Despite the tweeted denials by Trump himself, despite the protests of Trump's supporters, and despite the feckless attempts by many Republican leaders to continue coddling this president's ego and cowering before his supporters, Donald Trump, the nation's forty-fifth president, lost this election decisively!

While Trump flailed in his efforts to avoid conceding defeat, the result has spoken for itself. The incumbent president lost the popular vote by more than seven million votes. This was the largest spread in both raw vote total and percentage of total vote that a challenger has defeated an incumbent president since the 1932 presidential election—Franklin Roosevelt's defeat of Herbert Hoover. The electoral vote was 306 for Joe Biden, 232 for Donald Trump.

VOTER SUPPRESSION

This stunning defeat happened despite choreographed attempts in many states to suppress the votes of Black Americans. Voter suppression can include spreading misinformation about voting laws and voting requirements. It can also include taking actions to make voting a long and difficult process. Finally, it can include outright intimidation. According to Pew Research, White voters (based on 2019 figures) account for about 69 percent of total registered voters in the United States. White voters accounted for about 85 percent of registered voters in 1996.[229] This demographic change has been the reality behind modern voter suppression efforts of the Republican Party. Rather than adapt to the changes in voter composition in a dynamic, growing country like ours, by talking and, more importantly, listening to groups of new potential voters, the Republicans have taken the old path: voter suppression, but mostly with a more subtle twist. Because of various Supreme Court decisions and federal civil rights laws, they have been forced to move away from the violent voter suppression of the days of the Jim Crow laws (state and local laws that enforced racial segregation and limited voting rights and access, supported by the southern Democrats in the old South of the early and middle twentieth century).

In a Center for Public Integrity article, "Barriers to the Ballot Box. Analysis: New and Age-Old Voter Suppression Tactics at the Heart of the 2020 Power Struggle," dated October 28, 2020, by Matt DeRienzo, the author pointed out that a Republican Party threatened in 2020 by demographic shifts and backlash to a deeply unpopular president resorted to the following brazen and unjust efforts to suppress the votes of Democrat voters (particularly Black voters).[230]

SLOWING DOWN THE MAIL

Donald Trump appointed Louis DeJoy to head the US Post Office in May 2020. He was one of the Republican Party's largest fund-raisers.

After he assumed the job, he immediately began instituting cost-cutting measures such as banning overtime, forbidding late or extra trips to deliver the mail, removing and dismantling hundreds of high-speed mail-sorting machines, and removing some mail collection boxes from our streets. The changes caused obvious and significant delays in mail delivery and resulted in investigations by congressional committees and the USPS inspector general. Fortunately, in August DeJoy was forced to announce his changes would be suspended, and in October, the USPS agreed to reverse those changes.[231]

SPEEDING UP THE RECENT SUPREME COURT APPOINTMENT

The stunning appointment of Amy Conant Barrett to the Supreme Court approximately one month before the election was the most brazen, most hypocritical naked political power grab our country witnessed in a long time. Despite having denied President Obama the right to appoint a Supreme Court justice nearly a year before a presidential election and promising that this would be a forever precedent, Republicans reversed themselves and pushed through this appointment after early voting in the presidential election had already begun. Wow! Can we say this was brazen, undisguised, shameless hypocrisy? If we are honest with ourselves, I think the answer is a resounding yes.[232]

SHUTTING DOWN POLLING PLACES
IN BLACK COMMUNITIES

Since 2016, nearly twenty-one thousand polling places were shut down nationally, mostly in poor and Black neighborhoods. In Texas, the governor, Greg Abbott, limited voter drop-boxes to one per county. Harris County, where the city of Houston is located, was limited to one drop-box for a population of nearly five million people. That, alone, might have been the most egregious example of modern voter suppression the country has ever seen. That, by itself, forced voters who did not want to vote on Election Day, because of the fear of contracting coronavirus, to drive an hour in each direction to simply deposit his or her ballot.[233]

STOP COUNTING PEOPLE OF COLOR IN THE 2020 CENSUS

The Trump administration stopped counting the census on October 15, 2020, where previous courts ordered the counting through October 31, 2020. This was an attempt to reduce representation in Congress and to reduce federal dollars being spent in the districts of Black citizens because they knew fewer Black citizens mailed in their census forms, and thus they needed to be counted via other canvassing methods.[234]

STOP COUNTING THE ACTUAL BALLOTS

This was nearly beyond belief. President Trump wanted only the ballots cast on Election Day to be counted. As nearly everyone knew, Republicans cast a much higher percentage of their vote on Election Day, whereas Democrats cast a much higher percentage of their vote before Election Day (either early voting on-site or early voting by mail). The president apparently thought you should only count the votes of your voters and thus stop the count when you have a significant early lead as reported on election night (often referred to as the red state mirage). In many states (red states, mostly those with a Republican tilt), the early on-site votes and the mailed votes were counted last. How could anyone of sound mind with a sense of fairness possibly believe and support this? This point of view, shared by President Trump and his supporters, was the underpinning of an authoritarian government, the precursor to a twenty-first century age of fascism.

LIES AND BRAINWASHING

Donald Trump repeatedly told his base of voters that the election was rife with fraud and that he would have won if it had been fair, thus stirring the pot of grievance and resentment with his base of supporters. With no evidence to support his ridiculous claims, he continued his mission of spreading lies and misinformation. In fact, before the election, he stated on multiple occasions that if he lost, the election was a fraud and invalid. Has any American presidential candidate in our history ever made such a claim? The answer is no because no other presidential candidate has been a serial liar; a vicious, selfish demagogue; and a traitor to our fundamental democracy. His relationship with his base was the relationship between a cult leader and cult followers. It was tantamount to brainwashing, and it was the most dangerous threat to our democratic republic most of us will ever see in our lifetimes.

RELIEF AND JOY OF FOREIGN LEADERS

Congratulations were sent to Joe Biden and Kamala Harris from around the world after the election. Most of our allies were happy to see America return to sanity after seeing us staring at the abyss for the last four years. They were happy to see America return to its place of leadership in the world. They were happy that they could deal with a competent government, that they could depend on mutual agreements, and that they could work together on common problems and seek reasonable solutions. They were happy that they could depend on shared intelligence and not worry about being shut out on critical information or dismissed entirely.

REPUBLICAN COLLABORATORS

Sadly, most Republican leaders were either missing in action or spreading Trump's false narrative about the election and transfer of power. A few have spoken out tepidly about the need to proceed with the transition of power, but only a few. Even those, who spoke about the need to proceed with the briefings and transition meetings, failed to congratulate the incoming president and vice president. Of course, neither the president nor his children showed the class or the dignity to congratulate President-elect Biden or Vice President-elect Kamala Harris. Until these last four years, I held the Republican Party in high esteem. I thought it held the high ground on so many issues of conse-quence. I thought it was the party that believed in American values of fairness, honor, and decency. I was wrong. The Republican Party surrendered the high ground. They were no longer the "shining city on the hill" referred to in speeches by former President Ronald Regan. They abdicated their civic responsibility out of a misplaced loyalty to a ruthless, selfish, wannabe tyrant/king. Worst of all, they became col-laborators in Trump's lies who aided and abetted the insurrection on the US Capitol. They can be described either as outright traitors or as cowards, blackmailed and extorted to do Trump's traitorous bidding.

I often asked myself why. I think the answer came down to two related motivations. The first reason was a generalized unease and simple fear of Donald Trump's base of voters. They feared losing the support of these voters in future elections. Their lust for maintain-ing their spheres of power overwhelmed their sense of patriotism, their sense of honor, and their sense of fairness and decency. Their stirred-up passions of hatred toward Americans who rejected Trump overwhelmed their ability to think clearly with a perspective toward history and the future. The second reason was a creeping cynicism that required them to stroke Trump's ego. They often behaved like little puppies around his pants legs. They wanted to be picked up, cuddled, stroked, and fed treats. They needed to feed Trump's ego, but they also needed their egos to be fed and acknowledged, even if it was just in a small, pitiful way. They no longer were their own persons. They were weak creatures willing to watch democracy slip away, as long they did not slip away from their "dear leader's care and comfort."

In my entire lifetime, I have never seen so many leaders within a political party succumb at the same time to cultlike worship of a malignant narcissist. This has happened in plenty of other countries and empires throughout world history, but never in the United States until now.

Their cynicism also was on full display in the battle for control of the US Senate that took place in Georgia in the runoff elections for two US Senate seats. Their ad campaigns were full of lies and out-of-context photos and statements, some from their opponents many years ago. Also, the unwillingness of Republican David Perdue to debate Democrat Jon Ossoff just screamed cowardice. In their previous debate before the runoff, Perdue looked for the exits nearly in tears from the political thrashing he was being given by Ossoff. And then there were Republican Kelly Loeffler's ads. In the primary election, she compared herself to Attila the Hun, claiming she was the most pro-Trump member of the US Senate. In the runoff with Raphael Warnok, she went back to an old playbook and tried to link him to Jeremiah Wright, Barack Obama's old pastor in Chicago. It was sad and ridiculous! Reverend Warnok was the epidemy of decency and grace. He was the head pastor at Ebenezer Baptist Church in Atlanta, where Martin Luther King once was the head pastor before his assassination. It was a shameful political hit job by Kelly Loeffler! To attempt to win an election by sowing the seeds of guilt by association was beneath contempt. She was a complete fraud and a coward, just in a more malicious way than David Perdue was. She was the epidemy of a self-righteous, entitled, spoiled brat. Most of the players on the WNBA team she owned, the Atlanta Dream, neither liked nor respected her. Her single-minded need to win her race for Senate no matter the cost to her character and integrity, was the polar opposite of the dignity, grace, and desire to serve displayed by her opponent, Reverend Raphael Warnok. She was a woman with more money than she would ever need, but she appeared to be a woman with an empty soul. I hope people pray for her. She appears to really need it.

The lies, the cynicism, the cultlike worship of Donald Trump and the sad clinging to power at all costs disqualified the Republican Party in my mind from any future consideration for my vote. As Mr. Wonderful (Kevin O'Leary) on the television show *Shark Tank* liked to say, "You are dead to me." My relationship with a political party sadly lacking in brains, heart, and soul is also dead to me.

The Republican Party of Donald Trump discounted the value of the votes of Americans of all races and religions by trying to negate the clear results of this election. Fortunately, these votes all counted the same, and more of these votes, despite ridiculous legal challenges by the Trump campaign and the Republican Party, prevailed and sent Trump packing. The ex-reality star had to face the fact that he was *fired*! He was not only fired for cause. He was fired with righteous indignation by a nation reeling from his ugly, mendacious tenure. He was fired by a nation wanting to move on from his assaults on democracy and the rule of law. He was fired for his lack of human decency and empathy. He was fired because of his corrupt incompetence and his selfish need to always be the center of attention while Americans suffered and died during the worst health care crisis in one hundred years. He was fired for his traitorous actions and his manifest dereliction of duty. He will be remembered by most Americans as the worst president in our history, something he more than earned! Finally, he was fired because, and I know it's rough to hear, his dedication to only himself. He was willing to start an insurrection to keep himself in power, and he and the Republican Party own the results—the deaths, the destruction, and the shame and dishonor.

FAILURE OF LEGAL CHALLENGES

Next, we review Trump's empty legal challenges to the results of the 2020 election. Jake Tapper of CNN took apart Trump's and the Republican Party's legal strategy to reverse the election he clearly and convincingly lost. Tapper referred to the efforts by Trump's lawyers as futile and embarrassing, and he described the president's legal team as the "gang that couldn't sue straight."[235] While Trump repeatedly and baselessly alleged that President-elect Biden stole the election from him via widespread election fraud, the desperate lawsuits filed by his lawyers were almost all thrown out of court for lack of evidence (no merit). On CNN's, *State of the Union*, Tapper highlighted several of the cases that were dismissed by both Republican-appointed and Democrat-appointed judges in several states. He pointed out that Trump lawyers were forced to admit that Republican election observers (often referred to as poll watchers) were allowed in Pennsylvania ballot-counting rooms, directly contradicting Trump campaign claims otherwise. Tapper also referred to other cases that were tossed out of court because they relied on inadmissible hearsay (basically conspiracy misinformation). Several groups of lawyers (including one team in Arizona) retained by the Trump campaign walked away from their representation of the Trump campaign because they realized the fact-free desperation allegations (spread by rumor mongers) seeking to overturn a free and fair election might not be résumé enhancing. On a Friday, shortly after the election, nine cases pushed by Trump and his allies were rejected or dropped.[236]

During the broadcast, Tapper said: "Nine! So, what now? Well, now the president of the United States is literally embracing a deranged conspiracy theory that millions of votes were changed using software." With lawyers jumping off the ship of fools, Trump announced that Rudy Giuliani, his personal attorney, would now head his legal efforts. Almost immediately, Giuliani began his tour of right-wing news (propaganda outlets) like Fox News and others to peddle fact-free, evidence-free software conspiracies. At the same time, the Trump administration's cybersecurity agency released a statement rebuking the president's unfounded claims of voter fraud saying, "there is no evidence that any voting system deleted or lost votes, changed votes, or was in any way compromised." The problem, as Tapper pointed out, was that Republican officeholders arguing that Trump had the right to present his evidence in court was that the president's efforts had nothing to do with presenting evidence. Tapper said, "They have to do with hearsay and rumor and insinuations and lies and conspiracy theories. Once these efforts have been rejected by every court, outgoing President Trump will likely continue to make them." He added, "How long is the Republican Party going to continue to defer to unhinged mendacious desperation led by the gang that couldn't sue straight?"[237]

In Michael Kang's article in *Think* on November 15, 2020, "Donald Trump's legal strategy makes no sense for winning the vote count. So, what is he doing?", the author speculated on other motivations beyond Trump's futile efforts to overturn the election. Kang said, "Almost all of the objective experts and election lawyers from both major parties agree Biden has won enough battleground states by sufficiently large margins." Despite the failure of his legal challenges with its highly questionable claims, many of which will affect only a small number of ballots, Trump and his allies pressed forward with their implausible challenges.

They knew that recounts would not change the outcome. Recounts rarely result in significant changes. Over the last twenty years, the average recount vote margin was 282 votes. Unlike the Bush versus Gore recount in 2000, which only involved the state of Florida, Joe Biden's victory did not depend on only one state. Nor was the margin in any of the battleground states as close. Only one of his legal challenges out of a smorgasbord of claims yielded any positive results. He only prevailed once In Pennsylvania, where a deadline had passed for a small number of newly registered to provide identification.[238]

POLITICAL MANEUVERING TO STAGE A DE FACTO COUP

Instead, what Trump was pursuing was a longshot political maneuver rather than a serious legal challenge. Trump and his followers were hoping to delay certain states with Republican state legislatures from certifying the vote counts and convincing those legislatures to directly appoint Trump electors to the Electoral College instead of Biden electors. The *Atlantic* reported an early sign of this strategy in September when Republican leaders in Pennsylvania admitted discussing among themselves and with the Trump campaign the idea of overriding the state's election outcome in case it went against the president. By dragging out the process and not conceding the election, Trump was attempting to give certain state legislatures the political cover to consider a cynical ploy to basically overturn the election. The Trump campaign through its efforts in their sympathetic propaganda media (Fox News, One America News Network, and News Max) did succeed initially in convincing 70 percent of Republicans that Joe Biden's victory was only the result of election fraud and irregularities. They were hoping a vote would then be taken in Congress to determine which set of electors to the Electoral College it would accept. Although the Democrats held the numerical advantage in the House, each state delegation in the House gets one vote. Because the Republicans controlled more state delegations than the Democrats, they would have the advantage if the House decided the next president under the provisions of the Twelfth Amendment to the Constitution.[239]

Fortunately, this nefarious strategy failed. Immediately after the election, the Pennsylvania Senate leader again stated that his state legislature would not appoint its own electors. Michigan, Arizona, Georgia, and North Carolina followed suit shortly thereafter. Moreover, this complicated plan would not likely have succeeded from a legal standpoint because the legislatures of every state long ago dictated that their electors to the Electoral College would only be selected by the voters within their respective states. The bottom line is this: Seizing back the appointment of electors after an election because the legislature did not like the voters' decision violated state law and basic due process. After a similar version of this strategy played itself out in the election of 1876, Congress passed the Electoral Count Act of 1887 to deal with this possibility. This implementation and enforcement mechanisms of this law favored Joe Biden. The set of electors appointed under settled state law recognizing the election result must be seated in the Electoral College. Even if a claim of election fraud was made, this 1887 law directed Congress to only recognize the set of electors certified by the governor of the state, not electors chosen by the state legislatures. The certification timeline was so important because if election results were certified by December 8, the election result was conclusive. By attempting to drag out the process past this certification deadline, the Trump campaign tried unsuccessfully to create more chaos and doubt. Even if they were successful in this regard, the courts would likely have stepped in and stopped this charade in its tracks. Finally, two more safeguards were in place. First, Michigan, Wisconsin, Pennsylvania, and Nevada all had Democratic governors who would have refused to approve a set of Trump electors with the popular vote clearly showing Biden won in each of these states. Second, the terms of the president and vice president both end on January 20, 2021. At that time, if there was not a final result, the speaker of the House would become the acting president.[240]

Any serious attempt like this to stage a coup and remain in office for a second term would have been met by a massive outcry throughout the country. It would have caused extreme backlash and a crisis of unimagined proportions for our democratic, constitutional republic. It was beyond the realm of possibility that Donald Trump would have been able to overturn this election result.

In addition to the failure in the courts, Trump and his army of zealots were rebuffed by the secretaries of state of Arizona, Pennsylvania, Wisconsin, Michigan, Georgia, and Nevada. Some were Republicans and some were Democrats. They universally took umbrage with being called cheaters, and they defended the people diligently counting and recounting the audited ballots. In Maricopa County, Arizona, these people had to be walked to their cars after dark by law-enforcement personnel because a sad, pathetic, deranged, ugly mob of Trump supporters (some armed with guns) were yelling and threatening to enter the building. This deplorable state of affairs had the possibility of turning our nation's partisanship from a "cold war" into something far more savage and sinister.

I personally knew someone who should be smarter than to fall for charlatans like Donald Trump and Jesse Ventura (yes, him, too) openly state that he hoped the United States went to civil war. Well, he got his wish on January 6, 2021, when a huge mob of vicious traitors stormed our Capitol. This reinforced my conviction that the Trumpist takeover of the Republican Party was the most dangerous movement to hit our country since the American Civil War and the rise of the Ku Klux Klan. It was, and perhaps still is, a movement in the grasp of many crazy potential domestic terrorists and traitors. Trumpism could be a rising storm of potential violence that still hopes to decapitate our institutions and destroy our democracy. Several people who left the Department of Homeland Security have spoken out about their concerns over the rise of White supremacy groups in the United States. The FBI has also raised concern about the strength and viability of these groups operating in the country.

The Trumpists do not want our votes to count equally. They want theirs to count more. They want their minority of hate and grievance to subjugate the rest of us. Fortunately, I do not believe they will be successful because they are far outnumbered by people of good faith, people of conscience, and people united to see that their ugly, evil vision for America is thoroughly rejected and defeated. Some Trumpists think Donald Trump will run again for president in 2024. I say, bring it on. I cannot see enough Americans voting for him again. Most of us just wanted he and his family to go away, to leave us in peace. Now most of us want him removed from office; we want him to never again be able to hold federal office; and we want him and his family punished to the full extent of the law for their instigation of violent insurrection. These seditionists, these traitors, who breached the Capitol during this insurrection, need to be punished to the full extent of the law. Their evil deeds need to be remembered so that others will think twice before ever embarking on such a murderous, violent, terrorist assault on our institutions and our representative government.

Perhaps the worst, most flagrant attempt at sabotaging our votes came recently when the Texas attorney general filed a lawsuit suing four other states (Georgia, Michigan, Pennsylvania, and Wisconsin), claiming they were going to cast unlawful, fraudulently tainted votes in the Electoral College. There has been no widespread evidence of voter fraud to back up this ridiculous claim. What is astounding and frightening is that 125 out of 195 Republican members of Congress voted in support of this action by the Texas attorney general. This action by an overwhelming majority of Republicans in the House puts the Republican Party squarely in the position of ignoring reality, supporting an authoritarian coup, and spitting on American democracy. This GOP action also amounted to giving the middle finger to every voter who voted for Joe Biden for president. It basically said that the vote of anyone who voted for Joe Biden was worthless, that only Trump votes should count, and that the Republican Party is the only political party that should be viewed as legitimate in the United States. This, in and of itself, is the most widespread traitorous act of any political party since America's Civil War. Fortunately, the US Supreme Court dismissed this hollow, worthless lawsuit, saying Texas had no standing to bring this case before the court. No standing, no evidence, and nothing but misinformation and contempt for our democratic traditions and values, so this lawsuit died a quick death.[241]

Perhaps the most damaging evidence of Donald Trump and his Republican enforcers was revealed on July 30, 2021, by multiple sources, including NPR Politics Podcast titled "Notes Show Trump Pressed The Justice Department To Declare The 2020 Election Corrupt," by Ryan Lucas. The basis for this reporting was from notes prepared by Richard Donoghue who was one of the participants in the December 27, 2020, phone call with Donald Trump. In this phone call, Trump attempted to influence the Justice Department to make a declaration that the election of 2020 was corrupt despite pushback from acting US Attorney General, Jeffrey Rosen, and acting US Deputy Attorney General, Richard Donoghue. They warned the

President that the claims of voter fraud that he was hearing and seeing on the internet and from other sources were not true. After being told by Rosen that the Justice Department could not snap its fingers and change the outcome of the election, Trump acknowledged that he understood that, but that he still wanted them to just make a statement saying that "the election was corrupt and leave the rest to me and the R. Congressmen." At this point Trump does not specify which congressmen, but later in the call he mentions three Republican lawmakers by name: Representative Jim Jordan of Ohio; Representative Scott Perry of Pennsylvania; and Senator Ron Johnson of Wisconsin. Representative Carolyn B. Maloney (Democrat from New York) and Chairwoman of the House Oversight and Reform Committee said the notes "show that President Trump directly instructed our nation's top law enforcement agency to take steps to overturn a free and fair election in the final days of his presidency." Trump also suggested that he might replace Rosen as Acting Attorney General, even mentioning the name of a possible replacement, Jeff Clark. Surprisingly, Trump did not attempt to stop the release of the notes.[242]

These notes provide shocking evidence of overwhelming pressure put on the Justice Department to assist in the overthrow of the election of Joe Biden. This was comparable to the pressure Trump put on the President of Ukraine in attempting to bribe and manipulate him into making a statement about potentially starting an investigation into Hunter Biden's activities as a member of the Board of Directors of a Ukrainian gas utility company. As most people will recall, this resulted in Donald Trump's first impeachment by the U.S. House of Representatives. Trump, in both cases tried to put pressure on someone to make a press statement that would help him politically, the first, by smearing the son of a political rival, and the second, by tainting that same political rival's victory.

Trump was taking his "Big Lie" a much dangerous step further. In addition to using Republican representatives (including Minority Leader, Kevin McCarthy) and senators to spread his malicious lies about the 2020 presidential election, he was now actively recruiting others in the Justice Department to support and participate in an active conspiracy to mislead the American people and to motivate his supporters to come to the Capitol to help overturn the election. After they arrived in Washington DC, Trump then lit the match with his incendiary rhetoric and deceitful exhortations on January 6th. For his "Big Lie" about the election and for his attempt to spread the conspiracy to include members of the Justice Department, Donald Trump should stand trial as a vicious selfish seditionist. This writer hopes that the House Committee investigating the insurrection can, at a minimum, damage Trump's political brand so thoroughly that he is never taken seriously as a political candidate ever again.

SABOTAGING A SMOOTH TRANSITION OF POWER

This chapter has so far focused directly on Trump's willingness to sabotage our democracy by his direct broadside attacks on our cherished democracy and right to vote. I would like to next discuss his ugly willingness to hold up the briefings and transition activities necessary to put our new president-elect, Joe Biden, in position to deal with the problems and opportunities ahead for our country. The willingness and determination of Donald Trump to "swamp the boat" and harm our country's preparedness cannot even charitably be described as anything other than traitorous.

We needed the Biden administration to be ready for the myriad challenges we would face to our national security. Without the briefings and other shared information, the people chosen for cabinet-level national security positions (secretary of defense, secretary of state, secretary of Homeland Security) and other key positions like national security adviser were not going to be able to get up to speed as quickly. It offered our adversaries more time and ability to operate against our interests around the world. Russia, China, North Korea, Iran, and others were no doubt happy with this transition stiff-arm that Trump gave our president-elect. This sideshow by Trump also prevented the timely installment of the key national security team because this team must be approved by Congress.

In the past, the General Services Administration (GSA) always moved forward quickly with approval of commencement of the transition. This provided for office space and funding of all transition activities and meetings. This year under the petty and dictatorial lame-duck president, the GSA withheld this key declaration pending official vote certifications or a concession by Trump. Our traitorous president was willing to hold up vital intelligence assessments and briefings from the incoming president. Most Republicans went along with President Trump for far too long, but at least a few recognized the dangers of not proceeding to start the transition. President-elect Biden initially powered through this refusal by Trump to assist in the transition, calling the president's refusal to concede an "embarrassment."

Not only did Trump fire key national security personal with about two months remaining in his tenure in office, but he also notified military commanders to expect orders to begin significant drawdowns of troop levels in Iraq and Afghanistan before January 15. This left President-elect Biden to deal with the potential fallout from a collapse of the Afghan government in the wake of a resurgent Taliban offensive push. The *New York Times* reported recently that the president had sought options to strike Iran militarily during the lame-duck period to hurt its nuclear capacity. If he had initiated such an action, it would have made it nearly impossible for the Biden administration to revive the Obama-negotiated agreement with Iran and other international allies limiting Tehran's ability to jump-start its nuclear weapons program. Fortunately, advisers to the president persuaded him not to pursue a reckless attack that could have triggered a wider conflict and undercut one of his campaign promises—not to engage the United States in another war in the Middle East.[243]

The other major problem our country faced from Trump's steadfast refusal to cooperate in the transition process was the rollout of coronavirus strategy including the vaccine distribution efforts that would need to begin once the vaccines had been given final approvals from the Federal Drug Administration (FDA). This outright refusal to help our new president by the outgoing commander in chief was again the act of a vicious traitor.

What is wrong with the Trump supporters and other Republic leaders? Could they not see what was right in front of their eyes? Two vaccine trial results from Pfizer and Moderna were extremely promising, with initial results on efficacy over 90 percent and minimal side effects. There was serious concern that Trump's refusal to move forward with the transition could slow and seriously complicate the distribution efforts of these and perhaps other vaccine candidates currently in the testing protocols. This could result in unnecessary additional deaths from the coronavirus and more delay in pulling us out of the huge economic hardship faced by many Americans and their families. It could result in delaying Americans a chance to return to normalcy as quickly. People want to return to work. They want to see family and friends. They want to travel, dine out at restaurants, meet friends at bars, and attend concerts, plays, and sporting events.

The massive logistics operation of low-temperature storage and distribution of the vaccines needs to be rolled out in phases based on ranked priorities. Despite the appallingly selfish behavior of many Trump supporters, who refused to wear masks, who attended super-spreader events, and who made every effort to politicize this public health crisis, the biotech industry was able to come up with vaccine candidates that could stop this contagion in its tracks.

The national and international inoculation efforts will still require a high level of trust by the public and will require strong ethical debate over who should be prioritized to get the vaccines first. The whole program could be damaged if it is politicized. By Trump's refusal to cooperate, the Biden team was forced into a dangerous game of catch-up in dealing with the coronavirus before and after the vaccines were approved for distribution.

During the past year, the abject, willful failure of President Trump to take needed steps and to demonstrate leadership by rallying the American people to adopt measures to help slow the spread of the coronavirus was shocking for most of us to watch. With continued vacuous leadership during Trump's lame-duck period, it was even more important than ever to make the transition go as smoothly as possible to alleviate the mistakes and overall mismanagement of the past year. America needed Joe Biden and his team to be able to hit the ground running on January 20. The victims of Trump's negligence were thousands of Americans in the absence of a well-coordinated national response to the winter spike in infections. The difference between these two men regarding this pandemic could not have been clearer after witnessing the past two weeks since the election. Joe Biden had a sense of urgency to call for and coordinate a national response to mitigate this uncontrolled nationwide spike in new infections and the crippling impact on our nation's health, our economic well-being, and our national psyche.

Donald Trump, on the other hand, wallowed in self-pity, personal grievance, and uncontained rage over his humiliating electoral loss. Trump still could not grasp the moral imperative of being a good steward to his countrymen. He continued to boost unfounded conspiracy theories about imagined voter fraud simply to stoke the fires of anger and ill-will within his voting base in a vile attempt to maintain control of the levers of power within the Republican Party and to keep his followers in thrall to him. With the number of dead Americans climbing by over three thousand per day and millions of Americans out of work and needing economic support to keep their businesses from failing (particularly restaurants), Donald Trump gave us a real look inside his heart and mind. He demonstrated each day his single-minded determination to put his misplaced personal goals ahead of the national interest.

CHAPTER 8

LIES, MISINFORMATION, AND CONSPIRACY THEORIES

IN THE *WASHINGTON* Post, an article titled "President Trump has made more than 20,000 false or misleading claims," by Glenn Kessler, Salvador Rizzo, and Meg Kelly, dated July 13, 2020, highlights the total mendacity and shockingly brazen disregard for the truth exemplified by Donald Trump and his minions. It took Donald Trump 827 days into his presidency before he topped ten thousand false or misleading claims in the Fact Checker's database, an average of twelve per day. By July 9, 2020, just 440 days later, he crossed the deceit barrier of twenty thousand false or misleading claims, an average of twenty-three claims a day over a fourteen-month period.[244]

The coronavirus in early 2020 gave rise to a whole new category of Trump falsehoods. In just a few months, this category of lies and misleading statements reached almost one thousand, more than his false claims about his personal income taxes. Just prior to the coronavirus reaching our shores, during his impeachment investigation and hearings, Trump made another nearly twelve hundred false and misleading statements.[245]

When the *Fact Checker* started this project at the beginning of the Trump presidency, Donald Trump averaged fewer than five misleading or outright false claims in the first one hundred days in office. At that initial pace, he would have ended up with about seven thousand false or misleading claims in his four-year term in office. However, Lying Don picked up the pace, making even Pinocchio proud. As of July 9, 2020, the grand total of falsehoods reached 20,055.[246]

An appearance on Sean Hannity's show on Fox News put him over the twenty thousand mark. Below is a list of some of the falsehoods uttered during this interview with Sean Hannity, one of Trump's leading bootlickers.

➤ Former President Barack Obama "did not want" to give surplus military equipment to police. Obama scaled back the program but still allowed specialized firearms, manned and unmanned aircraft, explosives, and riot gear.

➤ Trump has tremendous support in the African American community. No polling shows this.

➤ Trump "insisted" the National Guard be used in Minneapolis to quell disturbances, and Seattle officials "knew" he was ready to act with force if the city did not shut down protests. Local officials say neither claim was true; they acted on their own.

➤ The United States has a "record" for coronavirus testing, and China has not tested as many people as the United States. The United States still lags several major countries in terms of tests per million people, the best metric for comparison. The United States has a higher per capita testing rate than China, but China in June said it had tested ninety million people- at the time, three times as many as the United States.

➤ Obama and former Vice President Joe Biden "spied" on his campaign and "knew everything that was going on." Trump has made allegations of Obama spying since 2017, based on little or no evidence.

➤ The jury forewoman in the Roger Stone trial was "disgraceful." The judge in the case rejected claims of bias. Tomeka Hart's political leanings and activities were clearly known during the jury selection process, and not even Stone's legal team tried to strike her from the jury pool.

➤ Paul Manafort, Trump's former campaign manager, was placed in "solitary confinement," while Al Capone "was never in solitary confinement." Manafort was in a "private, self-contained living unit" that was larger than other units, which included a bathroom, shower, telephone, and laptop access, according to court records. Capone was eventually sent to the infamous Alcatraz prison, where he was stabbed and got into fights and, according to some reports, ended up in solitary confinement as his brain deteriorated from untreated syphilis.

➤ "We're doing record numbers on the border." In 2020, no records were set, and border apprehensions spiked sharply in June.

➤ "We've rebuilt the military, $2.5 trillion." Trump frequently suggests this money is all for new equipment, but he's adding together three years of budgets, none of which is a record.[247]

Throughout his presidency, Trump's most repeated claim (360 times) is that the US economy today is the best in history. He began making this claim in 2018, and very quickly it became one of his favorite untruths. Whereas he used to say it was the best economy in US history, he now often says that he achieved "the best economy in the world." He could have legitimately taken some credit for continuing the economic growth that originated with the Obama administration, but he could not stop himself from trying to claim, greatest of all-time (GOAT status).[248]

"By most important measures, the precoronavirus economy was not doing as well as it did under Presidents Dwight Eisenhower, Lyndon Johnson, Bill Clinton, or Ulysses Grant. By that time, the Trump economy was also slowing, the result of his incessant trade wars. The manufacturing sector was tipping into recession. Trump managed to repeat his mantra of the 'best economy ever' over one hundred times after the coronavirus emerged in China and sent the US economy into a deep depression, crushing the retail, restaurant, and travel sectors of the economy."[249] Trump attempted to use the economy as a closing sales pitch for his reelection in 2020, but his mismanagement of the coronavirus undercut him and helped lead to his defeat.

"Trump's second most repeated claim, 261 times, is that his border wall is being built. Congress refused to fund his full-length concrete barrier wall, so the project evolved into the replacement of smaller older barriers with steel bollard fencing. New fencing has been put on very few miles of open land. The *Washington Post* reported that this bollard fencing is easily breached, with smugglers sawing through it, despite Trump's claims that it is impossible to get past. Sadly, the project has diverted billions in military and counter-narcotics funding to become one of the nation's largest infrastructure projects in US history. Not achieving its dubious purpose, and at the same time, causing the seizure of private lands, the cut-off of wild animal traffic corridors, and disrupting Native American cultural sites, the wall will eventually be remembered as America's biggest 'white elephant.'"[250]

"Trump has falsely said 210 times that he passed the biggest tax cut in history."[251] Before it was passed, he promised it would be the biggest, even bigger than Republican presidential icon Ronald Reagan's tax cut. Reagan's tax cut was 2.9% of Gross National Product (GNP). When the Trump tax cut finally was passed, it was 0.9% of GNP, making it the eighth largest tax cut in one hundred years. Still, when he trotted out this "whopper" at his rallies, it got cheers and applause.[252]

The database created by the *Washington Post* has gone through every statement the president made at press conferences, rallies, in TV appearances, and on social media. In partnership with *PolitiFact*, *Kaiser Health News* produced a news story entitled "Downplay and Denial of the Coronavirus," by Daniel Funke and Katie Sanders.

> A Florida taxi driver and his wife had seen enough conspiracy stories online to believe the virus was overblown, maybe even a hoax. So, no masks for them. They got sick. She died. A college lecturer had trouble refilling her lupus drug after the president promoted

it as a treatment for the new disease. A hospital nurse broke down when an ICU patient insisted his illness was nothing worse than the flu, oblivious to the silence in beds next door.

Lies infected America in 2020. The very worst were not just damaging, but deadly.[253]

President Donald Trump fomented confusion and incited conspiracies from the earliest days of the coronavirus pandemic. He clung to the idea that COVID-19 accounted for only a tiny percentage of thousands upon thousands of deaths. He undermined public health guidance from public health professionals like Dr. Anthony Fauci. Others inside the administration added to the idiocy spewed by Trump by offering up more junk science. Trump addicts, even some medical doctors, threw out accusations that hospitals were padding their coronavirus case numbers to generate bonus payments. Influential TV and radio opinion hosts told millions of viewers and listeners that physical distancing was a joke and that states had all the protective equipment they needed when they did not.

It was a symphony of counternarrative, and Trump was the conductor, if not the composer. The message: The threat to your health was overhyped to hurt the political fortunes of the president.[254]

Every year the editors at *PolitiFact* review the year's most inaccurate, untruthful statements to determine which to award the Lie of the Year. The award goes to a statement or a collection of claims that prove the most substantial at undermining truth and reality. It has become harder and harder to choose when cynical political pundits and politicians no longer pay much of a price for spreading even the most grievous lies and misinformation falsehoods. For the past month and a half, the president and his toadies in the Republican Party have continued to spread unproven claims of massive election fraud, testing our democratic institutions. These bald-faced lies certainly qualify as historic, but fortunately, they have been unable to topple our constitutional form of government or our democratic traditions. They sure tried, however, with their violent assault on our Capitol.

As of the evening of December 30, 2020, the coronavirus has killed over 341,000 Americans (projected to be over 400,000 by the end of January), a health crisis made more virulent by the reckless spreading of knowing falsehoods. Therefore, PolitiFact's 2020 Lie of the Year: any and all claims that deny, downplay, or misinform the American public about COVID-19.

As mentioned in a previous chapter, Donald Trump acknowledged during a taped interview with Bob Woodward on February 7, 2020, that the coronavirus was "more deadly than even your strenuous flus." On February 26, 2020, he told the public something else entirely when he appeared with the coronavirus task force briefing. He said, "I mean view this the same as flu." Three weeks later, on March 19, he acknowledged to Woodward the following: "To be honest with you, I wanted to always play it down. I still like playing it down. Because I don't want to create a panic."[255]

His political allies in the right-wing media told similar stories to their large audiences. Rush Limbaugh told his audience on February 24 that the coronavirus was being weaponized against Trump when it was "just the common cold, folks." This was so wrong, when in the very beginning it was known to have a much higher fatality rate than the common cold or flu. Steve Deace on Facebook claimed that only 6 percent of deaths blamed on coronavirus could be attributed to this virus. This was a gross misrepresentation. The CDC had always said that people with underlying health problems, comorbidities, such as diabetes, hypertension, and asthma, were more vulnerable if they caught coronavirus. Their report noted that 6 percent of the people who died from coronavirus had no underlying health conditions. This idea that only 6 percent of the people who caught COVID-19 and died had died from COVID-19 was peddled all over social media. These coronavirus deniers kept saying 94 percent of the people who caught COVID-19 and died, died from other factors or comorbidities. Dr.

Anthony Fauci addressed this claim on *Good Morning America,* on September 1, 2020. "The point that the CDC was trying to make was that a certain percentage of them had nothing else but just COVID. That does not mean that someone who has hypertension or diabetes who dies of COVID didn't die of COVID-19—they did."[256]

False and misleading information about the cause of death from coronavirus continued to move between social media, Donald Trump, and TV, creating this feedback loop. The same thing happened concerning the wearing of masks. At the very beginning of the pandemic, the CDC told healthy people not to wear masks, saying it was more important for health-care workers on the front lines treating coronavirus patients to wear masks. By April 3, however, the CDC changed its guidelines, saying every American should wear a mask in public. Trump announced the CDC recommendation and then immediately rendered it useless. At a press briefing he said, "So it's voluntary. You don't have to do it. They suggested for a period of time, but this is voluntary. I don't think I'm going to do it."[257]

Donald Trump, instead of promoting the best practices recommended by public health experts, turned mask wearing into a political calculation. Americans saw him time and again appear before the public without a mask. On the internet, countless others made wild, unsubstantiated claims to undercut the message of epidemiologists and public health experts. They would say things like: masks reduce oxygen, masks trap fungus, masks trap coronavirus, and masks just did not work. On Fox News, Tucker Carlson claimed that almost everyone, about 85 percent, who got coronavirus in July were wearing masks. He was wrong, making a claim based on a small sample of people who tested positive. Public health experts have been very consistent since April 2020, saying face masks are one of the best ways to prevent the spread of coronavirus. The combination of Trump's failure to lead by example, by not wearing a mask, false internet claims, and misinformation by alt-right media personalities worked together to send a message to Trump supporters that mask wearing was unnecessary and probably harmful.

On March 24 at the end of her shift, registered nurse Melissa

Steiner posted a tearful video talking about her experiences treating COVID-19 patients in the ICU of a Michigan hospital. Below is her emotional plea.

> Honestly, guys, it felt like I was working in a war zone. I was completely isolated from my team members, limited resources, limited supplies, limited responses from physicians because they're just as overwhelmed.
>
> I'm already breaking, so for f---'s sake, people, please take this seriously. This is so bad.[258]

Steiner's post was one of many emotional pleas by overwhelmed hospital workers, risking their own lives to try and save others. The virus deniers then mounted their counteroffensive. On the Laura Ingraham show on Fox News, Dr. Scott Jensen, a Minnesota physician, accused hospitals of overreporting coronavirus cases to collect more money from Medicare. He accused hospitals of fraud without any proof whatsoever, and his false claims got circulated on social media like they were true, when they clearly were not true. Trump cynically jumped all over this false and misleading reporting on the campaign trail and continued to minimize the climbing death toll.[259]

One of the most egregious examples of misinformation about the pandemic was made to look as if it was coming from the scientific community of health experts. In this video, "Pandemic: The Hidden Agenda Behind COVID-19," a former scientist at the National Cancer Institute claimed the virus was being manipulated in a lab, hydroxychloroquine was effective against coronavirus, and face masks made people sick. On July 27 on "Breitbart," a group called America's Frontline Doctors, standing in front of the US Supreme Court, discouraged mask wearing and claimed hydroxychloroquine (a drug used for rheumatoid arthritis and lupus) was already a cure for coronavirus. This misinformation about hydroxychloroquine created a shortage of the drug for people with lupus and rheumatoid arthritis.[260]

On September 26, Trump hosted a Rose Garden ceremony to

announce his replacement for the late Ruth Bader Ginsburg on the US Supreme Court. More than 150 people attended the event. There was no social distancing, and few people wore masks. About six days later, Trump announced that he tested positive for coronavirus along with his wife, Melania, and several others including three US senators. Trump, who should have been sobered by contracting the virus, began minimizing it almost immediately upon returning to the White House after leaving Walter Reed Hospital. Instead of accepting responsibility for his poor judgment about the large White House gathering, he bragged about his quick recovery. On the morning after his return to the White House from Walter Reed Hospital, Trump tweeted that COVID-19 was far less lethal for most age groups than flu in a typical flu season. This claim was false. Within every age group, the mortality rate from COVID-19 was much higher than the mortality rate from seasonal flu. When Trump left the hospital, the death total in the United States was more than two hundred thousand. While the death total climbed above 380,000, Trump moved forward with a group of holiday parties in the White House and daily golf outings.

The vaccine misinformation campaign started in the spring of 2020, and it is still under way. Blogs and social media users were claiming that Democrats and Bill Gates wanted to use microchips to track which Americans had been vaccinated. One blogger claimed that Pfizer's head of research said the coronavirus vaccine could cause female infertility, which was totally false. Another website claimed the vaccine could cause a wide array of life-threatening side effects, and that the FDA knew about this. The list included all possible, not confirmed, side effects. Social media users speculated that the federal government would force Americans to receive the vaccine. Neither Trump nor Biden has advocated mandatory vaccination, and for that matter, the federal government does not have the power to universally mandate vaccines. "Most polling has shown far less than universal acceptance of the vaccines with about 50% to 70% of Americans willing to take a vaccine. The Institute for Health Metrics and Evaluation projected that without mask mandates and a rapid rollout of the vaccine, the death toll could rise to more than 500,000 by April 2021."[261] As of May 15, 2021 the actual death total is above 585,000.

This sad, deplorable misinformation campaign with its outright spread of lies and falsehoods certainly contributed to more deaths than necessary from the coronavirus. Unfortunately, the people in the United States are now living in two separate informational realities, one based on truth and logic, and the other based on falsehood and political propaganda.

At campaign rallies, which have been the primary tool of his campaign, Trump unloads so many lies, so much misinformation, and so many gross exaggerations on his easily deceived audiences that they no longer recognize truth. In the *New York Times* in an article titled "Rallies Are the Core of Trump's Campaign, and a Font of Lies and Misinformation," dated October 26, 2020, by Linda Qiu and Michael Shear, they document a litany of lies at a campaign rally in Janesville, Wisconsin. In his ninety-minute appearance, Trump made 131 false or misleading statements.[262]

Early into the rally, Trump asserted that the United States was doing very well compared to Europe and other countries in controlling the coronavirus. This was so false as to almost deserve no other comment. The truth is that the United States has more cases and more deaths per capita than any other country in Europe except Belgium and Spain. I mentioned previously, but I still think it is worth repeating, that the United States has 4 percent of the world's population, but more than five times the number of deaths from Covid-19.

Below, the authors of this article summarize the scope and scale of Trump's deceit. The president's pattern of speech is at times so inarticulate that it often sounds like a discordant cymbal at a violin concerto. His audience might at times become so confused trying to understand his "word salad" that many of the lies fly under the radar.

> Over the course of the next 87 minutes, the president made another 130 false or inaccurate statements. Many were entirely made up. Others were casual misstatements of simple facts, some clearly intended to

mislead. He lied about his own record and that of his opponent. He made wild exaggerations that violated even pliable limits of standard political hyperbole.[263]

While it is certainly true that past presidential candidates have used political speech to occasionally bend the truth, Donald Trump is different. His falsehoods form the basis of his campaign rallies. The lack of truth is integral to ginning up and motivating his audience. A detailed review of his statements in Janesville by the *New York Times* found more than 75 percent of his assertions were either false, misleading, exaggerated, disputed, or lacked evidence. Less than 25 percent were true.[264]

The rally in Janesville was not unique. Since Inauguration Day, the president has held more than 125 rallies around the country, mostly in states where the electoral outcome would be determined. Trump loved to do rallies because it made him feel comfortable and validated by his adoring crowds. He can be nearly totally disconnected from the truth and still bask in the adoring applause and shouts of support from the audience. After Trump was released from Walter Reed Hospital where he was treated for Covid-19, he delivered similar stump speeches at rallies in Florida, Georgia, Iowa, Michigan, Nevada, North Carolina, and Pennsylvania. In each place, he repeated many of the same lies, often verbatim, despite being challenged by fact-checkers.

Let's look at twelve particularly inaccurate statements he made at the Janesville rally.

1.   Trump claimed to have enacted the "biggest tax cut in history" and that Joe Biden was "going to raise your taxes substantially, like quadruple."

REBUTTAL

As mentioned previously, Trump's tax cut was about one-third the size of Ronald Reagan's tax cut and was the eighth largest in the last one hundred years. Joe Biden promised no tax increase for anyone making less than $400,000 per year. For those making over $400,000 per year, their taxes would only increase at the marginal tax rate. Their tax rate on the first $400,000 of income would be the same as it is now and the same as everyone else's.

2. Trump claimed that "everybody owns stocks."

REBUTTAL

This claim is totally false. Only about half of all Americans own stocks.

3. Trump claimed that "we cut more regulations than any administration in history."

REBUTTAL

There is no evidence of this.

4. Trump claimed that Joe Biden would "ban fracking."

REBUTTAL

Joe Biden never said he would ban fracking entirely. He said he would ban fracking only on public lands, not on private property.

5. Trump claimed that Democrats would reduce the child tax credit.

REBUTTAL

Joe Biden, in fact, said he would expand it.

6. Trump claimed that "it used to take 18 to 21 years to get a highway built" and that he reduced it to two years.

REBUTTAL

The average has been between three and six years and recently has been three years.

7. Trump claimed that Joe Biden would implement a nationwide economic lockdown to combat the coronavirus.

REBUTTAL

Joe Biden has said he would follow the recommendations of public health experts. If they felt it was necessary, he would do it, but otherwise, he would just focus on promoting social distancing and mask wearing.

8. Trump claimed several times to have "rebuilt a depleted" military.

REBUTTAL

This is a huge exaggeration. Most military members, based on preelection polling and exit polling, voted against Donald Trump. The numbers were especially bad for Trump among the officer corps.

9. Trump told the crowd that his policies had "brought back many car plants" and that the previous administrations "had not brought back a plant in over 42 years."

REBUTTAL

This again was totally false.

10. Trump promised to protect people with preexisting conditions, a vow that he has made throughout his entire presidency.

REBUTTAL

This again was totally false. He pushed Congress to overturn the Affordable Care Act that provides this protection.

11. Trump said repeatedly that Joe Biden and the Democrats "don't want to have a border."

REBUTTAL

This again is totally false. Joe Biden's immigration plan includes border screening. Biden has said, "Like every nation, the US has a right and a duty to secure our borders."

12. Trump continued to insist that his border wall was being built and that Mexico was paying for it.

REBUTTAL

This again was totally false. Almost all 371 miles of barriers were replacement barriers, not new barriers on open land. Mexico has steadfastly refused to pay anything for building this wall. There has been no border fee.[265]

Trump did cite data at times during these rallies to promote his accomplishments, but he often changed the numbers to make the results look better than they really were. In Janesville, he claimed the unemployment numbers for Black Americans, Hispanic Americans, and Asian Americans, women, and people without a high school degree to be the "greatest." All of that was true, but then he also claimed that employment numbers were the greatest for "people with a diploma," and "people that graduated first in their class at MIT." In fact, unemployment rates were lower for high school and college graduates before he took office.[266]

Trump then claimed to have the support of every single police union in the United States, even in New York City. He was correct in saying the New York City police union endorsed him; however, many other police unions and law enforcement groups did not. He then said that Joe Biden did not have the support of law enforcement, when in fact, 190 law enforcement officials endorsed him. He also claimed that Joe Biden refused to use the words *law and order* during their first presidential debate. That, of course, was a lie.[267]

The president then claimed in the rally to have "saved your suburbs, your house, and the American dream." This might have been a reference to an Obama-era housing rule regarding a more rigorous process to reduce housing discrimination. It did not impose low-income housing or any zoning changes on local municipalities. If Donald Trump's claims of rescuing the suburbs were true, why did the suburban vote in the 2020 election go so heavily to Joe Biden?

Many of Trump's deliberate lies serve to support caricatures of his opponents, a tactic he used in both 2016 (remember lying Ted, Little Marco, Sleepy Joe) and 2020. He continued to suggest to the crowd that Joe Biden was sitting in his basement throughout the campaign and that Joe Biden was losing his edge mentally. The first debate put an end to the mental capability issue. Joe Biden looked dignified, confident, and presidential compared to Donald Trump, who appeared rude, combative, and ill-informed.

Donald Trump could never stop himself from taking jabs at his predecessor, Barack Obama. Near the end of the Janesville rally, he referred to "hydrosonic missiles; I call them superduper missiles; they go seven times faster than a normal missile. Now President Obama let that get away." Again, Trump offers nothing but falsehood and misinformation. Efforts to revamp the US nuclear arsenal began under President Obama. President Trump also confused a hypersonic missile with the name of a toothbrush.[268]

Before wrapping up his remarks in Janesville, the president in promising to "make America great again," bragged about saving a plant in Lima, Ohio, that manufactures and assembles M1 Abrams tanks for the army. There were no plans to shutter this plant, and Congress has authorized millions to fund continued production at this plant.[269]

The people in the crowd applauded and screamed approval. The wrecking ball of lies will no doubt continue even after the president leaves office. He appears determined to maintain control over his followers, even out-of-office. He wants, dare I say, needs, the adulation from this group of ill-informed but pliable base of supporters.

Trump talks about buying or starting a news operation to compete with other conservative news outlets. This would be a twenty-four-hour Trump cable news operation, featuring everything "Trumpy"— himself, his family, his acolytes, and his fawning, weak-minded supporters. It would facilitate keeping him in the news, and it would be a way to keep his options open for a potential 2024 run for president.

The new cable outlet could be another way for his corrupt family of grifters to raise funds through selling advertising to finance another run for president in 2024 for himself or one of his children. After his dastardly instigation of violence and rebellion at our Capitol, that might now be impossible. It simply could be the ultimate propaganda machine, the most disingenuous attempt to spread lies and misinformation and to traffic in crazy conspiracy theories that our country has ever witnessed.

Although he paints himself as a conservative, he is neither a conservative, nor a moderate. He is an authoritarian, mentally ill narcissist, who has sunk this country into a deep well of unabashed dishonesty and pathetic failure. Despite their MAGA hats and MAGA flags, many of his seventy-four million followers are eager to sabotage America's greatness and cripple America's leadership in the world to feed their compulsion to worship at the feet of Donald Trump. They are deeply uninformed about our history, our collective character as a nation, and what it really means to be a conservative. They are selfish, more concerned with their tax cuts and more concerned with their lust to remain in power at all costs. Many of the people who sacrifice the most for the rest of us, members of our brave military, also have the most insight into the heart and mind of Donald Trump. As mentioned previously in this book, polling among active-duty members of the military revealed considerable dissatisfaction with Trump's leadership. I pray that over time more and more Trump supporters will shake themselves of their fetishlike allegiance to this dishonorable, dictatorial, ignorant, and dangerous narcissist.

Writing this book and reviewing some of the work of others of like mind has been a labor of love. I have many family members and friends who cannot seem to shake themselves of this cultlike addiction to a man of no honor, a man with a shameless desire to remain in power, no matter the cost to his country and its citizens. I have heard family members speak of civil war and question early voting as fraudulent. I have heard friends speak of Trump's rants and tweets as though they are nearly gospel truth. I have seen people who should be smarter than this caught up in a web of denial and anger. I care deeply for them all, but I am deeply afraid that they are not going to be able to pull themselves out of this conspiracy-laden rabbit hole of deceit. This obsession with Trump has caused many to believe things that are obviously untrue.

So many political ads financed by the Republican Party or so-called independent political action committees are rife with demonstrable untruths. Claiming the Democrats are going to eliminate employer-sponsored health insurance, defund police departments and the military, eliminate gun owners' rights and the Second Amendment, and turn the country into a socialist state are so ridiculous. Marginal taxes going up for those making over $400,000 is not socialism. The takeover of ownership and control of all private industry is socialism, not slightly higher tax rates. The stock market did very well under the Obama administration. The well-to-do are not going to lose their homes, their cars, their boats, their 401(k) plans, or their other assets. This clinging to scare-tactic fictions makes the Trumpists and the Republican Party look angry, selfish, and desperate.

They need to grow up and accept that elections have consequences. By putting their faith in a liar and a con man, they have only themselves to blame. The fact that many Republicans and Independents (me included) were unable to hold their noses and vote for Donald Trump should have been a clue about the character of this indecent human being. Unfortunately, many of them seemed to miss this clue because of their willful adulation and worship of this racist, traitor tyrant. When someone selects a person without moral character just to keep their taxes low, they are not exhibiting patriotism or ethical judgment. When they demonize political opponents, lie, and exaggerate about their positions and records, and treat them as enemies, they are placing their wants and needs above their country's well-being. Sadly, they are getting exactly what they deserve! They need to grow up and accept the better judgment of most American voters. More than seven million more voters preferred Joe Biden to the radioactive, self-absorbed fascist traitor in the White House. While the pandemic raged, Donald Trump raged. He was more concerned with remaining in power for four more years than he was in using his remaining days in office to protect and defend the American public, or to keep his legacy from being indelibly stamped as a sore loser, a spoiled brat, and now a shameful seditionist. People need to think carefully about their choices. They were willing to place a traitor ahead of their countrymen. Many in this deranged political party want to move on from this ugly subversion of American values in the name of unity, hoping that the rest of us will forgive and forget this wicked treachery.

There can be no unity until these traitors pay for what they have done and the disgrace of Trumpism is purged from American hearts and minds. After the murderous reign of the Axis powers before and during World War II, there was no forgive and forget by the rest of the world. In the hope that this would never happen again, the perpetrators were swiftly tried and punished. Many senior level Nazi government officials and top military officers were executed or imprisoned for life. With the exception of the German officers and officials who tried to assassinate Hitler (Operation Valkyrie in 1944), others in Germany and elsewhere in Europe who attempted to save as many Jewish people as possible by hiding and smuggling them to safety, by working in the underground, or by serving as spies for the Allies to help shorten the war and bring this criminal regime to justice (Carl Lutz, Freddie Oversteegen, Johan van Hulst, Virginia Hall, and the famous Lutheran pastor Dietrich Bonhoeffer), many of the German people would bear collective guilt for generations by supporting and enabling a mass murderer and his evil cartel of associates.

This stubborn clinging to Donald Trump, a man so unworthy, so unfit for office, and so selfish, evil, and traitorous more than borders on pathological delusion. Under Trump our country has not reached the level of murderous madness that occurred under Hitler and his henchmen before and during World War II, but our country witnessed the inhumanity unleashed on our Capitol that had been percolating in the hearts and minds of hate-filled Trump legions. If they want to be welcomed back into the community of American citizens, they must denounce and vote to punish the traitors immediately. Otherwise, they own this treachery, themselves. They must do this to regain even a modest amount of credibility, a modest amount of self-respect, and a modest amount of respect from non-Trump people who realized early on what an existential threat this man has been to our democracy, our civility, and our national security.

In an article in *The Conversation*, titled "Trump's lies about the election show how disinformation erodes democracy," dated November 29, 2020, by Chris Tenove and Spencer McKay, the authors refer to recent polls that found about 70 percent of Republican supporters believe President Donald Trump was defeated in an unfair and fraudulent election. Numerous legal challenges by the Trump campaign have been defeated in court across the country, and rumors about election fraud have been thoroughly debunked. Not one secretary of state, Republican or Democratic, questioned the validity or accuracy of the vote. Even several journalists at Fox News said that the election was won by Joe Biden, and that it was won fair and square by a wide margin without fraud.[270]

Nevertheless, most Republicans cling to the belief that the election was illegitimate. This, as discussed previously, caused a problem for a smooth transition of power, and it turned our political and civic life into an ugly farce. To function smoothly, the authors point out three things that must exist for a democratic political system to work:

➤ It must include citizens in its political processes.
➤ It must incorporate high-quality information into decision-making.
➤ It must ensure a baseline of mutual respect and acceptance.[271]

Instances of dangerous disinformation can be successfully challenged in the public market, but the volume and persistence of concerted attacks on our nation's institutions and norms that enable political discourse provide opportunity for serious and lasting damage. Disinformation is communication that deliberately promotes misunderstanding through lies, misrepresentations, deceptive sourcing, or other tactics. Disinformation campaigns are organized efforts to use disinformation to achieve political or economic goals.

Russia was a primary source of disinformation in the 2016 election, and Russia and other countries like North Korea and Iran continue to target the United States with disinformation. In 2020, however, American partisan elites were the primary source of disinformation. The originators of disinformation campaigns might be a small number of people, but they can have a disproportionate impact when their lies or false claims are increased in scope and volume by high-profile influencers and others on social media.[272]

Three harmful forms of disinformation were identified and will be discussed.

> The first is corrosive falsehood. This is much worse than typical garden variety lying. It involves an attempt to undermine institutions that typically provide high-quality information or correct false beliefs, such as professional news media and government information agencies. Russian government information agencies, conservative commentators, and Trump have consistently attacked the credibility of professional journalists, accused news organizations of spreading "fake news" and created actual fake news organizations to push partisan messages. Social media platforms did little to push back against the false information pushed in the 2016 election. They have made a stronger attempt in the 2020 election campaign to push back against this reckless spread of false, malicious libel.[273]

Unfortunately, libel laws and court precedents protect free speech above the integrity of public officials. Repeated forms of corrosive falsehoods can result in overwhelming cynicism that leads citizens to distrust accurate sources of information, regularly dismiss claims based on partisan commitments, or cease to believe in any shared reality.

> The second is moral denigration. Disinformation cam-
> paigns regularly make false or misleading claims to vilify
> individuals or misrepresent their beliefs. The best ex-
> ample might be Trump and his allies spending months
> promoting conspiracy theories about Joe Biden and his
> family using the #Biden Crime Family hashtag. It also
> includes efforts to portray leading Democrats as sup-
> porters of shadowy global cabals, or child-trafficking
> and pedophilia rings. Such claims provoke antipathy
> and disgust, and if believed, justify total disregard for
> anything the accused individuals say.[274]

This strategy attempts to destroy the character of the partisan opponent without any evidence or truth. These ugly, vicious attacks say more about the integrity and character of the attacker than the person being attacked.

Even though Joe Biden received more votes in Arizona and Georgia as well as more votes in the national popular vote, the so-called "Stop the Steal" campaigns emerged on right-wing media outlets. These disinformation campaigns used the same baseless rhetoric, implying that political opponents were so undesirable that they could only win by cheating, which they were willing to do because they were corrupt. This type of attack, many psychologists would say, is classic projection. Project your corruption on your opponent and hope nobody is paying attention.

The third is unjustified inclusion, when people without rights to participate in a democratic process do so at the expense of legitimate participants. Foreign disinformation campaigns do this by using fake accounts or bots claiming to be American citizens. Domestic and foreign agitators have used fake accounts to be members of groups hated and despised by Republicans, such as Antifa or Black Lives Matter, to misrepresent their views and widen societal divisions. "Unjustified inclusion often leads to unjustified exclusion, such as when the voices of real citizens are drowned out, or when real individuals are labeled as fake. This too, is a common strategy of disinformation campaigns."[275]

> There have also been widespread, false accusations that anti-racism protestors or victims of gun violence were actually paid actors or that millions of fake people were voting by mail. Over time, such allegations can produce a situation of fake inauthenticity, when many people believe that fake or illegal participation in their democracy is widespread.[276]

While elections and the peaceful transition of power are typically seen as minimal conditions in a democracy, it is becoming clear that a healthy, knowledgeable public is the foundation to the proper functioning of elections and hope for "Making America Great Again," or simply "Enabling America to be Sane Again."

> If citizens do not believe the institutions that count ballots and the organizations that accurately and credibly report those results, if they see political opponents as unworthy of being heard, if they dismiss the voices and votes of other citizens as fake or illegal, then it will be impossible to agree on what a legitimate election looks like.[277]

Without being willing to talk to non-Trump voters and willing to share differing views in good faith, it does not matter to most Trump voters which candidate gets the most votes and wins the election. To them, facts are not important. They will only accept victory for their candidate.

On *CNN Politics*, a segment by Daniel Dale, dated September 2, 2020, titled "Fact check: A guide to 9 conspiracy theories Trump is currently pushing," Dale lists and then refutes each of nine recent conspiracy theories Trump was pushing. By no means is it an exhaustive list covering all his peddled conspiracy theories; it provides typical baseless samples.

THUGS ON A PLANE

On a Fox interview, Trump told a story about what he claimed was a plane flight to Washington loaded with thugs wearing black uniforms, bent on causing destruction and chaos on the streets. He repeated the story the next day, but this time he said the flight was from Washington.

"Facts First": Neither Trump, nor anyone in his inner circle, has presented any evidence to corroborate this story.[278]

WEALTHY FUNDERS

In another interview, Trump suggested violent protesters were being funded by "some very stupid rich people." This was a similar claim to one he made in August when he alleged antifa activists were being funded by Democrats, George Soros, and other people.

"Facts First": There is no basis for the claims that Democrats, George Soros, or other wealthy individuals funded antifa or violent protesters. Some famous or wealthy people have donated to the Black Lives Matter racial justice movement, but that is not what Trump was insinuating.[279]

CORONAVIRUS

Both on Twitter and in a Fox News interview, Trump promoted a QAnon conspiracy theory that said the CDC had admitted that only

6 percent of reported COVID-19 deaths were people who actually died from COVID-19.

"Facts First": Trump was incorrectly describing the 6 percent statistic. The CDC simply said that 6 percent of victims' death certificates listed only COVID-19 as a cause of death. The other 94 percent of death certificates included other conditions as well (comorbidities), but the presence of comorbidities does not mean COVID-19 did not cause the death. Without COVID-19, the person would still be alive. The CDC's chief of mortality statistics, Bob Anderson, said on CNN that people with hypertension, diabetes, or other chronic conditions could live normal lives for years with treatment for these conditions until COVID-19 struck them down. Both Anderson and Dr. Anthony Fauci said the presence of comorbidities does not mean that COVID-19 did not kill them. They both said COVID-19 was the cause of death, the trigger that killed them.[280]

THE 2016 POPULAR VOTE

Trump, who earned nearly three million less votes in the 2016 election for president than his opponent, Hillary Clinton, claimed that he won the popular vote. Trump claimed there was a tremendous amount of cheating in California and New York.

"Facts First": This is false. There was no evidence of mass fraud in California or New York in the 2016 election.[281]

THE GENERAL FAIRNESS OF THE 2020 ELECTION

In a speech to the Republican National Convention, Trump said, "The only way they can take this election away from us is if this is a rigged election."

"Facts First": This is false. There is no evidence the election was rigged or that any significant fraud occurred. The president was decisively beaten both in electoral votes and in the national popular vote.[282]

MAIL VOTING IN THE 2020 ELECTION

The president has repeatedly alleged that the increased use of mail-in voting this year would produce a rigged election. He cast doubt on the use of mail-in drop boxes. He claimed foreign countries could easily interfere with mail-in voting. He suggested that only through cheating could he have a lead on election night, but then turn out to lose after the mail-in ballots are counted.

"Facts First": All of Trump's allegations were undeniably false. Mail voting was not rife with fraud; drop boxes were secure; and US intelligence agencies said unequivocally that foreign powers were not able to penetrate the ballot collection or counting process. There was nothing rigged about states counting every legitimate ballot, mailed or in person.[283]

JOE BIDEN'S INDEPENDENCE

Trump has time and again tried to portray Joe Biden as a puppet of the far left. He claimed in a Fox News interview that Biden's strings were being pulled by people we never heard of, by people that were in dark shadows.

"Facts First": This is absolute rubbish. Biden's staff is comprised of Democrats, many of whom have been involved in Democratic politics for decades. Most are well-known, respected people with public records, not shadowy figures of the far left.[284]

BIDEN AND SPYING

Trump dragged Joe Biden into his frequent allegation that Barack Obama spied on Trump's campaign in 2016. He said both Obama and Biden spied on his campaign, and they both were caught.

"Facts First": There is no evidence that either Obama or Biden had any role in ordering FBI surveillance of Trump's campaign. The campaign was investigated by FBI counterintelligence personnel, and justifiably so, as several members of the campaign staff, including Trump's idiot son, Donny Jr., met with Russian operatives. His campaign manager at the time, Paul Manafort, even shared polling data with a Russian intelligence agent. The Trump campaign Russia investigation began in July 2016 when the FBI learned that a Trump campaign aide may have had advance knowledge that Russian intelligence operatives had stolen Democratic emails. A diplomat revealed that the aide, George Papadopoulos, had boasted to him that he had heard Russia had damaging information on Democrat Hillary Clinton that it could release to harm her campaign. That conversation tripped alarms within the FBI. The Russian hacking operation eventually resulted in public disclosure of thousands of emails through Wikileaks.[285]

BIDEN AND DRUGS

Trump alleged in a Fox interview that Joe Biden was taking performance-enhancing drugs. He said Biden could not have improved so much in his final debate with Bernie Sanders without this help.

"Facts First": This again was more nonsense without any basis in fact. Trump made the same baseless claim about Hillary Clinton during the 2016 campaign.[286]

In this chapter, the case has been made that Donald Trump is a liar. My review of recent articles provided many examples of lies and misinformation and outright kooky conspiracy theories promulgated by Donald Trump. These examples are by no means the only ones available. His litany of lies could fill an encyclopedia. What is so disturbing about this retreat from the truth is not that Trump was doing it; it was that about 70 percent of Republicans were believing it. Friends and family members supporting this president have surrendered their common sense, have celebrated behavior and actions by Trump they never would have accepted from anyone else, and have become angry, embittered people whose addicted love for Trump is only exceeded by their hate for the Americans who rejected Trump at the polls.

CHAPTER 9

TRUMP SUPPORTERS, IT IS TIME TO LEAVE THE CULT

AFTER WATCHING BROADCAST and cable news from a variety of sources and reading numerous articles and books about the hostile takeover of the Republican Party by Donald Trump, a man who spent most of his life as a Democrat, I admit that the most baffling part of the Trump years has been watching people who should know better, who should be smarter, and who should have more backbone, character, and honesty, fall for this man with cultlike devotion. This chapter explores the reasons for this strange, unhealthy attachment of his followers and speculates on the future after this sad chapter in American history.

In his book *Traitor, A History of American Betrayal from Benedict Arnold to Donald Trump*, the author, David Rothkopf, includes a quote from H. L. Menken, made during the 1920 election that put Warren Harding into the office of the presidency. The quote, beyond being providential, revealed a deep understanding of the risks of populism. "Instead of embracing his freedoms, the average person, 'He longs for the warm, reassuring smell of the herd, and is willing to take the herdsman with him. The demagogue is one who preaches doctrines he knows to be untrue to men he knows to be idiots.'"[287]

In this book, David Rothkopf quotes himself from an article he wrote in *Foreign Policy* magazine.

Donald Trump, champion and avatar of the shallow state, has won power because his supporters are threatened by what they don't understand, and what they don't understand is almost everything. Indeed, from evolution to data about our economy to the science of vaccines to the threats we face in the world, they reject vast subjects rooted in fact to have reality conform to their worldviews. They don't dig for truth; they skim the media for anything that makes them feel better about themselves. To many of them, knowledge is not a useful tool, but a cunning barrier, elites have created to keep power from the average man and woman.[288]

In this book, Rothkopf says,

While this might sound like just another condemnation of the 'deplorables' from someone comfortably living in an ivory tower, it is not. It is a desire to zero in on the fact that the first war waged by demagogues is against the truth, as sage observers from Hannah Arendt to Michiko Kakutani have reminded us. After all, it is only by creating the idea of fake news that a man who has endured six bankruptcies can persuade voters he was a master businessman; a man whose finances were unknown but who, according to the New York Times, during one year in the 1990s, lost more money than any other man in America, can sell himself, without a shred of evidence, as a billionaire; a man without a moment of his life spent in public service can persuade millions that he cares about their plight; or a man without any policy competencies can convince voters of his competency to govern.[289]

What it leads to, of course, is the elevation of a man who was a traitor from before he was in office and has been an ever-greater catastrophe as president with every day he was in office.

Rothkopf points out in his book that the problem is not Trump, per se, but the problem is his rabid supporters. He says, "It's not one man but the tens of millions who support him. If you dare not say that for fear of offending them, you also will not address the root causes of this societal disease."[290]

"Those causes begin with alienation, fear, frustration, and anxiety. Those problems are exacerbated by inherent prejudice and by the license to hate given by Trump, the GOP, evangelical ministers, Fox News, and the rest of the right-wing grievance-amplification machine."[291]

"What is different in the America of Trump is that hate has not only become more permissible in public, it is that the grievance machine has turned it into a bond among the disaffected, a rallying cry. It is no longer left versus right in America. It is the changing demographic and economic realities of 21st century America versus what we might call the far white."[292]

"We are approaching a great national decision—in the election ahead and in the years that immediately follow—about whether the American experiment will succeed or fail, whether the moment does what two world wars, a civil war, and countless past mis-judgements and missteps could not."[293]

What faces the country now that Trump has been defeated is more of a challenge than anything the country has faced in a long time. We defeated the most corrupt, despicable, incompetent, disloyal president in the history of the country, but now we need to build a foundation of decency, patriotism, competence, and honesty. We need to immediately marginalize Trumpists and to eventually destroy their wicked, crippling movement. To do that we need to analyze what went wrong and who bears the responsibility for metastasizing this cancer on our political system and our previously shared values. If this sounds too strong, too harsh, consider again what occurred at our Capitol on January 6, 2021.

RISE OF TRUMP AND THE ALT RIGHT

Let us begin by looking at some of the issues raised in a book by Charles J. Sykes, *How the Right Lost Its Mind,* one of the best books I have ever read. Just to provide some background, Charlie Sykes was a popular, articulate, and very thoughtful morning talk show host on WTMJ radio in Milwaukee. My wife and I listened to him regularly while we were living in southeast Wisconsin before we retired to North Carolina and later to Georgia. He left WTMJ and joined "The Bulwark," a news network launched in 2018 dedicated to providing political analysis and reporting, free from the constraints of partisan loyalties and tribal prejudices. It is a project of Defending Democracy Together Institute, a 501(c) (3) organization. All donations are tax deductible. He also appears regularly on CNN and MSNBC.

I refer to and quote him extensively in this chapter. His dedication to truth, not to expediency, is rare in the "age of Trump." Moreover, his book on the rise of Donald Trump and the takeover of the Republican Party by the Alt Right is the most thoughtful, penetrating analysis about this period of recent American history that I have ever read.

In this book, Sykes provides the road map on how the Republican Party became the populist vessel for Donald Trump. In his chapter the "Perpetual Outrage Machine," Sykes discussed the firebrands and the purists within the Republican Party who pushed for government shutdowns and major cuts in federal spending. He correctly identified the reality that while this group (many former Tea Party conservatives) insisted America was a center-right country that wanted ever larger federal spending cuts, they were never a majority within the country, or even within the Republican Party. They were the loudest and most frequent critics of other more moderate voices within the GOP. Their perpetual outrage was magnified on right-wing networks such as Fox News and News Max.[294]

These networks and their opinion stars and guests created what Sykes referred to in the title of his next chapter, "Alt Reality Media." In the last ten years, citizens on the right side of the political spectrum have to a nearly universal degree separated themselves from a variety of news sources and opinions. By isolating themselves, they have created an alternate reality with their own set of facts, narratives, opinions, and, yes, truths. This loud echo chamber has magnified divisions and dislikes, sometimes bordering on hate. In fairness to conservatives, the mainstream media sources in the past have often displayed bias in reporting on conservative ideas and candidates. However, I think there has been some improvement in recent years because many of these mainstream sources have heard the criticism and acted accordingly. I believe that some have made sincere efforts to try and get more responsible conservatives (including Never Trumpers) on their shows. However, I also believe that they have had a difficult time getting Trump or his hard-core acolytes to come on their shows.

Charlie Sykes points out that social media sites are a special problem unto themselves. People seeking people with like-minded political views reinforce their own views and amp up their own and others' anger. He stresses that the result is a perpetual feeding frenzy of post-truth politics. Misinformation and eventually outright false conspiracy theories spread through the Alt Right crowd at dizzying speed. Anything they have heard from others outside their chosen media and social media sites are discounted or discarded. Consequently, objective norms and standards are ignored. Anything that challenges their self-imposed reality is referred to as "fake news," even if it is clearly and demonstrably true. The bottom line is this: depending on their source, some or most of their Alt Right news is false (fake news), and again depending on the source, some or most of the news they claim is fake news is instead true. Sykes asks why so many people are willing to believe false news. People want to confirm their biases, their belief systems, and their circles of trust. They believe false news because they want to believe it and because it is so easy to believe it.[295]

This post-truth politics of the right is reflected in the ad campaigns of political candidates and their supporting political action committees. The best example I can think of is here in Georgia where we had two Senate races in the same year, the result of Republican Senator Johnny Isakson retiring in the middle of his term. Both

Republican candidates, Kelly Loeffler and David Perdue, kept running TV ads accusing their Democratic opponents, Raphael Warnok and Jon Ossoff, of supporting defunding the police and defunding our military. The two Republicans showed that they were devoid of personal integrity because they knew that neither of their opponents supported defunding our police or defunding our military. In one particularly egregious example, they took a small part of a sermon from Raphael Warnok where he quoted Jesus from the Gospel of Matthew. They then used this quote from Jesus about not serving two masters and always prioritizing God in your life and twisted this out-of-context portion of his sermon into an attack on our military, trying to paint US Senate candidate and head pastor of the Ebenezer Baptist Church, Raphael Warnok, as a radical leftist.

In his sermon, where one or two sentences were taken out of context, Reverend Warnok read from Matthew 6:24:

> No one can serve two masters. Either you will hate the one and love the other, or you will be devoted to the one and despise the other. You cannot serve both God and money.

Reverend Warnok was making the point that serving the will of God and loving your neighbors should always be the highest priorities of any Christian. I do not for a minute believe that he was saying that it was wrong to serve in the military. He was simply saying put all your faith in God. For that matter, many pastors serve as commissioned officers in all branches of the US military.

How shameful of Kelly Loeffler! A man of God, giving a sermon to his congregation, using the words of Jesus, was portrayed in a desperate political ad by Republican Kelly Loeffler as someone he was not. I do not think I would like to be disputing the obvious meaning of the words of Jesus to unfairly and irresponsibly misrepresent the views of her opponent to win an election. Fortunately, enough voters in Georgia were repelled by her false and robotic attacks on Reverend Warnok that he won, and she lost. I only can say that I hope in the future I never support a candidate like Kelly Loeffler. Contributors and supporters of Republican Kelly Loeffler should feel a sense of deep remorse, but, of course, they will not. They do this because they think they can get away with it. They think their voting base will believe them no matter what the truth is. Misrepresenting the views of a pastor chosen to lead the church once led by Martin Luther King does not seem like a good life choice or a way to seek the grace of God. Political ambition apparently has no boundaries for Kelly Loeffler or her Republican supporters.

Donald Trump has carried this post-truth campaign to a new supercharged level. *Time Magazine* and Sykes refer to this as Trump's "Grand Unified Campaign Conspiracy Theory." Examples include claims during the 2016 campaign that Hillary Clinton often met with international bankers to plot the destruction of US sovereignty to enrich global financial banks, her special interest friends, and her campaign donors. Trump also claimed the global power structure was responsible for economic decisions that robbed our working class, stripped our country of its wealth, and put money into a handful of favored corporations and political entities. Trump's birther claims that President Obama was not born in the United States and thus was not eligible to be president fall into this post-truth reality to many on the right.[296]

Sykes takes on other talk radio hosts and television pundits like Rush Limbaugh, Hugh Hewitt, and others. Their willingness to spread false rumors, conspiracy theories, and track in the politics of personal destruction is a sad legacy for them to leave behind. They used to pride themselves on educating the public and bringing new conservatives to their intellectual cause. That legacy looks more than a little tarnished now to me.

Sykes next discusses how the many years of liberal attacks on conservatives for being Nazi sympathizers, racists, and granny killers backfired on liberals in the mainstream media and with liberal politicians. He compared it to the dangers of the little boy crying wolf too often. When unfair rhetorical punches were thrown at Republicans like John McCain and Mitt Romney to paint them as racists, those attacks were not well-received by many independents or Republicans. It reminded people of all the attacks on Ronald Reagan and the Bushes for being warmongers. Sykes believed this created a climate of indifference within broad swaths of the general public that enabled them to "tune out" or completely ignore this type of rhetoric. By desensitizing large parts of the voting population, it created a climate where some in the Republican Party could now express racial animus more openly without fear of being called bigots.[297]

In another chapter, the "Rise of the Alt Right," Charlie Sykes talked about how in the past, the Republican Party excommunicated those people that openly expressed sympathy for White nationalism and antisemitism, like how the John Birch Society was isolated from mainstream conservative thought and influence in the 1960s. Sadly, this affinity for White nationalism and right-wing authoritarianism has increased, not only in the United States, but also in many European countries. The new leaders of the Alt Right, including Donald Trump and his supporters (including many in the conservative media), began a propaganda campaign targeting traditional conservatives and moderate Republicans for being weak on issues surrounding immigration and cultural identity within the White community.[298]

In the 1950s and the 1960s, William F. Buckley, through his television appearances on *Firing Line* and through his magazine, *National Review*, was able to keep the John Birch Society isolated from mainstream conservative thought and from infiltration of the Republican Party. Some excellent writers like Jonah Goldberg and Peter Wehner have denounced the authoritarianism and racism of the Alt Right. Unfortunately, these writers never had the reach and authority that William F. Buckley once had. Therefore, this infestation of authoritarianism, nativism, and racism has smoldered and now burns within the current-day Republican Party.[299]

Fear of the political left and fear of the Democratic Party has now caused Republicans to see everything as a binary choice. It has become us against them. Sykes talked about several key writers and thought leaders who let their fear of the opposition's ideas color their thinking to the point that everything was reduced to a battle between good and evil. For instance, Dennis Prager said, "Leftism is a terminal cancer in the American bloodstream and soul. So, our first and greatest principle is to destroy this cancer before it destroys us. We therefore see voting for Donald Trump as political chemotherapy needed to prevent our demise. And at this time, that is by far, the greatest principle."[300] An even bigger surprise to Sykes was the conversion of the man who wrote the *Book of Virtues*, William F. Bennett, who wrote "our character that supports the promise of our future—far more than particular government programs or policies" now minimized concerns about Trump's character as a sign of "vanity."[301] Historian and writer Victor Davis Hanson acknowledged that Donald Trump was crude and "mercurial," but said that his defeat would lead to left-wing control of the Supreme Court and the whims of left-wing bureaucrats. He expressed impatience and frustration with traditional conservatives unwilling to back Donald Trump.[302]

Years ago, the famous Austrian economist and writer Friedrich Hayek saw the potential for someone like Donald Trump and his brand of authoritarian populism infecting our free societies.

Hayek knew that it was the nature of free societies for people to become dissatisfied "with the ineffectiveness of parliamentary majorities," so they turn to "somebody with such solid support as to inspire confidence that he can carry out whatever he wants."

Hayek then lays out the preconditions for the rise of a demagogic dictator: a dumbed down populace, a gullible electorate, and a common enemy or group of scapegoats upon which to focus public enmity and anger. The more educated a society is, Hayek says, the more diverse their tastes and values will be, "and the less likely they are to agree on a particular hierarchy of values." The flip side is that "if we wish to find a high degree of uniformity and similarity of outlook, we have to descend to the regions of lower moral and intellectual standards where the more primitive and common instincts and tastes prevail." But in a modern society, potential dictators might be able to rely on there being enough of "those whose uncomplicated and primitive instincts" to support their efforts. As a result, Hayek said, he "will have to increase their numbers by converting more to the same simple creed."[303]

Charlie Sykes's book provides great insight into the fertile birthing ground for the Alt Right movement led by Donald Trump. Now, we need to examine in more detail some of the actions, compromised values, and psyche of Trump supporters. Let us begin with the evangelical community. What follows, I expect to be difficult for them to read and accept.

SPIRITUALLY UNHEALTHY RELATIONSHIP WITH EVANGELICAL CHRISTIANS

Some important insights are contained in an article in the *Atlantic* by Emma Green, dated November 15, 2020, titled "The Evangelical Reckoning Begins." This article takes the reader on a life journey of the pastor Andy Stanley, the leader of one of the largest megachurches in the country. Andy Stanley is the son of well-known pastor and televangelist, Charles Stanley, the former president of the Southern Baptist Convention. Unlike his very right-leaning father, Andy Stanley has spent his career in the ministry consciously avoiding politicizing his church. His goal was to reach people beyond the conservative Christian world by spreading the gospel of resurrection and salvation to the unchurched. As a result, he rejected his culture-war inheritance and blazed a new path.[304]

The rise of Donald Trump has made it much harder than ever to separate evangelicalism from politics. Exit polls showed that about three-quarters of White evangelicals voted for Donald Trump in the 2020 election, a slightly smaller share than in 2016. In this article, Andy Stanley had some interesting comments concerning most evangelical voters. "To his credit, he's figured out how to leverage that group. I mean he's not evangelical. But he owns them. And they've loved him."[305] He compared the relationship between Trump and many evangelical voters to a lyric from Bob Seger's song "Night Moves": "I used her, she used me, but neither one cared."[306] Long after President Trump has left office, the judges he has appointed will still be fixtures in the judicial review system. In turn, the evangelicals will have gotten what they wanted.

While Andy Stanley largely stayed out of ministering on behalf of Donald Trump, he did not join the active resistance movement either, preferring instead to comment selectively on issues. His goal was to remain a pastor to his flock, not a headline-making firebrand.[307] He struck me as someone who was caught somewhat betwixt and between.

Other pastors, however, have been much more vocal in their support of Donald Trump. Many have professed that their faith is completely aligned with Trumpism. This has created a difficult position for Andy Stanley and some of the pastors like him who want to remain above worldly politics. They are now linked with an image of evangelicalism they did not want, and they did not create. They are stuck with the political baggage and the political choices of the remainder of the evangelical movement. Stanley has said that the alignment with Trump by many in the evangelical movement will hurt, going forward, the ability to reach people outside the church, at least for some time. He also said that in time, this association will fade. Others are not so sure. Mark Galli, the former editor in chief of *Christianity Today*, said, "We Christians have a lot of ground to make up now against those evangelical Trump followers whose devotion to him bordered on the idolatrous."[308]

Returning to Andy Stanley, he suggested in this article that Christians put their faith filter ahead of their political filter. Stanley has a theory about why so many evangelicals backed Trump. Most evangelicals believe that Jesus is going to come back, judge people, and send everyone who doesn't follow him straight to hell. Stanley thinks that there is a large group of evangelicals "who are excited by that prospect, they can't wait." He posits that as many evangelicals get older, they realize that Jesus is unlikely to return during their lifetimes, "they get a little bit desperate" and want to use policy and legislation to bring the world closer to the time of Jesus's return. "That kind of thinking makes you vulnerable when somebody comes along and says, by golly, all of your dreams are going to come true."[309]

According to Andy Stanley, the biggest way in which Trump has damaged the reputation of the church is in his endless willingness to engage in name-calling and in his willingness to engage in belittling people. Examples included mocking a reporter with a disability and calling people from Mexico criminals and rapists. He also believed Trump's ongoing threats on journalists were awful and were usually one of the first actions totalitarian leaders implemented to silence the media. By aligning themselves so closely with Trump, Stanley believed these leaders opened themselves up to the public perception that they were fine with Trump's authoritarian impulses. He acknowledged the possibility that Black people might be hurt or aggrieved over some of Trump's words and actions, but he did not think it would have a lasting impact on the future growth of evangelicalism.[310]

Others, me included, are not so sure. In Charlie Sykes's book *How the Right Lost Its Mind*, an entire chapter, titled "What Happened to the Christians," is devoted to the recent strange behavior of evangelical Christians. Sykes makes the point that for decades, at least going back to 1980, a bedrock principle of the Christian right was that character mattered and that personal morality and ethics were essential requirements of political leadership. "The stunning thing about the Christian Right in 2016 was not its support of Donald Trump in the election of 2016, it was the stunning transformation of its value system, and even its core standards of personal conduct."[311] In October 2016, a poll was released that found that 76 percent of White evangelicals no longer believed that a candidate's morals were that important.

While other voting groups had also become more tolerant of personal immorality, no group had changed as much as the evangelicals.[312]

Jerry Falwell Jr., one of Trump's earliest supporters in the Republican primary election season, explained his support for Trump: "Look at the fruits of his life and the people he's provided jobs, that's the true test of somebody's Christianity."[313] Conservative commentator Eric Erickson responded, quite appropriately, in my opinion, "I did not know the truest test of somebody's Christianity was being an employer. I thought humbling yourself, putting your needs behind those of others, and repenting of sin were more characteristics of faith than putting people on the payroll."[314]

Sykes wrote: "Evangelical support of Trump was especially surprising given how indifferent he was toward, and ignorant of, the basic tenets of the faith."[315] In an interview with Cal Thomas, Trump was asked, "You have said you never felt the need to ask for God's forgiveness, and yet repentance for one's sins is a precondition to salvation. I ask you the question Jesus asked Peter; Who do you say He is?"[316] Trump's response was sad, but also illuminating.

> Trump: "I will be asking for forgiveness, but hopefully I won't have to be asking for much forgiveness."
>
> Thomas: "Who do you say Jesus is?"
>
> Trump: "Jesus to me is somebody I can think about for security and confidence. Somebody I can revere in terms of bravery and in terms of courage and, because I consider the Christian religion so important, somebody I can totally rely on in my own mind."[317]

Apparently, this was good enough for most evangelicals even though there was no reference to Jesus's divinity in his answers.[318]

Included in this chapter of Sykes's book is another revealing look at Jerry Falwell Jr.'s defense of Trump's personal conduct, including a comparison of Trump to King David.

God called King David a man after God's own heart even though he was an adulterer and a murderer. You have to choose the leader that would make the best king or president and not necessarily someone who would be a good pastor. We're not voting for pastor-in-chief. It means sometimes we have to choose a person who has the qualities to lead and who can protect our country and bring us back to economic vitality, and it might not be the person we call when we need somebody to give us spiritual counsel.[319]

Charlie Sykes's response is a direct rebuke: "Comparing Trump to King David was beyond absurd, because Trump felt no need to repent or seek forgiveness."[320]

James Dobson described his vote in the 2016 election in very binary terms: "If anything, this man is a baby Christian who doesn't have a clue about how believers think, talk, and act. All I can tell you is that we have only two choices, Hillary or Donald. Hillary scares me to death."[321] Dobson's comments are the ultimate example showing how fear dominated evangelicals' decisions in what most of them thought was a life or death, binary choice.

Sykes refers to an essay, "The Uncomfortable Truth about Christian Support for Trump" by Jonathon Von Maren, that explained how so many Christians had surrendered some of their most cherished and deeply held values. Likely, Maren conceded, Trump did not care about religious liberty, right to life, or other concerns of social conservatives.

At the end of the day, virtually every criticism of Trump is true. He's a huckster. He doesn't care about most, if any, of the issues that are important to Christians. He's probably just making promises to ensure that Christians show up and vote for him in November. But on the other hand, Hillary Clinton is passionate about these issues. She's passionate about the ongoing destruction of human life by abortion, and she's passionate about furthering the secular progressive agenda that has been backing Christians against the wall for eight years. So that when people point out that Donald Trump will probably do nothing, many Christians respond that yes, that's the point. He probably won't. She definitely will.[322]

While not trusted as one of us, most White evangelicals were persuaded to vote for Trump because he was not one of them.

ACCEPTANCE OF DICTATORS, BIGOTRY, AND SCAPEGOATING

What is also truly baffling to me is the acceptance of outright racism and bigotry by Trump's supporters and their strange acceptance of his promotion of the views and policies of America's enemies. In his book *The Corrosion of Conservatism*, Max Boot, in the chapter titled "The Surrender," says, "While scapegoating Mexicans, African Americans, and Muslims, Trump had nothing but praise for an actual enemy of America. In an interview on *Morning Joe*, on December 18, 2015, Trump praised Russia's dictator, Vladimir Putin, as a better 'leader' than President Obama. When Joe Scarborough asked him about allegations about Putin killing journalists and political opponents, Trump replied, 'I think our country does plenty of killing also, Joe, so you know.'"[323]

Boot then points out that not only did Trump express admiration for Putin, but Trump also stated clearly that he wanted to emulate him and his authoritarian impulses. Boot goes on by quoting Trump. "Be careful," Trump often told anyone speaking out against him, as if he were a dictator or at least a mob boss.[324]

Trump instituted Muslim travel bans and referred to Mexicans as criminals and rapists.

ALWAYS AT WAR WITH THE MEDIA

He expressed a desire to change the libel laws so that when journalists wrote negative articles about him, "we can sue them and win lots of money."[325]

INSTIGATING VIOLENCE AT HIS RALLIES TO
STIR UP HIS MOBS OF SUPPORTERS

"Trump would routinely instigate violence at his rallies against protesters. At a February 2016 rally in Las Vegas, Trump said, from behind a phalanx of Secret Service bodyguards, that he'd like 'to punch a demonstrator in the face' and lamented that the man 'wasn't carried out on a stretcher.' The parallels with fascist rallies in the 1930s were inescapable and alarming—even if 'see no evil' Republicans purported not to notice them."[326]

OUTDATED, INCONSISTENT POLICIES AND PROPOSALS
THAT ACTUALLY HARMED HIS SUPPORTERS

Boot goes on to say, "To the extent that Trump had coherent policy proposals, they were a throwback to the isolationism and protectionism of the 1930s—and a repudiation of the free trade and internationalism that the Republican Party, and the conservative movement, had championed since World War II. Trump threatened to pull US troops out of Germany, South Korea, and Japan, and to impose massive tariffs on our trade partners."[327]

These dangerous, weak, and discredited policies are not fully understood by his base of supporters. In this book's chapter on trade policy, the negative impacts on many of his supporters are described, but those supporters apparently either do not understand the impacts of those policies on their employment and standard of living or simply do not care because their worship of Donald Trump overwhelms their common sense.

My son, Matthew Moore, passed on to me a quote from a Trump supporter he knew: "He's not hurting the people he needs to be hurting." Matt had an interesting take on this, which he paraphrased as follows: "People who vote for the GOP don't necessarily want what's better for them, but rather what's worse for those they hate."[328] I think this is a very instructive and insightful look into the mind of this Trump voter. My experience talking with most Trump voters is that they are not inspiring people. They are profoundly ignorant and self-defeating for our country and its future.

In early 2016, Max Boot wrote in one of his columns that Trump was "a liar, an ignoramus, and a moral abomination."[329] The result has been a chaos candidate and a chaos president. Conservatives, in their panting desire to get tax cuts and conservative Supreme Court justices, forced our nation to pay the huge costs of racism, nativism, collusion with foreign powers, fake news, misinformation, war with the media, fiscal irresponsibility, and the beginning of the end of American world leadership, global engagement, and the rule of law.[330] Again, we can never forget what happened at our Capitol on January 6, 2021.

GOP FALLS IN LINE WITH THE HOSTILE TRUMPIST TAKEOVER

Again, in his chapter called "The Surrender," Max Boot describes the Republican reaction to Trump's takeover of the party:

> As Trump began to emerge as the inevitable nominee, something ominous occurred: Republicans genuflected before their new master. This could be explained by the Republicans' demonization of Democrats; by their knee-jerk loyalty to the GOP

brand, regardless of whether its nominee shared any of their professed principles or not; by their fear of the Republican masses, whose passions Trump had shown a disturbing skill in whipping up; and by the sheer lust for power that is unfortunately characteristic of most officeholders and seekers. As countless toadies have done with demagogues of the past, so now most Republican leaders showed that they were willing to discard their principles as mindlessly as a Styrofoam fast-food container if by doing so they could enhance their own positions and avoid the wrath of a powerful and vindictive leader.[331]

TALK SHOW HOSTS ALSO FALL INTO LINE

Similar pressure fell on radio talk show hosts and television opinion show hosts. Of course, Fox News Channel with its lineup of Sean Hannity, Jeanine Pirro, and Bill O'Reilly were onboard and all-in with their sycophantic support of Donald Trump. Later, Laura Ingraham, Tucker Carlson, and Lou Dobbs joined the party, each trying to outdo the others in their worshipful attitude and over-the-top praise of anything Trump. Even Hugh Hewitt, who had been tough on Trump during the primary season and had earned the wrath of "the Donald," became an eager, enthusiastic supporter. Max Boot, who had often been a guest on Hewitt's radio show, and who had found him to be a smart, well-informed interviewer, "a cut above the Fox rabble rousers,"[332] was shocked and disappointed by the complete capitulation by Hewitt.

Only a small group of conservative radio hosts resisted, for example, Charlie Sykes in Wisconsin and Erick Erickson in Georgia. They took principled stands against the malignant narcissist Donald Trump.

Fortunately, the birth of the Never Trump movement yielded

some other principled people (beyond Charlie Sykes, Max Boot, and Erick Erickson) who fought the principled fight against this thoroughly unprincipled man. Republican operatives, campaign managers, writers, and pundits like Nicole Wallace, Mathew Dowd, Jennifer Rubin, Joe Scarborough, Evan McMullin, Steve Schmidt, Rick Wilson, George Conway, Jennifer Horn, Ron Steslow, Reed Galen, Mike Madrid, Stuart Spencer, William Crystal, Jason Johnson, Jeff Flake, Charlie Dent, Michael Salter, Michael Murphy, Bret Stephens, Mia Love, Larry Hogan, Charlie Baker, John Kasich, Ana Navarro, Ross Douthat, Robert Kagan, David Brooks, Anne Applebaum, Amanda Carpenter, Michael Steele, Tom Nichols, and George Will also come to mind. Some were founders or involved with the Lincoln Project. The ads they generated were excellent and helped mobilize some Republican voters to turn away from Donald Trump in the 2020 election. These ads baited Donald Trump and caused him to get off message throughout the campaign. The founding of the *Bulwark* in 2018 also gave people a new place to find news and analysis, not thoroughly corrupted by crazy conspiracy theories, lies, and disgusting propaganda. These people stood up when their country needed them.

I would like to take this opportunity to comment on a famous athlete who has done a huge amount for charity, and who is well regarded by family, friends, and people throughout the world of golf. I am speaking about Jack Nicklaus. Shortly before the recent presidential election, he came out and endorsed Donald Trump. He had every right to do that, but we also as fans and fellow Americans have the right to criticize him for it. What disappointed me the most about his endorsement was that after the election, when asked about why he endorsed Trump, or if he regretted endorsing Trump, he no longer wanted to talk about it. It just struck me as thin-skinned and rather selfish. He felt he could send out a tweet of support to thousands of fans, right before an election to influence votes, but after the election, he does not want to hear a peep from any of us. Too bad, so sad. Our votes and our thoughts about the direction of the country are every bit as relevant and important as his. Like I said, I have no problem with his endorsement. I do have a problem with his smug, high-maintenance, self-important attitude toward the rest of us. If you insert yourself into the realm of politics and public opinion, you need to be man enough to answer some questions and maybe listen to a little well-deserved criticism.

Two other famous golfers, Annika Sorenstam and Gary Player, deserve criticism for accepting Presidential Medals of Freedom from President Trump on January 7, 2021, the day after the insurrection at the Capitol. Gary Player's own son, Marc, was deeply critical of his father for accepting this award from Trump. Annika Sorenstam expressed "no regrets" over accepting this award, and she told her detractors that "it was time to move on." At least, Bill Belichick, the head coach of the New England Patriots, had the fundamental decency to not accept this award from Trump. While I will always respect the accomplishments in professional golf of Annika Sorenstam and Gary Player, I will also respect them less as human beings for their acceptance of these awards from our traitor-in-chief.

Too many others sold out their principles and let their country down. These cowards, too many to name them all, will not be forgotten. The corrupt leadership of the Republican Party—Kevin McCarthy and Mitch McConnell—and the deceitful propaganda machine, fueled by Fox News Channel, Rush Limbaugh, and the rest of the sad, unprincipled cohort of Trump toadies, will be long remembered. The wreckage they left in the wake of Donald Trump can never be ignored. The damage to our democracy, to our place in the world, and to our values and traditions has been too large and too disfiguring to our country to be forgiven. These people deserve the condemnation of history that collaborators in the Vichy government in Nazi-occupied France and the quislings in Nazi-occupied Norway deserved.

They put their selfish interests and the selfish interests of a despicable megalomaniac ahead of the interests and desires of the American people. They've shown us nothing but defiance, tweets, and lies while the coronavirus has ravaged friends and families across the country. This negligence, in the face of an attempted naked power grab by some in the Republican Party, could ultimately cripple, if not outright destroy, the GOP. This poisoning of the hearts and minds of their voters and supporters to push a false belief and a false narrative by President Trump that the election was rigged will live in infamy. It is understandable that some within the Trump coalition would fall for this lie, but polls showed about 70 percent of Republicans believed this nonsense. That is more than a little sad and more than deeply troubling. I beg, beseech, shame, and pray that people I know will let go of this unhealthy, spiritually crippling attachment to this lying traitor.

It is a modern-day, classic example of the "Big Lie" theory. Joseph Goebbels, the propaganda minister of Hitler's Nazi Party, said that if you condition the population through an ever-growing series of lies, they will come to believe, accept, and act upon even larger lies until they finally believe even your biggest lies. I used to believe that Americans, particularly Republicans, were too smart to be manipulated in this way. After listening to many Trump supporters (including some prominent Republicans), since the election, parrot Trump's false narrative about the election being stolen, I have changed my mind. Armed with an unrelenting propaganda machine, a charismatic, dangerous leader can shape an alternate reality, even here in the United States of America. Max Boot describes this sad reality: "The Republican Party, as I have known it, is now dead. As far as I'm concerned, the anti-Trump holdouts are the real Republican Party, in exile."[333]

In a chapter called "Trump Toadies," Max Boot blames Trump supporters more than he blames Trump himself.

> Yet almost no Republicans are willing to speak out against him. It is hard to know who is worse: Trump or his enablers. I am inclined to think it is the latter. Trump does not know any better; he has no idea of how a president, or even an ordinary, decent human being, is supposed to behave. But many of his supporters do know better, and they are debasing themselves to curry favor with him because he controls the levers of power.

Before Trump won the presidency, here is some of what Republicans had to say about him, as compiled by the *New York Times*. They called him a "malignant clown," a "national disgrace," "a complete idiot," a "sociopath without conscience or feelings of guilt, shame, or remorse," "graceless and divisive," "predatory and reprehensible," "flawed beyond mere moral shortcomings," "unsound, uninformed, unhinged and unfit," "a character and temperament unfit for the leader of the free world," and "a bigot, misogynist, fraud, and a bully."[334]

Rationalizers and enablers, the Republican Party became an active force operating to upend decency, common sense, and the rule of law. Trump's supporters became willing participants in Trump's march toward the establishment of an authoritarian government and an authoritarian culture. Another Republican who refused to countenance Trump's behavior was the late John McCain. Prior to his death, McCain warned about the dangers of Trumpism, denouncing the "half-baked, spurious nationalism cooked up by people who would rather find scapegoats than solve problems."[335] The other senator from Arizona (before he retired from the Senate), Jeff Flake, believed this spell cast on Republicans would eventually break. Max Boot captured this sentiment, eloquently saying, "At least I hope he's right. And if he is, the judgement of history will not be kind to so many of my old friends and fellow-travelers who propitiated a man so unfit for the highest office in the land."[336]

EMBRACING ANTI-INTELLECTUALISM

This point in history is a huge warning shot across the bow. When people aspire to be something they are not, eventually they will become something they are not. Republicans have embraced populism, conspiracy theories, and xenophobia. Therefore, especially among younger people; the Republican Party is often referred to as the "Stupid Party." Rather than run away from this anti-intellectualism, the Republican Party has embraced it and added it to its arsenal of political weapons. A near perfect example was the rise of Sarah Palin. When she was the running mate of John McCain in 2008, she was asked during the campaign what were her sources for news. She could not answer the question other than to say that she had many sources, none of which she cited. Too many Republican voters now wear this anti-intellectual label as a badge of honor.

Viewing Fox News Channel demonstrates this embrace of the anti-intellectual within the world of Republican Trump voters. Fox News Channel personalities regularly pushed conspiracy theories such as: President Obama was not born in the United States, Obamacare would create "death panels," Hillary Clinton sold America's uranium to Russia, and the "Deep State" is plotting to overthrow Donald Trump.

Perhaps the most revealing criticism of Fox News came from Ralph Peters, a retired army intelligence officer, who in 2018, resigned in disgust as a regular Fox News commentator.

> Fox has degenerated from providing a legitimate and much-needed outlet for conservative voices to a mere propaganda machine for a destructive and ethically ruinous administration. Four decades ago, I took an oath as a newly commissioned officer. I swore to "support and defend the Constitution," and that oath did not expire when I took off my uniform. Today, I feel that Fox News is assaulting our constitutional order and the rule of law, while fostering corrosive and unjustified paranoia among viewers. Over my decade with Fox, I long was proud of the association. Now I am ashamed.[337]

In an op-ed by Paul Waldman in the *Washington* Post, dated November 23, 2020, titled "Trump will Go, but Trumpism will

Remain," describes what very well could happen to the future GOP after Trump leaves office.

CONTINUED SPREADING OF CONSPIRACY THEORIES

Spreading conspiracies will be even more commonplace among a large group of GOP voters. Having been served a steady diet of conspiracies run by dark-minded cabals controlling events, this large group of pliable voters do not believe in coincidences. Anything they do not like, or anything that they think works against them is, in their minds, prima facie evidence of menacing forces operating against them and their interests.

One of the worst conspiracy theories held by many of Trump's craziest supporters is the belief in QANON, a thoroughly disproven and discredited far-right conspiracy theory. This group of lunatics allege that a secret cabal of Satan worshipping, cannibalistic pedophiles is running a global child-trafficking ring and plotting against former president Donald Trump. QANON asserts that Donald Trump has been planning a day of reckoning against this group referred to as "the Storm." QANON supporters allege that many liberal Hollywood actors, Democratic politicians, and high-ranking government officials belong to this secret cabal. They also believe a high-ranking government official referred to as Q provides them with marching orders and inside information on various electronic message boards.

QANON supporters were actively involved at the insurrection on our Capitol as news video showed supporters with QANON signs, T-shirts, and sweatshirts. After being taken into custody by the FBI, several QANON supporters provided testimony about the group and its involvement in the insurrection.

Marjorie Taylor Greene, a newly elected Republican representative from Georgia, is a strong believer in this insane conspiracy theory. When a "nut-bag" like her is elected to Congress and accepted into the Republican caucus, the Republican Party is in deep trouble—intellectually, morally, and spiritually. When crazy people and crazy conspiracy theories become acceptable and relatively mainstream to a significant share of voters within a political party or political movement, the days are numbered for that political party to be taken seriously by a vast majority of Americans. Why these kooks have not been denounced and disavowed by the Republican Party is beyond me. This woman encouraged on Facebook threats to execute Democrats and federal agents. Her reward from Kevin McCarthy, the Republican minority leader, was a seat on the House Education Committee. Fortunately, this committee assignment was revoked by a full vote in the House 230-199. Unfortunately, nearly all republicans supported her on this house vote. At a minimum, the Republican Party should have voted not to seat her until the Republican label was removed next to her name. Better yet, they should have made every effort to expel her from the House of Representatives. This woman should be publicly ostracized and disowned, not welcomed inside the Republican tent.

"Now that actual supporters of QAnon lunacy can be elected to Congress, the GOP's elite will wink and nod to every conspiracy theory that comes along, from stolen elections to pandemic hoaxes to the machinations of the 'deep state.' We'll continue to see a vicious cycle in which politicians and conservative media feed conspiracy theories to the Republican masses. As they become more convinced, they're true, the politicians and media will continue pandering to them with still more."[338]

CELEBRATION OF VIOLENCE

The celebration of violence when directed at liberals will continue. Let us not forget about Trump's response to protesters during the 2016 campaign when he said, "I'd like to punch him in the face." Also, let's remember his praise for a Republican congressman, just elected governor of Montana, for assaulting a reporter, or for his recent promotion of the Proud Boys.[339] Again, we can never forget his whipping up of supporters to assault our Capitol. We should all be thankful that more people were not murdered by Trump's storm troopers. We should also be thankful for the ten Republican members of the House of Representatives who had the courage to stand up and vote to impeach this ravenous beast of a president. Unfortunately, it has been reported that other Republicans wanted to vote for impeachment but did not because they were afraid of retribution by Trump thugs. These representatives should resign from office because they have been corrupted by fear. If they cannot vote their consciences and vote to represent their country, not its traitors, they have no business being in the House of Representatives. Their cowardice and dereliction of duty will be remembered for a long time. The unwillingness to be a profile in courage is just another sign of a country in deep trouble because one of its major political parties has largely abandoned honor and courage.

DISPLAYS OF FAUX-MASCULINITY

Also, expect comical displays of faux-masculinity. On T-shirts, toys, and action figures, do not be surprised to see Trump's face superimposed on the body of a muscled action figure. Waldman continues: "Thus the obese septuagenarian who has never in his life displayed an instant of physical courage is transformed into a cartoonish version of manhood that lives in the dreams of teenage boys and the adults who are still teenage boys at heart."[340]

ENDLESS WHINING ABOUT VICTIMIZATION

Most politicians and certainly every president has had to endure criticism. It is the nature of the job that many voters on the other side and many in the media will point out shortcomings and failures. No president, however, whines about it so much as Donald Trump. His supporters take their lead from him. They whine and moan like little babies claiming they are "society's victims, always struggling under the bootheel of government, of the culture, of the media. With a Democrat in the White House, this complaining will only intensify."[341]

IRRELEVANCE OF POLICY

Republicans know that many of their policies are very unpopular, including attempting to destroy the Affordable Care Act. Most Americans are happy with the protections it provides for those with preexisting conditions and the coverage it provides children up to age twenty-six under their parents' health care plan. Republicans used to believe that their policies would be much more popular if they had a better chance to explain the policies to voters. Trump has now convinced them that policy is irrelevant. According to Waldman, "Trump voters did not rally to him because of economic anxiety, but instead they rallied to him because of cultural anxiety. Many Trump voters feared being displaced in a rapidly changing country. He gave them voice for their resentments, their nostalgia, and their contempt for people who aren't like them. Outcomes from Trump policies did not matter to most of them. What mattered was the channeling of their feelings."[342]

OWNING THE LIBS

Waldman stresses in this op-ed that this might be the entire core of Trumpism: "a politics defined not by what you want to change or the country you would like to create, but by the people you hate. The way to elevate your profile and gain support is to troll your enemies, to antagonize them, to make them cry their liberal tears."[343] They feel no shame or fear regarding lying. No story fed to Trump supporters is too ridiculous. They simply get great pleasure from defining themselves by the petty squabbles they start. The 2024 nomination process will be a unique and detestable circus to watch. The contenders will vie to be the biggest jerk insulting their opponents, spewing hatred toward Americans with different points of view, and telling voters to nurture their most toxic feelings.[344]

The Trump presidency has presented the Republican Party with a difficult choice going forward. Do Republicans leverage a politics of grievance and try to summon a coalition (Trump's base of voters) and grow it into a majority status? Many in Trump's voter base stuck with him through scandal after scandal, through controversy after controversy, and through chaos followed by more chaos. It was not a majority, but it was close enough to a majority that with shrewd maneuvering, it could suffice and govern.

The problem for Donald Trump, in governing strictly to consolidate his base, was that he galvanized an anti-Trump base of voters every bit as determined and solid in their opposition. Donald Trump demanded and received deep and fervid support from his loyal fans, but he also stirred up ferocious antipathy among a larger group of voters. This arms race of political mobilization caused voting participation to break records in 2018 (midterms) and in 2020. Since his defeat in the 2020 election, some of Trump's supporters are pondering political life after Trump. Many would like to pursue a Trumpist collection of populist domestic ideas and isolationist retreat from the world, but they would like to serve it to voters without all the self-sabotaging statements, ugly personality traits, and grudges embedded in the Trump brand. Many also want to continue down the path of more and more tax cuts. Republicans used to care about the budget deficit and national debt as well as low taxes. Now, not so much. Tax cuts, in my opinion, are the key driving force behind support for Donald Trump among his higher income supporters. It is their holy grail. They are willing to overlook his traitorous behavior, his racist behavior, his lawless behavior, his constant lying, and his corruption to keep their tax cuts. Oh, by the way, they also like his authoritarianism.

David Frum, in his November 15, 2020, article in the *Atlantic*, "Populism without Popularity," describes two paths forward. He posits that Trumpism apart from Trump's personality and grudges is not much of anything. He said if you remove Trump's resentments and the myth of him being a business genius (and I do stress *myth!*), there is not much left. He asks the question: Are immigration restriction, trade war with China, and sabotaging NATO really all that compelling to base a new age of politics upon? While he agrees that there are potential contenders for the resentment vote in Tom Cotton, Dan Crenshaw, Josh Hawley, or Marco Rubio, none of them have the connection Trump has with his base of support. None of them have the myth of business success attached to themselves either. Other potential contenders for the resentment vote would be Don Jr. and Tucker Carlson. Their problem is that they overdo the resentment and, again, that neither offers the myth of business success.[345] Another problem for little Donnie Jr might be the law. His attempts at ginning up the crowd before the attack on the Capitol could put him in jail for many years.

The second problem is that Trump was defeated by the reality of basic math. He polarized American politics in a way that trapped him on the side with less people. The anti-Trump vote exceeded the pro-Trump vote by about three million votes in 2016, by nearly two million in the off-year election in 2018, and by over seven million in the recent presidential election. Trump's inflated ego was his blind spot. He lived in a world inside his head that thought his campaign was brilliant and that he would win easily. To this day, he still believes he could not lose to Joe Biden. He still believes the election was stolen from him despite no evidence to support him. Donald Trump is delusional, and he still controlled the nuclear codes until January 20, 2021. That sobering thought should terrify Americans.[346]

Trumpism without Trump, unfortunately for his die-hard believers, will have to eventually face the test of reality. Trumpism without Trump is partially comprised of a dull, dimwitted group of people railing against socialism, when most of them do not even understand that many of Trump's policies were far closer to socialism than many of the policies prescribed by Joe Biden. Trump was opposed to free trade and the economic benefit of letting nations with "competitive advantages" produce certain goods and services to offer lower costs to consumers. Trump proposed price controls on the pharmaceutical industry rather than seriously negotiate better deals for drugs purchased under Medicare and Medicaid. Trump threatened companies to force them to manufacture everything in the United States when doing so would reduce profits, in some cases lock in losses, and increase prices, reduce output, and ultimately lower the wages and standard of living of not only their workers, but also consumers throughout the country.

Trumpism without Trump is an even more rudderless movement dominated by anger, grievance, and rage. Without Trump, his voters' level of excitement is bound to be diminished. Logic and common sense cannot quite capture the incredulity this writer feels as to how anyone of sound mind could have fallen for this charlatan. I guess it comes down to this: blind allegiance to an authoritarian fool and an ugly, vicious traitor. While Trumpism without Trump lowers the excitement of his base, it does nothing to quell the utter, complete distaste and disgust most voters have for his policies. Trumpism without Trump has no answer to shrink the gender gap or to return sufficient percentages of college-educated, mostly suburban voters to the Republican Party. It has no answer except louder, less subtle appeals to racism, conspiracy theories, and lies.

The GOP has no coherent policies on health care or on controlling college tuition costs. The GOP without Trump will probably be sucked into a black hole of trying to appeal to only angry grievance mongers. Trump dismissed everyone who voted against him as dumb, radical, and socialist. We fired him for incompetence, lawlessness, chaos, corruption, negligence, racism, lack of human decency, and a host of other reasons, perhaps none more important than his traitorous acts.

The ironic behavioral characteristic of Donald Trump and many of his supporters is a distrust of highly educated people. He needed to listen to the public health officials and scientists, but instead of relying on their expertise during a pandemic, he demeaned them to the delight of his base. The more these experts were trusted by most Americans, the smarter they were, the more Trump needed to demean them. If he had listened to them and followed their recommendations, he might have stood at least a slight chance of being reelected. David Frum referred to Trumpism as the political equivalent of losing money on each sale and hoping to make it up on volume. The harder Trumpists tried, the worse was their electoral result.

Trump's successors are left with two possible strategies to follow. The first is to recognize the post-Trump Republican Party is likely to remain a minority party. With that acceptance, the goal would be to maximize the powers of that minority. With control of enough state legislatures in red states, Republicans have been able to maintain control of redistricting through gerrymandering, helping to ensure another decade of relative minority strength. If a Democratic president is nonwhite or female or highly educated, or all three, the Republicans can gin up cultural resentment until it becomes a strong weapon of partisan recruitment and media propaganda. This reminds me of how southern Democrats operated before Republicans began to make major inroads in the South beginning in the late 1960s.

There is a second way forward for the Republican Party, should they choose to take it. "Over the course of the past decade, the share of adult non-Hispanic whites with a college degree has increased from 33% to 40%. This proportion will likely continue to increase in this decade. The Republican Party would need to recognize and would need to accept that it is education more than immigration that is turning these southern red states purple."[347] We can see evidence in recent election results in Virginia, North Carolina, Georgia, and Texas. We can also see this happening in Arizona. To compete in the southern and other sunbelt states, the Republicans must adapt to the more educated, more diverse, and more secular electorate. Under this strategy, they would need to become a modern center-right political party emphasizing fiscal conservatism, international leadership, and military strength.

They also would need be more willing to accept female leadership and become much less divisive on cultural issues.

To go forward on this second path, the Republican Party would need to accept the victory of Joe Biden and Kamala Harris. They would need to quit the gerrymandering business and to recommit themselves to equal voting rights. Furthermore, they would need to compete to win over voters, not disenfranchise any of them. Otherwise, the United States is headed back to the politics of the Jim Crow era with the Republican Party ensconced as a minority party seeking to manipulate antidemocratic rules to slow the tide of history.[348]

TRUMP'S HOLD ON RANK AND FILE

Ed Kilgore, in an article dated November 20, 2020, in *New York Magazine*, discusses the power Trump holds over his supporters regarding his claims of a fraudulent election. Most Republican officeholders and insiders privately acknowledge that Trump lost this election "fair and square." They rationalize and explain their silence to confront him as like having to deal with a toddler who needs to wear himself out screaming and crying before bedtime or naptime. What is so shocking is the millions of his voters who believe the nonsense coming out of the mouths of this toddler, his far-right media allies, and some of his lawyers. "According to a new Monmouth University poll, about 75% of Republicans doubt the fairness of this election without any significant evidence to support these claims."[349] Even though many Democrats were disillusioned with the outcome of the presidential election in 2016, they were not perpetual sore losers. They did not doubt the accuracy of the votes counted, and they remained committed to American democracy. They channeled their frustration with Donald Trump and the way he governed to mount a comeback in 2020. Their standard-bearer, Hillary Clinton, conceded on election night. There is only one way to look at this undermining in confidence among overwhelming swaths of GOP voters. The ringmaster, the cult leader, the master rabble-rouser, Donald Trump is the person responsible for inciting insurrection among his voting base. His lust for power and their lust to please him supersede their reason, fairness, honesty, and devotion to country. Before the election, Trump demonized voting by mail as inherently fraudulent. As a result, about twice as many Biden voters voted by mail or early in person. When the results were reported on election night, in most states, the heavily Trump same- day voting tallies were reported first. Some states were not even allowed by state law to count or report early votes until Election Day polls closed. Trump conditioned his voters that perfectly legal votes cast early, whether in person or by mail, were illegitimate and fraudulent. By engineering a contested election well in advance of Election Day, Donald Trump convinced millions of his voters that the inevitable shift in vote totals that occurred when all the remaining and, yes, legitimate votes were counted, constituted proof of fraud and a stolen election by Joe Biden.

Ed Kilgore summed it up by stating the following in this article:

> But if Trump's original plans to contest the election were limited by a legal strategy that was initially narrow, technical and ultimately incapable of challenging enough votes to matter, he's thrown enough chum in the troubled waters of a deeply polarized electorate to create a feeding frenzy in right-wing media and among MAGA bravos everywhere. As he mulls his future, including a possible 2024 comeback, his demonstrated power to convince his supporters that democracy is "rigged" against them is a bankable political asset.
>
> No wonder Republican elites are afraid to call Trump's election challenge itself a massive fraud.[350]

PSYCHOLOGICAL MAKEUP OF HARD-CORE TRUMP SUPPORTERS

In an abstract printed in the *Journal of Social and Political Psychology* by Thomas Pettigrew in 2017, several factors were identified among Trump supporters. No one factor, by itself, describes Trump supporters, but this array of factors can explain the rise of loyal devotion to Trump by his supporters. This loyalty to Trump in my opinion outweighs loyalty to our country, to its long-held values, and to its fellow citizens.

- ➤ Authoritarianism
- ➤ Social Dominance Orientation
- ➤ Prejudice
- ➤ Relative Deprivation
- ➤ Intergroup Contact[351]

Many people, when asked what most defines Trump voters, would answer "white, uneducated, poor, and racially prejudiced." While many Trump supporters do fall within these parameters, the common most statistically significant is a strong attraction to authoritarianism. This characteristic is common to lower income, less educated Trump voters and to higher income, more educated Trump voters. I should stress, however, that within the entire electorate, more highly educated voters voted for Joe Biden. That can be explained by the fact that more highly educated voters were repulsed by the deep-seeded attachment to authoritarianism by Trump and many of his voters.[352]

There are three major types of authoritarians. The first group, the traditional authoritarians, are conventional authoritarians who strongly believe in legal authorities and processes. They believe in legitimate authority and support law and order, but they are not particularly attracted to demagogues. They believe in elections and constitutional law.[353]

The second group, the passive authoritarians, believe leaders should be followed unquestionably. They are not, however, activists.

These are the lazy, frightened authoritarians who want to go along just to get along.[354]

The third group, the aggressive (also referred to as the punishing) authoritarians, are the frightening group that needs to be watched closely. This is the group of Trump's earliest and most fervent supporters. They have a strong desire for security, order, power, and status. They demand from others unquestioning obedience to their leader, and they display hostility toward anyone or any group that deviates from their sense of loyalty. They tend to be openly hostile to groups (people of color, people of different religions, people from the other political party—Democrats) that they disagree with, and to use those groups as scapegoats, particularly because of their perceived sense of grievance. They do not just disagree with their political opponents; they demonize and depersonalize them. They are willing to believe political ads that make statements about their opponents that are not true. They grossly exaggerate their opponents' place on the political spectrum by calling mainstream, center-left Democrats, socialists. This allegation in Republican ads is almost laughable. I challenge the people making this claim to look up the total stock market returns during the terms of Bill Clinton and Barack Obama and compare them with other recent presidents. They are also willing to overlook almost anything their preferred leader does or says. They will deny facts, they will deny statements, they will deny objective reality. These are the true cultists. They see no evil and hear no evil despite evil being demonstrated right in front of them each day. They refuse to read or listen to other sources of news or opinion beyond their go-to sources, Fox News, One America News, or News Max. Nearly a century ago, these were the people that joined the SA "brownshirts" early during Nazism's rise and then became the SD and the SS later during the rise and subjugation of the German people, and then later most of Europe.

In a recent interview on CNN, former President Obama was asked what the seventy-four million votes for Donald Trump said to him. His answer was very straightforward: our nation was very deeply divided and polarized. He went on to say that the Republican

Party operated on a different set of facts in an alternate reality. During most of my days as a Republican, I would have been offended by his interpretation, but the reality I have come to accept is that President Obama was right. Republicans now accept and routinely distribute false claims, outright unfounded conspiracy theories, and ruthless, bitter attacks on their opponents. In my opinion, they have allowed themselves to become consumed with anger and fear, which manifests in distrust and hatred. They masquerade this overwhelming sense of foreboding within themselves, with MAGA hats, MAGA rallies, and MAGA parades. They are cocky and dismissive of other people's views, but sadly they are often unhappy on the inside—with themselves and with conditions in their own lives.

They are the ultimate "control freaks." At a gathering of family or friends, these are often the people who monopolize the conversation and interrupt before anyone else of a differing opinion can elicit a single sentence, let alone a full rebuttal. They drone on and on, drifting from one lazily constructed, factually inaccurate point after point. If anyone has the audacity to challenge them, they then play the anger card and try to discount the character of the challenger rather than truly debate the points or evidence raised. Usually surrounded by other Trumpists, who nod and drool at their spread of misinformation, they continue to drone on and on until people leave the table to watch football, to open presents, or to go home. They are often insecure, passive-aggressive people who only feel temporarily good about themselves when surrounded by other weak-minded authoritarians.

Despite my disparaging comments about this subset of Trump voters, the behavior of this group of punishing authoritarians is something for this country to pay attention to and to fear. Authoritarians obey. They are attracted to, and they follow, leaders they perceive as strong. They respond aggressively to outsiders, especially when they feel threatened. It is time, now before it's too late, for those Americans who believe in our better angels to recognize this rising attraction to authoritarianism and to do everything in our power to stop it in its tracks. What happened in Europe in the 1930s led to secret police, concentration camps, mass murder, and World War II. Donald

Trump and many of his supporters want to build the wall, shut down mosques, prohibit Muslims from entering our country, deport eleven million illegal immigrants, and establish a database that tracks Muslims. They also want to separate children from their parents at the border. This widespread attraction to authoritarianism should terrify most Americans. The fact that the FBI believes White supremacy is now the greatest terrorist threat to our democracy and our way of life should terrify true patriots everywhere. These "MAGA patriots" are anything but patriots. They are the followers and enablers of evil authoritarianism, tied together only by their devotion to evil authoritarians.

Before I close this chapter with some comments about the future, I need to include the headlines (titles) of a few articles that appeared on Smart News on my I-phone today. No comments need to be made. The titles speak for themselves. They reveal the sad, depraved, reckless disregard for the truth by the cowardly Republican Party of Donald Trump and perhaps one of the worst years of recent history. Let me list them, and let me make a recommendation to the readers of this book to read them. They reveal the squalid lack of character, selfishness, and deep-seated moral decay that has infected most members of the disgraceful version of today's Republican Party.

First, I will list the "good" articles by the patriots, the truth-tellers, and the media who are unafraid to reveal the rot within the GOP and its pathetic acolytes.

> *CNN Politics*: "Battleground states issue blistering rebukes to Texas lawsuit to invalidate millions of votes"

> *San Diego Union Tribune*: "Readers React: Brave Republicans who stand up to Trump deserve to be honored"

> *People*: "Meghan McCain Calls Out 'Stupid and Embarrassing' Tweets from Arizona GOP: 'Really Guys? Really?'"

Vanity Fair: "Apparently Deborah Birx Wants to Join Biden's COVID Team"

Vanity Fair: "The Trump Denialism Doctrine is a Grim Preview of Coming Era of Republican Politics"

Politico: "Relax, A Trump Comeback In 2024 Is Not Going to Happen"

MSNBC: "Karl: Trump's looking, not just like a loser, but impotent"

MSNBC: "Ludicrous Texas anti-election lawsuit jolts Republican politics"

The *Washington Post*: "Opinion—The danger is growing that Trump's lies about the election will lead to violence"

The *Washington Post*: "Opinion—The risk of right-wing terrorism is rising dramatically"

CNN: "Georgia becomes ground zero for election misinformation ahead of Senate runoff"

NBC News: "'Seditious abuse of judicial process': States fire back at Texas' Supreme Court election challenge"

Second, I will list "good" articles about the liars, the deceivers, the minority media (the 700 Club, Rush Limbaugh Show) who are propagandists for, hopefully, a dying political party (if it doesn't find its soul soon).

Newsweek: "Pat Roberson Says God Will 'Intervene' in Favor of Texas SCOTUS Lawsuit"

Newsweek: "Rush Limbaugh Says Conservative States Are 'Trending Toward Secession'"

CNN: "GOP senators ready to acknowledge Biden won but struggle with Trump's refusal to concede"

The *Washington Post*: "Trump pressures congressional Republicans to help in his fight to overturn the election"

FORFEITURE OF CREDIBILITY

Recently, my wife, Louise, and I had a phone conversation with a couple we have been friends with for over a decade. We mostly talked about our families, but near the end of our conversation I asked them how they thought the second impeachment trial would turn out. These avid Trump supporters would not answer my straightforward question. All they said, quite brusquely, was, "We don't talk about politics anymore."

Two years earlier while out to dinner with them and another pro-Trump couple, they went on and on about their love for everything about Donald Trump, both his policies and his style. I spoke up and made several negative comments about their "dear leader." I remember saying that the Trump presidency was not going to end well for the Republican Party and the country. One of them got extremely angry, and his face got very red.

Many Trump backers, who were very vocal in their support for him, now seem very reluctant to talk about recent events like the Capitol insurrection and the second impeachment trial. This angry and bitter refusal to talk about current events reveals a character weakness. It forfeits their credibility with me. While I would like to regain respect for them, I find it difficult to do so because they refuse to admit mistakes of judgment about the character of Donald Trump and the direction of the Republican Party. Louise thinks they were uncomfortable with the actions that took place at the Capitol. She also thinks, however, that they wholeheartedly believe those actions were justified.

THE FUTURE

What becomes of the Republican Party? Where do Never Trumpers go in the future? The answer is probably different for each person. Max Boot answered this personal question near the end of his recent book.

> I respect Never Trumpers such as Bill Kristol and Tom Nichols who have remained Republicans because they hope to wrest that party back from extremists. But I have concluded that the battle is lost, at least for the time being. Sadly, David Horowitz and Laura Ingraham, Dinesh D'Souza and Jack Posobiec, Donald Trump and Devine Nunes are far more representative than I am of the right today—and quite probably in the past too, even if it's taken me a long time to realize it.[355]

Near the end of his book, *How the Right Lost its Mind*, Charlie Sykes suggests a much-needed exorcism of the forces that possessed the Republican Party and perverted its mission and its values. In his numbered list below, he said conservatives need to:

1. Address the legitimate grievances that buoyed Trump with the white working class, but to find a way to separate them from the toxic elements of Trumpism, including its authoritarianism, racism, misogyny, and isolationism.

2. Return to first principles and revive classical liberalism as an alternative to progressivism on the Left and authoritarian nationalism on the Right.

3. Revitalize a policy agenda that has grown tired and nostalgic. While conservatives need to reclaim the optimism of Reagan, simply repeating the mantras of the Reagan years is no longer enough, and demanding ideological purity is a self-defeating strategy. The alternative may include taking a fresh look at what so-called Reformicons and others have been saying for the last decade.

4. Be willing to tell hard truths, about the importance of limited government (even if it means we do not get everything we want), free markets, why governments should not pick winners and losers, and the need for American leadership in the world (despite the siren call of the new isolationism).

5. Break free from the toxic thrall of corporate cronyism and K street lobbyists. Recognize that being pro-business is not the same thing as being pro-market if it means handing out favors and goodies to special interest moochers. The 2016 election was a revolt against this kind of rigged, insider-dealing culture. The GOP had it coming.

6. Realize the demographic bomb that Trump planted in the GOP. The appeasement of Trump may have alienated Hispanics, Asian Americans, Muslim Americans, African Americans, and women for a generation. Restoring the party's ability to appeal to these groups will require more than a cosmetic makeover, but failure to do so will consign the party to political oblivion.

7. Drain their own swamp, starting with the Alt Right and its bigoted, anti-Semitic minions. Lines must be drawn, lest the GOP morph into a European-style National Front party.

8. Confront the conservative media that boosted and enabled Trumpism and created a toxic alternative reality bubble that threatens the credibility and sanity of the conservative movement. Conservatives cannot continue to outsource their

message to the drunk at the end of the bar or the cynical propagandists on the internet.[356]

On a more personal level, Charlie Sykes offered some modest advice for conservatives to better equip them to move through this harrowing cycle of history. Again, in his own words:

➤ Be worthy of the movement but make sure the movement is worthy of you. The conservative movement is (or ought to be) about ideas. When the movement ceases to be about those things, question your allegiances.

➤ As the Psalmist reminds us, "Put not your faith in princes." Do not sacrifice your principles on the altar of other people's individual ambitions. Ultimately, our politics cannot simply be about politicians; they come and go, dissemble, flip-flop. There is a fundamental difference between movements based on ideas and cults of personalities. Princes will inevitably let you down. This is not a glitch; it is a feature.

➤ You should care about what other people think, but only those people whose opinions you respect. The troll who writes in all caps, not so much. A corollary (one that applies to our lives outside of politics as well): The loudest voice in the room is not always the one you want to listen to; the most extreme opinion is not always the most honest and cogent.

➤ Develop a well-honed BS meter. To be effective, you need to know what is real, because your credibility is one of your most important and precious assets. But it is also essential in this brave new world where we are inundated with "facts" and information that are often completely bogus. Ask questions: What is the source? How do we know this? Is it credible? Do not suffer crackpots lightly. Do not forward chain emails.

➤ Be willing to step out of the bubble. Our politics have become increasingly tribal, with each tribe having its own facts and its own reality. But if we are to succeed politically, we need to reach beyond those tribal loyalties. The sad truth is that it is easy to get trapped in the alternative reality silos that we have created. If you take your view of reality and your facts from *Infowars* or *Breitbart* or other alternative reality sites, you will eventually find yourself in a corner, isolated from people you need to persuade. (P.S. If your Facebook feed is your primary source of news/opinion, you need to reexamine your life choices.)

➤ Fight against political correctness, recognizing what the term really means. Sometimes boorishness and vulgarity are just boorishness and vulgarity.

➤ Do not become what we despise. If the other side abandons all pretense of ethics and values, that is not an excuse for us to do the same. Otherwise, we become indistinguishable from what we fight against.

➤ Be willing to be unpopular. You know this because you are conservatives, so you know what it is to be marginalized, despised, and unpopular in the broader culture. But I mean something more: be prepared to lose friends on our side. Be willing to challenge the conventional wisdom, even among your friends. Stand up for what you believe and decide whether what you believe is worth the price you sometimes must pay.

➤ Politics is a team sport, but you are still an individual who can think for yourself. Of all areas of American life, politics may be one of the very few where you can get booed by saying that people should follow their consciences. Any movement that tells you to ignore your conscience is a movement that should be met with skepticism.

➤ Be willing to take the long view. In the end it will be far more important that you preserve your personal integrity, and fight for what you believe, than that you win this or that election. Every used-car salesman, every fund-raising pitch tries to convince you that you must make the deal right now; politicians insist that the apocalypse is upon us. Be willing to step back. As unfashionable as it may be to say these days, there are no permanent victories and no permanent defeats. Which leads to ...

➤ Winning is great, but always weigh the cost. My father always used to say that sometimes the only fights worth fighting for were the lost causes. I never really understood that, but as I have gotten older and seen more, I have come to appreciate it. There is nothing dishonorable about losing, but there is something shameful about abandoning your principles. After all, what profits it a man to win the whole world, if he loses his soul? But for an election? Any election?"[357]

The famous Russian dissident and author Aleksandr Solzhenitsyn once wrote: "Let your credo be this: Let the lie come into the world, let it even triumph. But not through me."[358]

What America desperately needs is a center-right party, either a reborn, reformed GOP or an entirely new political party. What it does not need is a Republican Party smelling of the stench of Trumpism. It does not matter so much if it is a new center-right party, or a completely overhauled Republican Party. What does matter is that the traitorous elements within the current GOP are marginalized and, for practical purposes, made impotent. People like that that attempt a rebirth of Trumpism in the future, or long after Trump has departed, must never be allowed to gain power again, or ever even gain a foothold. Whatever emerges as the center-right coalition must never compromise or short shrift honesty, the rule of law, or opposition to racism, sexism, xenophobia, and other forms of prejudice. Given the deeply entrenched history of the two-party system in the United States, rehabilitation and reclamation of the Republican Party might be the easiest approach to offering people a center-right choice going forward. Until the Trumpist movement is completely uprooted and removed, however, the Republican Party needs to be cleansed by a series of defeats. This author will never again vote Republican until all vestiges of Donald Trump and the worst of his enablers are gone or impotent.

By comparison, the new third-party option looks less likely but not impossible. Certainly, it would face structural challenges. While the inertia of the two-party system would be an impediment, our history, nevertheless, does include the death of various major political parties and the rise of new ones (remember the Federalists and the Whigs).

DEMOGRAPHIC CHANGES ARE AN ANCHOR ON GOP GROWTH

Republicans should be able to win elections for a few more years in selected states by relying on a base of older, less educated White voters, but that strategy will have diminishing returns as the number of people of color continues to grow.

EMPOWERING TO LEAVE THE TRIBE

Staying in the GOP tribe, when my conscience was telling me it was well past time to leave, was uncomfortable, both intellectually and psychologically. Sure, there was going to be enormous social pressure from some family members and from some Republican friends to either remain in the tribe or to face being ostracized. The pressure to conform to tribal political expectations has grown much stronger in recent years as more and more Americans are comfortable with identifying only with people who think alike, particularly in the spheres of politics and religion.

I would like to address Trump supporters with a bit of tough love. Fortunately, polling conducted after the insurrection reveals that independents and, more slowly, Republicans are starting to break from the president. In both the Real Clear Politics Polling Average and the 538 Polling Average, President Trump's job approval is exceeded by his disapproval by 17 percent as of reported on January 14, 2021. This shows me that the stench of his incitement to insurrection and his second impeachment is beginning to dawn on some of Trump's supporters. Many Trump supporters now realize that their reputations and judgment are being seriously called into question, and they are trying to head for the exits. I still say that without a cathartic admission of guilt, none of you deserve much credit for your abandonment of him. Why is it so hard to admit you were wrong about this man? It would demonstrate to me some strength of character to admit your mistake in judgment instead of continuing to half-heartedly justify your vote and your past support. The man is a traitor, a serial liar, a racist, and a fascist. Just admit it! You will look less weak-minded if you do this. Trying to make yourself feel good inside by hanging on to ridiculous rationalizations is not only an insult to others but also an insult to you. Give yourself permission to admit you were wrong. In our pasts, all of us are wrong at times. For goodness' sake, we are all human beings. By letting go of stubborn justifications and ridiculous rationalizations, you will free yourself from psychological guilt. It should not be as hard as it seems to you right now. Honestly, you will feel better about your self if you drop the defensive attitude and move on from this serious lapse in judgment. Supporting Trump was a colossal mistake; distancing yourself only half-heartedly makes you look even weaker and even worse. Leaving this tribe of fear and becoming true to yourself will feel better emotionally and spiritually. It cannot feel good protecting a self-consumed traitor above your country and your conscience. As for others in the Trump/Republican tribe who might get angry, simply tell them in a straightforward manner that you cannot put the interests of an authoritarian narcissist ahead of loyalty to your country and the rest of its citizens.

Despite pressure on social relationships, the feeling of liberation from tribal politics was so strong and so spiritually awakening. By closing myself off to other ways of thinking, my sense of self-worth and peace of mind were in a constant state of agitation. This state of cognitive dissonance needed to be resolved. Becoming a free agent, no longer beholden to other people's agendas, attitudes, and prejudices, was the greatest gift I could give myself. When we all look back on our lives and on our political choices, we all want to know whether we made a positive difference in our marriage, in our family, in our church and social groups, and in our country at large. You want to know you stood for what you believed to be right. As a campaign volunteer, as a paid campaign professional, or as an ordinary voter, each of you will be involved in elections where your side won and other elections where your side lost. The most important thing is not the win-loss tally; it is whether you sincerely tried, with all your heart and mind, to stand on the side of truth.

THE WAY FORWARD

I have never written a book before. What drove me into this challenging pursuit was a sense that our country was going down a dangerous path, that a large percentage of our citizens (mostly Republicans) were desperately misinformed and angry, and that our nation's shared democratic and constitutional values were being corrupted by a malignant narcissist with radical authoritarian views. Instead of "Making America Great Again," this wicked man was prepared to make America weaker, more divided, less decent, more insular and withdrawn, and less a leader in the world.

His willingness, no eagerness, to manipulate his easily manipulated voter base, both Republicans and some others, was driven not by altruistic purpose to achieve great things for the country. Instead, it was driven by his enormous ego, his need for money, his need for power, and his need for worship by his followers.

History will no doubt render a swift verdict on the Trump presidency. I believe the verdict will be that his presidency was the worst in our nation's history, and that it was dictatorial, authoritarian, criminal, and traitorous. While he is a terrible human being, devoid of honor and moral character, he cannot be blamed for everything that occurred during his time in office. His senior staff, Republican leadership in Congress, rank and file legislators, ordinary Republican voters, and other supporters bear responsibility for this sad chapter in American history.

In trying to come to grips with the hold Trump has maintained over his supporters, I have reached a sobering conclusion. These people are not without substantial blame, not without substantial responsibility, and not without substantial disgrace for willingly enabling, following, encouraging, and justifying his reign of terror against basic American values and many of their fellow citizens. While I cling to the hope that some of these supporters will eventually throw off their cultish attachment to Donald Trump and leave behind the prejudices that drive some of it, I am less than enthusiastic that most will. Although my hopes and prayers are with them all, my willingness to absolve them of their complicity in creating the "age of Trump" is gone. Without acknowledgment and admission of their substantial, grievous errors in judgment, my respect cannot return, at least in the areas of politics and civil affairs.

I am at this point quite pessimistic. One relative recently echoed Rush Limbaugh in an apparent willingness to move down a path of secession and perhaps including civil war. Well, he got his wish when our Capitol was assaulted, and five people were killed. Another relative, when we mentioned we had voted early in the Georgia Senate runoff election, claimed our vote was fraudulent and got so angry he hung up the phone. I told a few friends who are Trump supporters that I was writing this book. The reaction I received was mostly less than enthusiastic—no curiosity, no congratulations for the hard work and effort, no interest whatsoever. One person was very dismissive and discounted my efforts by referring to many books written by new authors as vanity books. Fortunately, when someone puts me down or attempts to discourage me, I tend to react in the opposite way that the person putting me down probably expected. It makes me a bit angry, and it motivates me. I stubbornly refuse to allow someone else to discourage me.

An opinion editorial in the *Washington Post* by Jennifer Rubin, dated December 20, 2020, titled "John Kelly is wrong. These were not good people," described the rationalizing of Donald Trump's former chief of staff, John Kelly. Her conclusion matches mine exactly. Her writing is graceful yet powerful. It captures the righteous indignation many of us feel over the people who powered the destructive policies of the Trump administration.

John Kelly told the *Atlantic*:

> The majority of the people who worked in the White House were decent people who were doing the best they could to serve the nation. They've unfortunately paid quite a price for that in their reputation and future employment. They don't deserve that. They deserve better than that because they kept the train from careening off the tracks.[359]

Jennifer Rubin said emphatically that this was dead wrong, and these were not victims. She said their reputations were besmirched for exceptionally good reasons. They participated in corruption, nastiness, racism, and authoritarianism unparalleled in American history.[360] I would add that they were collaborators.

Their excuse that it would have been worse without them is a demonstration of sophistry. She asks these questions: Would we have lost even more than the over 460,000 Americans lost to date from COVID-19? Would we have been even more lax in failing to respond to Russia's interference in our elections, its payment of bounties to the Taliban for killing our troops, or its hacking into our government's computer systems?[361]

These people John Kelly is referring to did nothing to stop the child separation policy at our border. Most of them did nothing to stop Trump from trying to delegitimize the 2020 election. They did nothing to stop Trump from lying about paying hush money to a porn actress. They did nothing to warn the public early on about the coronavirus pandemic and its real danger. They did nothing to discourage Chinese President Xi Jinping from placing millions of Uighurs in concentration camps or extorting the president of Ukraine to dig up political dirt on Trump's political rival and president-elect, Joe Biden. They did nothing to stop him from defaming our intelligence community or from using tear gas on peaceful protesters outside the White House.[362]

The number of senior officials who quit on principle was close to zero. The number of former cabinet officials who came forward during the impeachment hearings to testify was zero. In numerous cases, Trump's aides broke norms and laws to support this sorry excuse for a president.

In fairness, a handful of officials behaved commendably and prevented greater harm. Foremost, Christopher Krebs, the former director of the Department of Homeland Security's Cybersecurity and Infrastructure Security Agency, made valiant efforts to stop disinformation about the election and call out efforts to discredit the results. The reward for his honesty and fairness and his efforts to keep Americans informed about what was truly going on was termination by Donald Trump. Jennifer Rubin called the termination a badge of honor. I concur. Doing the right thing, when the wrong thing would have been easier, puts him far above the lackies and stooges who for the most part were either afraid of Trump or who were willing to put personal ambition above honor and love of country.[363]

Other honorable public servants who stepped forward and stepped up to their responsibilities to honor the Constitution and the rule of law were Fiona Hill, Alexander Vindman, and Marie Yovanovitch. They each, at the expense of their jobs, were willing to testify to Donald Trump's impeachable and traitorous conduct in office. Christopher Wray also performed with honor as director of the FBI.[364] My father, James Moore, who served as a special agent in the FBI, died in 2016. Rest in peace, Dad. I know you would be proud of the people in the bureau who stood for truth under the withering rhetorical guns of Donald Trump and his deceitful, dishonorable senior officials and his pathetic horde of disgusting followers. The racists, the White supremacists, the authoritarians all would have disgusted my father; my mother, Paula Moore (who died in 2018); and my brother, Scott Moore (who died in 2010). My mother and father were former Republicans. They were Reagan supporters, as was I. My brother was a Democrat. Scott and I disagreed over some issues, but I loved my brother dearly. Each of them loved their country. My son, Matt, and his wife, Brittany; my wife, Louise; and I all are disgusted and fearful for the future of this country after this period of lawless treachery.

The idea that aides, even those with lower levels of power and authority, should be exempt from criticism and, yes, condemnation for the moral outrage of this radioactive presidency is simply out of the question. This would be like excusing lower-level fascists in Italy, Germany, and Japan, whose only jobs were record-keeping for regimes that brought war and destruction upon the world and systematic death to the racial and religious groups they deemed undesirable and detestable. When a regime attempts to undermine democracy and establish hate toward others who disagree with them, all employees that further the regime's goals and implement its policies are accountable for the results. There is no hiding from the ugliness, the incompetence, the corruption, the craziness, the indecency, the lies, the lawlessness, the racism, the authoritarianism, or the willingness to fail to protect or defend the nation against all enemies, foreign or domestic.

Regimes depend on lower and middle level aides to carry out tasks required by higher-ups. Hitler depended on Himmler and Heydrich to carry out his racial and religious extermination policies. They, in turn, depended on SS and SD officers to carry out their orders, who in turn, required soldiers and concentration camp guards to murder and bury Jewish victims. None of them, top to bottom, could deny responsibility. In the US military, officers and soldiers cannot use the excuse that they were just following orders. Illegal and unjust orders are not to be followed. Soldiers are not allowed to execute civilians or prisoners without just cause. The Uniform Code of Military Justice is quite clear on this subject.

While the United States under Trump did not execute people in concentration camps, Trump and his supporters did talk openly about arresting political opponents. They were responsible for stirring up the White supremacist and anti-government hatred that signaled right-wing militias to defy the Michigan governor, Gretchen Whitmer, and plot to kidnap and potentially execute her. Trump got away with what he did and said as president because of the Mark Meadows, Kayleigh McEnanys, Kellyanne Conways, and others too numerous to list.[365]

These people deserve nothing but contempt from Americans who believe in democracy, who believe in the Constitution, and who believe in truth, not lies. The fact that they might suffer damage to their reputations and credibility is something they should have thought about before they threw their moral compasses into the trash. Hopefully, at least some of these accomplices will awake to their wicked words and corrupt, condemnable actions. Maybe some attempt at repentance and honest reflection could at least partially save them from the overwhelming guilty judgment by their fellow citizens. However, the parodies about "Don the Ly'in King" will never go away.

His pardons of crooked congressmen, Doug Collins for inside trading and securities fraud, and Dana Rohrabacher for spending campaign funds on personal expenses, and the pardons of several people on his campaign staff—George Papadopoulos, Roger Stone, Paul Manafort, and others—are symptomatic of the rot and corruption that infiltrated everything Trump touched. He also pardoned four military contractors convicted of killing fourteen unarmed Iraqi civilians in Baghdad in 2007.

In an article in the *Atlantic* titled "Engaging with Trump's Die-Hard Supporters Isn't Productive," dated December 21, 2020, by Tom Nichols, the author argues forcefully that Trump loyalists who cling to conspiracy theories should be deprived of the attention they seek. He makes a very articulate and strong case for ignoring these people.

President-elect Joe Biden made unity a major theme at the heart of his campaign. Most Americans would like to move on from the reckless, heartless, selfish four years of Donald Trump. True patriots want to begin to take on the tasks and challenges Donald Trump ignored or minimized such as fighting the coronavirus, reestablishing respect for the rule of law, and restoring our alliances and leadership in the world. Still, millions of Americans, me included, are not ready to welcome Trump supporters, friends, neighbors, and family members back into a circle of trust. The prevarications, the unwillingness to admit colossal errors in judgment, and the distrust planted into our electorate are simply too much to allow a forgive and forget attitude to assuage the damage these four years have done to the country's collective psyche.

In this article, Nichols says Americans are not wrong to feel a profound anger, a sense of contempt even, for the people that brought us to this place. This might sound cold and harsh, but Democrats, independents, and what is left of remaining sensible Republicans should all try to move forward solving the nation's problems. We should never forget what the Trumpists in the Republican Party did to bring this nation to its knees. Seven weeks after the election, Donald Trump was still threatening to burn down our democracy. He was fighting with anyone and everyone not doing his shameful bidding to remain in office. He is still talking about primary challenges to Republicans who did not help him overturn the results of the election. His neglect of the American people in the remaining days of his lame-duck presidency was there for all to see. Other than focusing selfishly on his need to remain in power, he checked out of all other responsibilities and duties of his office.[366]

Ordinary Americans, who have lived through these four years of chaos, dysfunction, and neglect, have every right to refuse to take the Trumpists seriously ever again. In this referenced article, Nichols states that he is not talking about all seventy-four million people who voted for Trump. Some of these voters that supported him in 2016 and 2020 might have done so with some degree of hesitancy. Some may have focused on a single issue, such as abortion, or a self-interest in keeping their tax rate low.

Some Republicans, however, were able to separate themselves from focusing solely on a single issue or a self-centered lust for lower taxes. They saw the existential threat Donald Trump was to their political party, to their country, and to the entire world. These are the Republicans, or dare I say it, former Republicans, who showed the strength of character and intellect to not be fooled by this corrupt charlatan.

In this article, Nichols refers to the people who continue giving Trump their full-blown support to the very end. These are the deadenders, the people willing, metaphorically speaking, to die on the hill with him. They are willing to accept his efforts to attempt a military coup, to consider martial law, and to believe all his untruths and conspiracy theories. They have moved beyond reasonable support and loyalty into the realm of addiction and mass delusion. It seems nearly impossible to engage with them in civil discourse or any type of reasonable discussion. Because they only accept what they hear on a limited number of right-wing media outlets, Fox News, One America News, and News Max, and through the echo chambers of social media, and from other friends and family similarly in thrall to Donald Trump, they are too far gone to ever really be taken seriously again. To argue with them is a waste of time and energy. It only legitimizes their toxic beliefs and weakens our resolve going forward.

Nichols is not in favor of treating the Trumpists with open contempt, or of confronting or berating them. He instead argues that they should be treated with silence. The people who cannot let go of conspiracy theories, and who cannot extricate themselves from Trump's cult of personality, should simply be deprived of the attention they seek. They should be ignored, minimized, and discounted. They should be shunned for their disrespect of other voters, who outvoted them, at the ballot box.[367]

What we have learned about Trumpism, according to Tom Nichols, is this: no content anchors it; no motivating ideology stands behind it or justifies it; no programs or policies come from it. Trumpism is the invention of one man—Donald Trump. It is built on general grievances and a hatred of cultural and intellectual elites. When a movement's views are incoherent and its beliefs are rooted in crazy, incomprehensible ideas, the ability to discuss and compromise with loyalists of this movement is impossible. According to Nichols, further engagement is not only not warranted; it is counterproductive and not worth the effort.[368]

Therefore, Nichols sees no need to start a national conversation with these people and no need to reach out to them in any way. Trump gave voice to ethnic and regional grievances, social resentments, economic insecurities, and authoritarian impulses that were dormant for quite a while. He then was able to construct a bizarre web of theories and conspiracies that made sense to a group of people looking for excuses for their problems and wanting a strong figure to articulate and reflect those problems. Trump did not offer answers or solutions; what he did offer was a window into their emotional state of being. He made them feel better about themselves by reflecting their insecurities onto him. He became their whisperer.

Those Americans who were not caught up in his orbit and who were not fooled by him will lose their own sense of well-being if they continue to engage with Trump's hard-core base. Non-Trump voters must turn off the noise and stop listening to or trying to understand what makes these people tick.[369]

The only people who need to engage such voters are political strategists because enough of these voters reside in swing states that can drive the Electoral College off the cliff or into a ditch. Nichols says the rest of the country no longer needs to worry about what they really want or why they seem unable to grasp reality. He says we must move forward as a nation. He gives us permission to love and to pray for our family members and friends caught up in Trump's world and unwilling to leave it. The millions of die-hards do not, however, deserve our engagement or interest. He states unequivocally that the sooner we refuse to continue these conversations with the Trump die-hards, the sooner we will return to being a serious nation.

On January 2, 2021, it was reported that eleven additional US senators planned to join Senator Josh Hawley, US senator from Missouri, and that up to 140 Republican members of the US House of Representatives, planned to vote against ratifying the Electoral College victory of President-elect Joe Biden on January 6, 2021. Included among this group was Senator Ron Johnson of Wisconsin. As a former resident of Wisconsin and a former Republican voter in the Badger state, I was shocked to see this reported by several media outlooks. Ron Johnson, someone I used to respect, has officially thrown his hat in the ring with a group of cynical, political hacks. This attempt to undermine our democratic traditions and our US Constitution demonstrates that the collective mental health of a huge percentage of elected national legislators from a once proud major political party is dangerously delusional and more than close to seditious. This political party is positioning itself as the party of crazy, the party of traitors, and the party that can no longer be taken seriously by most Americans. Ron Johnson is only setting himself up for a likely political defeat in 2022 and for a sad verdict of history. He might very well be mentioned in the same vein as the controversial and destructive former US senator from Wisconsin, Joseph R. McCarthy.

After the carnage of the January 6 insurrection, some of these senators changed their minds and did not object to the Electoral College results, including Senator Ron Johnson. However, they still cannot escape completely from their torturous justifications and rationalizations of Donald Trump's policies, his lies, and his traitorous incitement to insurrection. They still own these.

This motley crew has been referred to as the "Sedition Caucus." They describe themselves as conservatives, but they are anything but conservatives. In an NBC opinion editorial, dated January 6, 2021, the writers, Robert S. McElvaine and Elizabeth Chisholm, eloquently explain why none of these traitors should ever be considered conservatives or Republicans.

> Actual conservatives value responsibility, self-reliance, tradition, norms, law, truth-telling, morality, manners, knowledge, loyalty, success in business, self-control, religious values, patriotism, stability, maturity, marital fidelity, a sense of history, the checks and balances of constitutional government, deliberation, fiscal restraint, accountability, ordered liberty, justice, principle, humility, and compassion.

> There is no way to justify continuing the false designation of radical rightists as "conservatives" and people willing to end the republic as "Republicans." The dozen-plus elected members of the Republican Party in the Senate and more than a hundred in the House who announced that they would vote to overturn various states' electoral votes Wednesday should not,

despite their nominal party membership, be referred to as "conservatives" or "Republicans."[370]

These men and women are nothing but fringe radical rightists, Trump enablers, and propagandists. They are the worst examples of character deficient politicians seen in my lifetime. Their cynical, craven attempts to curry favor with Trump's gullible, authoritarian base of supporters is beneath contempt. They should all be recalled by the voters in their respective states. They are cowardly opportunists that history will render a swift and harsh verdict upon. Never in my lifetime did I expect to see within the political party I supported for so many years, such a den of vipers. These cultlike Trump zombies shame their party, their families, and their nation. If I sound over-the-top appalled at their detestable antics, it is because I am. I used to expect profiles in courage from members of my previous political party. Now I see too many profiles in vanity, treachery, and deceit!

In closing this book, I did not expect that the first weekend of 2021 would reveal so many Republicans infected with cynical character disorders or delusional psychoses. How so many people could sell their political souls to the worst narcissist in American history is something that is more than hard to explain. There seems to be a state of stubborn denial within the mind of the Trump supporter. Despite overwhelming evidence of corruption, lying, incompetence, and traitorous acts, the Trump supporters cling to him with unwavering allegiance. Unfortunately, their allegiance to Trump exceeds their allegiance to the rule of law, to the US Constitution, to their country's national security, and to their fellow citizens.

They resent those Americans who voted Trump out of office. This radically dangerous, stubborn state of denial and this refusal to seek out or believe the truth, portends ill for the future of the United States. Their unwillingness to accept the election results despite no evidence of significant fraud and their unwillingness to believe anyone other than Donald Trump or his acolytes appears to be the result of brainwashing. They refuse to seek out or listen to other Republicans who have dismantled Trump's claims of voter fraud. They refuse to listen to other sources of news and opinion. They are dug in and willing to watch their political party—the Republican Party—commit collective political suicide. This Trump era will end very badly for them and their party. When individuals or groups of individuals make Faustian bargains to achieve certain goals, it never ends well.

I have been very harsh on Trump supporters in this book, and I considered toning down the criticism as I was writing it, but after much deliberation, I have concluded that if anything, I have not been harsh enough. The damage to our institutions, to our civil affairs, and to our international standing in the world are just too much to overlook. The people who are unwilling to see what is right in front of their eyes need to be held to account. They need to be shamed and ridiculed for their cocky, obnoxious support of an obviously dangerously incompetent authoritarian. Their attachment to and belief in falsehood is an affront to every other American. Their willingness to try to shove their minority share of the vote (electoral and popular) ahead of our majority vote is seditious. This can never be tolerated in a free and democratic constitutional republic. History will be very unkind to the fracturing Republican Party, and it will be especially unkind to those Trumpists unwilling to admit their mistaken judgment. Americans are a forgiving people, but to be forgiven, people need to admit their mistakes and ask for forgiveness. Without clear and full admission of their role in rationalizing, enabling, supporting, and justifying the presidency of Donald Trump, they and their views should be, metaphorically speaking, excommunicated from serious consideration because they have not behaved like serious adults. Their votes, their ridiculous parades, their attendance at rallies and elsewhere without masks, their lies and misinformation, and their stubborn refusal to seek truth from sources other than their party's propaganda machines disqualifies them from anything other than political exile. They need to be corrected promptly when they spew falsehoods, and then if they continue, they need to be completely ignored and shunned.

There is always a chance (a slim chance) that I might return to a Republican Party purged of the Trump influence. There is a likelier chance that I might join a new political party should circumstances warrant. The most likely outcome for me, however, is this: I will park myself in the Democratic Party at least until the Republican Party pays a severe price for its mendacity, for its craziness, for its coordinated assault on democracy, for its attacks on the rule of law, and for its traitorous acts defending the indefensible.

Until the Republican Party's leaders and most of its voters condemn the assault on our Capitol and place blame where it should be placed, at the feet of Donald Trump, the Republican Party deserves nothing but scorn from the rest of us. Democrats have reclaimed the high ground on many of the issues now facing the country, especially national security, and foreign affairs.

While not a perfect fit for me on some issues, the Democrats at least behave like the adults in the room. As a result, now is a time for choosing. Many Republicans are changing their political affiliation by registering as Independents or Democrats across the country. So far, nearly ten thousand registered voters in Arizona have denounced their former party since the insurrection on the Capitol. If only more Republican House representatives and senators could find their spines, we could end Trumpism here and now. Too many of them fear being challenged in primaries by Trump toadies. While they might avoid a primary challenge by staying loyal to their former traitor in chief, Donald Trump, they will face a much tougher general election fight. Most Americans want to move on from Donald Trump, his pathetic family, and the kooks and traitors that now inhabit the Republican Party.

A special recognition needs to be given to the four men who testified before the House Committee investigating the January 6th insurrection at our Capitol. Pfc. Harry Dunn and Sgt Aquilino Gonell of the U.S. Capital Police and Michael Fanone and Daniel Hodges of the Washington DC Metropolitan Police are examples of true patriots and dedicated public servants. They spoke passionately for their compatriots who defended our Capitol and shed blood (some of whom died) to save the lives of both Republican and Democratic representatives and senators (as well as the vice president) on this tragic day in our history. They also spoke for most Americans who cast their ballots in a free and fair election, who want to move their country forward, not backward.

Laura Ingraham and Tucker Carlson, both Fox News opinion hosts, mocked the riveting testimony of these heroes. Tucker Carlson's snickers and Laura Ingraham's patronizing awards for "best political performances" showed how low this network could stoop in denying and minimizing the insurrection. Their shameful behavior reflects on them, their cable news network, and ultimately their viewers and advertisers. Nothing could be further from the truth than their despicable characterization of these heroes. These witnesses from the Capitol Police and the DC Police were honorable, decent men who held the line against an onslaught of real traitors on January 6th. They suffered horrific injuries, emotional and physical, holding the line against vicious, wicked traitors. Officer Fanone suffered a heart attack after being tasered by members of Donald Trump's satanic army. Several policemen committed suicide in the days, weeks, and months after they fought for their lives and the lives of our elected officials. I believe these police witnessed horrors, up close and personal, inflicted on them and against the very fabric of our country and its institutions. I think the unbelievable evil that they witnessed on January 6th, combined with the excuses and the denials of Republican officeholders and their sycophantic media allies were deeply depressing and profoundly shocking to these loyal and brave men and women. The anger, sadness, and courage in the face of danger we witnessed in the testimony of these four men should stir the souls of all patriotic Americans. It should make us proud that these people would put their lives on the line for our freedom to vote, to select leaders, and to determine the destiny of our nation. These heroes endured racial and personal taunts on top of the physical threats, injuries, and the overwhelming shock of facing their own citizens engaging in unconscionable barbaric and inhuman behavior.

They were a modern-day version of the Spartans who defended Thermopylae pass for three days before succumbing to the Persian onslaught in August of 480 BCE. These four men and the others who defended our Capitol deserve the eternal thanks and respect of every

American. For those who died protecting democracy, our prayers are with them and their families. They represent the best in America, the honorable and the brave. The insurrectionists and their supporters represent the worst in America, the dishonorable, the lost, and the spiritually evil. Trump supporters who condone and minimize the insurrection and who mock the patriots who prevented this attempted coup and saved our democracy, deserve nothing but contempt from the rest of us.

I hope this book is educational, and I hope it opens some minds. To Trump supporters, this book is written with the intent purpose of administering tough love. I enjoyed writing it, and I am blessed to have found so many sources of information and opinion on the failures of the Trump administration. I have used many quotes throughout the book from some of the best writers and political thinkers in the United States. My sincere appreciation and thanks go out to each of them.

BIBLIOGRAPHY

Araatani, L. (2020, October 30). Oversight report calls Trump administration response to the pandemic a 'failure'. *The Washington Post.*

Ater, R. (2020, December 23). *IN MEMORIAM: I CAN'T BREATHE.* Retrieved from reneeater.com: https://www.reneeater.com/on-monuments-blog/2020/5/29/in-memoriam-i-cant-breathe

Barnes and Cooper, J. a. (2020, January 14). Trump Discussed Pulling US from NATO, Aids Say Amid New Concerns Over Russia. *New York Times.*

Bauer and Goldsmith, B. a. (2020, October 15). Six post-Trump reforms to help protect the rule of law. *The Washington Post.*

Beason, T. (2020, August 17). Trump and Biden couldn't be more different on the complicated issue of race. *The Los Angeles Times.*

Bernstein, J. (2020, May 29). A Presidential Primer on the Rule of Law. *Bloomberg News.*

Biskupic, J. (2020, October 27). *Amy Coney Barrett joins the Supreme Court in unprecedented times.* Retrieved from www.cnn.com: https://www.cnn.com/2020/10/27/politics/amy-coney-barrett-joins-supreme-court-unprecedented/index.html

Biskupic, J. (2020, February 22). Trump's unbroken pattern of disdain for the rule of law. *CNN Politics.*

Blackwill and Rappleye, R. D. (2017, June 22). Trump's Five Mistaken Reasons for Withdrawing from the Trans-Pacific Partnership. *Foreign Policy Magazine.*

BMJNewsroom. (2020, October 27). Fatal police shootings of unarmed Black people in US more than 3 times as high as in Whites. *BMJ.*

Bolton, J. (2020). *The Room Where It Happened.* New York City: Simon and Schuster.

Boot, M. (2018). *The Corrosion of Conservatism.* New York: Liveright Publishing Corporation.

Bruen, B. (2020, August 02). Trump Wrecked the International Order. It's Time to Start Thinking about what Happens when He's Gone. *Business Insider.*

Buchanan, M. J. (2020, September 27). Trump's Impeachable Conduct Strikes at the Heart of the Rule of Law: Part 1. *Center for American Progress.*

Cavanagh, J. (2020, September 17). Trump trade wars have led to lost US jobs and factories. We need a worker-centered recovery. *USA Today.*

CochrneFuchsVogelSilver-Greenberg, E. H. (2020, August 18). The New York Times. *Postal Service Suspends Changes After Outcry Over Delivery Slowdown.*

Collinson, S. (2020, September 09). CNN Politics. *Trump intensifies assault on rule of law as he fights for reelection.*

Colvin, J. (2020, May 28). Trump continures to claim broad powers he doesn't have. *AP News.*

DailyNewsEditorial. (2020, November 01). Lethal dereliction: Trump's failures in the COVID-19 pandemic. *New York Daily News.*

Dale, D. (2020, September 02). *Fact check: A guide to 9 conspiracy theories Trump is currently pushing.* Retrieved from www.cnn.com: https://www.cnn.com/2020/09/02/politics/fact-check-trump-conspiracy-theories-biden-covid-thugs-plane/index.html

DeRienzo, M. (2020, October 28). *Barriers to the Ballot Box. Analysis: New and Age-Old Voter Suppression Tactics at the Heart of the 2020 Power Struggle.* Retrieved from www.publicintegrity.org: https://publicintegrity.org/politics/elections/

ballotboxbarriers/analysis-voter-suppression-never-went-awa
y-tactics-changed/

Fallows, J. (2020, November 20). Trump's Indifference Amounts to
Negligent Homicide. *The Atlantic.*

Fong and Mohs, V. a. (2020). Exploring the Impact of Tariffs on
Foreign Direct Investment and Economic Prosperity.
Internation Journal of Accounting and Taxation.

Frum, D. (2020, November 15). Populism without Popularity. *The
Atlantic.*

FunkeSanders, D. a. (202, July 31). *Downplay and Denial of the
Coronavirus.* Retrieved from www.khn.org: https://
khn.org/news/article/lie-of-the-year-the-downplay-an
d-denial-of-the-coronavirus/

Gabbatt, A. (2020, September 30). Trump's refusal to condemn white
supremacy fits pattern of extremist rhetoric. *The Guardian.*

Gerson, M. (2020, October 27). Here are the Trump administration's
four most profound failures in the pandemic. *The Washington
Post.*

Goldberg, J. (2020, September 03). Trump: Americans Who Died in
War Are 'Losers' and 'Suckers'. *The Atlantic.*

Gomez and Gonzalez, A. a. (2020, November 13). Biden might need
years to reverse Trump's immigration policies on DACA,
asylum, family separation, ICE raids, private detention and
more. *USA Today.*

Gottschalk, N. (2020, April 30). *5 ways President Trump's xenophobic agenda has accelerated during the COVID-19 pandemic.* Retrieved from www.politicsofpoverty.oxfama-
merica.org: https://politicsofpoverty.oxfamamerica.or
g/5-ways-president-trumps-xenophobic-agenda-has-ac-
celerated-during-covid-19-pandemic/

Green, E. (2020, November 15). The Evangelical Reconing Begins.
The Atlantic.

Hamburger and Barrett, T. a. (2020, October 27). Former US
Attorneys - all Republicans - back Biden, saying Trump
threatens 'the rule of law'. *The Washington Post.*

Hamlin, M. J. (2020, November 10). How Trump Sold Failure to 70 Million People. *The Atlantic*.

Kang, M. (2020, November 15). *Donald Trump's legal strategy makes no sense for winning the vote count. So what is he doing?* Retrieved from www.nbcnews.com/think: https://www.nbcnews.com/think/opinion/donald-trump-s-legal-strateg y-makes-no-sense-winning-vote-ncna1247841

Kendj, I. (2020, September). Is This the Beginning of the End of American Racism. *The Atlantic*.

KesslerRizzoKelly, G. S. (2020, July 13). President Trump has made more than 20,000 false or misleading claims. *The Washington Post*.

Kilgore, E. (2020, November 20). *Trump's Hold on the GOP Rank and File Continues to Be Amazing*. Retrieved from www.nymag.com: https://nymag.com/intelligencer/2020/11/trump-mail-in-voting-election-fraud.html

Krugman, P. (2020, October). *Why Did Trump's Trade War Fail?" (Notes toward a proper paper)*. Retrieved from gc.cuny.edu: https://www.gc.cuny.edu/CUNY_GC/media/LISCenter/pkrugman/tradewarfail.pdf

Kumar, A. (2020, November 30). Behind Trump's final push to limit immigration. *Politico*.

Lamothe, D. (2019, October 15). 'I Can't Even Look at the Atrocities' US Troops Say Trump's Syria Withdrawal Betrayed an Ally. *The Washington Post*.

Leonnig and Rucker, C. a. (2020). *A Very Stable Genius*. London: Penguin Press for the US and Bloomsbury Publishing for the UK.

Leubsdorf, C. (2020, July 02). Trump's five major failures on coronavirus. *Dallas Morning News*.

Lucas, R. (2021, July 30). *npr.org*. Retrieved from Notes Show Trump Pressed The Justice Department To Declare The 2020 Election Corrupt: https://www.npr.org/2021/07/30/1022826068/notes-show-trump-pressed-the-justice-department-to-dec lare-the-2020-election-cor

Lutz, E. M. (2020, November 04). Report: Texas has closed most polling places since court ruling. *THE TEXAS TRIBUNE.*

Lynch, C. (2020, May 08). Dispite US Sanctions, Iran Expands Its Nuclear Stockpile. *Foreign Policy.*

Mahler, J. (2020, November 17). Can America Restire the Rule of Law Without Prosecuting Trump. *The New York Times.*

McCammon, S. (2020, September 30). *From Debate Stage, Trump Declines To Denounce White Supremacy.* Retrieved from npr.org: https://www.npr.org/2020/09/30/918483794/from-debat e-stage-trump-declines-to-denounce-white-supremacy

McElvaineChisholm, R. S. (2021, January 06). *Opinion | Republicans' efforts to end the American reublic makes them Republicans in name only.* Retrieved from www.nbcnews. com`: https://www.nbcnews.com/think/opinion/republican s-efforts-end-american-republic-makes-them-republica ns-name-only-ncna1252872

Michaels, A. (2020, October 27). *Trump and Race: How the president's rhetoric and policies divided us.* Retrieved from wash-ingtonpost.com: https://www.washingtonpost.com/pod-casts/can-he-do-that/trump-and-race-how-the-presidents-rhetoric-and-policies-divided-us-1/

Montanaro, D. (2020, June 5). Americans Say President Trump Has Worsened Race Relations Since Goerge Floyd's Death. (S. McCammon, Interviewer) Retrieved from npr.org: https://www.npr.org/2020/06/05/871083543/american s-say-president-trump-has-worsened-race-relations-si nce-george-floyds-death

Moore, M. (2020, October 25). phone conversation. (B. Moore, Interviewer)

Narea, N. (2020, October 15). *Trump's Obstruction of the 2020 Census, Explained.* Retrieved from www.publicintegrity. org: https://publicintegrity.org/politics/system-failure/ trump-obstruction-of-2020-census/

Nichols, T. (2020, November 04). A Large Portion of the Electorate Shows the Sociopath. *The Atlantic.*

Nichols, T. (2020, December 21). Engaging With Trump's Die-Hard Supporters Isn't Productive. *The Atlantice.*

Now, D. (2020, October 22). Columbia Researchers Say Trump's Failures Led to at Least 130,000 Coronavirus Deaths. *Democracy Now.*

Peters, C. (2020, June 08). A detailed timeline of all the ways Trump failed to respond to the coronavirus. *VOX.*

Pettigrew, T. (2017, March 02). *wwwjspp.psychopen.eu.* Retrieved from Social Psychological Perspectives on Trump Supporters: https://doi.org/10.5964/jspp.v5i1.750

PewResearch. (2020, June 02). *In Changing U.S. Electorate, Race and Education Remain Stark Dividing Lines.* Retrieved from WWW.pewresearch.org: https://www.pewresearch.org/politics/2020/06/02/in-changing-u-s-electorate-race-and-education-remain-stark-dividing-lines/

Phillips, D. (2019, December 27). Anguish and Anger from Navy Seals Who Turned In Edward Gallagher. *The New York Times.*

Platoff, E. (2020, December 12). U.S. Supreme Court throws out Texas lawsuit contesting 2020 election results in four gattleground states. *THE TEXAS TRIBUNE.*

QiuSheare, L. a. (2020, October 26). Rallies Are the Core of Trump's Campaign, and a Font of Lies and Misinformation. *The New York Times.*

Reid, T. (2020, October 27). Republican former US attorneys endorse Biden, call Trump threat to rule of law. *REUTERS.*

Rodgers and Bailey, L. a. (2020, October 31). Trump wall: How much has he actually built. *BBC News.*

Rosenzweig and Kannan, P. a. (2020, September 07). Repairing the Rule of Law: An Agenda for Post-Trump Reform. *LAWFARE.*

Rothkopf, D. (2020). *Traitor A History of American Betrayal from Benedict Arnold to Donald Trump.* New York: Thomas Dunne Books.

Rubin, J. (2019, September 09). Trump's Invitation to the Taliban was Disgraceful. So was Republican Silence about it. *The Washington Post.*

Rubin, J. (2020, December 20). John Kelly is wrong. These were not good people. *The Washington Post.*

Rubin, J. (2020, September 13). Trump's racism and xenophobia haven't caught on. *The Washington Post.*

RymanWagnerO'DellCrow, A. D. (2018). *The Wall.* Retrieved from www.usatoday.com: https://www.usatoday.com/border-wall/

Sacchetti, M. (2020, December 03). Feuds flare along Trump's border wall as construction ramps up during his final days in office. *Washington Post.*

SchmittHabermanSangerCooperJakes, E. M. (2020, November 16). *Trump Sought Options for Attacking Iran to Stop Its Growing Nuclear Program.* Retrieved from www.nytimes.com: https://www.nytimes.com/2020/11/16/us/politics/trump-iran-nuclear.html

Smith, A. (2018, January 16). 'An Absolute Disgrace': Republicans Blast Trump for his 'Disgusting' Press Conference with Putin. *Business Insider.*

Solnit, R. (2019, October 09). President Trump is at war with the rule of law. This won't end well. *The Gardian.*

Spegele and Ostroff, B. a. (2020, November 15). Trump Family Business Faces Post-Election Reckonig. *The Wall Street Journal.*

Sykes, C. J. (2017). *How the Right Lost Its Mind.* New York: Saint Martin's Press.

Talbot, M. (2019, May 05). Trump, Barr, and The Rule of Law. *The New Yoker.*

Tapper, J. (2020, November 15). *Jake Tapper: GOP "led by the gang that couldn't sue straight".* Retrieved from www.facebook.com: https://www.facebook.com/CNNReplay/videos/jake-tapper-gop-led-by-the-gang-that-couldnt-sue-straight/691783828382371/

Tapper, J. (2020, November 15). *Tapper: Trump can lie on Twitter, but judges need facts. State of the Union.* Retrieved from www.cnn.com: https://www.cnn.com/videos/politics/2020/11/15/

trump-failed-legal-cases-claiming-voter-fraud-tapper-en
der-sotu-vpx.cnn

TenoveMcKay, C. a. (2020, November 29). *Trump's lies about the election show how disinformation erodes democracy.* Retrieved from www.theconversation.com: http://theconversation.com/trumps-lies-about-the-election-show-how-disinformation-erodes-democracy-150603

Travers, R. (2020, October 02). Trump's COVID-19 record is the single biggest failure in US history. *USA Today.*

Trevizo and Schwartz, P. a. (2020, October 27). Records show Trump's border wall is costing taxpayers billions more than initial contracts. *Texas Tribune.*

Trump, D. (2015). *Republican primary debate.*

Trump, D. (2015). *Trump Tweet.*

Trump, D. (2016). *Declaring America's Economic Independence.*

Trump, D. (2017). *Presidential Memorandum.*

Turner, S. (2020, February 11). Trump's Firing of Vindman Epitomizes the President's most Harmful Act of All. *Newsweek.*

USATodayEditorial, B. (2020, October 29). Coronavirus response shows Donald Trump's failure of leadership. *USA Today.*

USATodayTrump, D. (2016, March 14). Disappearing Middle Class Needs Better Deal on Trade. *USA Today.*

Villarreal, D. (2020, October 27). Trump Chants 'COVID' 10 Times At Rally After Obama Accuses Him of Being 'Jealous' of Virus Media Coverage. *Newsweek.*

Waldman, P. (2020, November 23). Trump will Go, but Trumpism will Remain. *The Washington Post.*

Warrick and Denver, J. a. (2020, September 30). As Kim Wooed Trump with "Love Letters". *National Security.*

Woodward, B. (2020). *Rage.* New York: Simon & Schuster.

NOTES

1   (Nichols, 2020)
2   (Leonnig and Rucker, 2020)
3   (Goldberg, 2020)
4   (Goldberg, 2020)
5   (Goldberg, 2020)
6   (Phillips, 2019)
7   (Smith, 2018)
8   (Bolton, 2020)
9   (Warrick and Denver, 2020)
10 (Barnes and Cooper, 2020)
11 (Bruen, 2020)
12 (Lynch, 2020)
13 (Lamothe, 2019)
14 (Rubin, 2019)
15 (Turner, 2020)
16 (Turner, 2020)
17 (Rothkopf, 2020)
18 (Villarreal, 2020)
19 (Gerson, 2020)
20 (Gerson, 2020)
21 (Leubsdorf, 2020)
22 (Travers, 2020)
23 (USATodayEditorial, 2020)
24 (USATodayEditorial, 2020)
25 (USATodayEditorial, 2020)
26 (USATodayEditorial, 2020)

27 (Now, 2020)
28 (Hamlin, 2020)
29 (Hamlin, 2020)
30 (Hamlin, 2020)
31 (Hamlin, 2020)
32 (Hamlin, 2020)
33 (Hamlin, 2020)
34 (DailyNewsEditorial, 2020)
35 (DailyNewsEditorial, 2020)
36 (DailyNewsEditorial, 2020)
37 (DailyNewsEditorial, 2020)
38 (Fallows, 2020)
39 (Fallows, 2020)
40 (Fallows, 2020)
41 (Fallows, 2020)
42 (Fallows, 2020)
43 (Spegele and Ostroff, 2020)
44 (Buchanan, 2020)
45 (Bernstein, 2020)
46 (Bernstein, 2020)
47 (Colvin, 2020)
48 (Colvin, 2020)
49 (Colvin, 2020)
50 (Colvin, 2020)
51 (Colvin, 2020)
52 (Solnit, 2019)
53 (Solnit, 2019)
54 (Solnit, 2019)
55 (Solnit, 2019)
56 (Solnit, 2019)
57 (Solnit, 2019)
58 (Solnit, 2019)
59 (Talbot, 2019)
60 (Talbot, 2019)
61 (Talbot, 2019)
62 (Talbot, 2019)
63 (Talbot, 2019)
64 (Talbot, 2019)
65 (Biskupic, 2020)
66 (Biskupic, 2020)
67 (Collinson, 2020)

68 (Rosenzweig and Kannan, 2020)
69 (Rosenzweig and Kannan, 2020)
70 (Rosenzweig and Kannan, 2020)
71 (Rosenzweig and Kannan, 2020)
72 (Rosenzweig and Kannan, 2020)
73 (Rosenzweig and Kannan, 2020)
74 (Rosenzweig and Kannan, 2020)
75 (Rosenzweig and Kannan, 2020)
76 (Rosenzweig and Kannan, 2020)
77 (Rosenzweig and Kannan, 2020)
78 (Rosenzweig and Kannan, 2020)
79 (Rosenzweig and Kannan, 2020)
80 (Rosenzweig and Kannan, 2020)
81 (Rosenzweig and Kannan, 2020)
82 (Rosenzweig and Kannan, 2020)
83 (Rosenzweig and Kannan, 2020)
84 (Rosenzweig and Kannan, 2020)
85 (Rosenzweig and Kannan, 2020)
86 (Rosenzweig and Kannan, 2020)
87 (Bauer and Goldsmith, 2020)
88 (Bauer and Goldsmith, 2020)
89 (Mahler, 2020)
90 (Mahler, 2020)
91 (Mahler, 2020)
92 (Mahler, 2020)
93 (Mahler, 2020)
94 (Mahler, 2020)
95 (Mahler, 2020)
96 (Mahler, 2020)
97 (Mahler, 2020)
98 (Mahler, 2020)
99 (Mahler, 2020)
100 (Mahler, 2020)
101 (Mahler, 2020)
102 (Mahler, 2020)
103 (Mahler, 2020)
104 (Mahler, 2020)
105 (Mahler, 2020)
106 (Mahler, 2020)
107 (Mahler, 2020)
108 (Mahler, 2020)

109 (Mahler, 2020)
110 (Hamburger and Barrett, 2020)
111 (Reid, 2020)
112 (BMJ Newsroom, 2020)
113 (Ater, 2020)
114 (Kendj, 2020)
115 (Kendj, 2020)
116 (Kendj, 2020)
117 (Kendj, 2020)
118 (Kendj, 2020)
119 (Kendj, 2020)
120 (Kendj, 2020)
121 (Kendj, 2020)
122 (Kendj, 2020)
123 (Kendj, 2020)
124 (Kendj, 2020)
125 (Kendj, 2020)
126 (Kendj, 2020)
127 (Kendj, 2020)
128 (Kendj, 2020)
129 (Kendj, 2020)
130 (Kendj, 2020)
131 (Kendj, 2020)
132 (Montanaro, 2020)
133 (Montanaro, 2020)
134 (Montanaro, 2020)
135 (Montanaro, 2020)
136 (Michaels, 2020)
137 (Michaels, 2020)
138 (Michaels, 2020)
139 (Michaels, 2020)
140 (Michaels, 2020)
141 (Michaels, 2020)
142 (Michaels, 2020)
143 (Michaels, 2020)
144 (Michaels, 2020)
145 (Michaels, 2020)
146 (Michaels, 2020)
147 (Michaels, 2020)
148 (Michaels, 2020)
149 (Michaels, 2020)

150 (Beason, 2020)
151 (Beason, 2020)
152 (Beason, 2020)
153 (Beason, 2020)
154 (Beason, 2020)
155 (McCammon, 2020)
156 (McCammon, 2020)
157 (McCammon, 2020)
158 (Gabbatt, 2020)
159 (Gabbatt, 2020)
160 (Fallows, 2020)
161 (Gottschalk, 2020)
162 (Gottschalk, 2020)
163 (Gottschalk, 2020)
164 (Gottschalk, 2020)
165 (Gottschalk, 2020)
166 (Kumar, 2020)
167 (Kumar, 2020)
168 (Kumar, 2020)
169 (Kumar, 2020)
170 (Gomez and Gonzalez, 2020)
171 (Gomez and Gonzalez, 2020)
172 (Gomez and Gonzalez, 2020)
173 (Gomez and Gonzalez, 2020)
174 (Gomez and Gonzalez, 2020)
175 (Gomez and Gonzalez, 2020)
176 (Gomez and Gonzalez, 2020)
177 (Gomez and Gonzalez, 2020)
178 (Gomez and Gonzalez, 2020)
179 (Gomez and Gonzalez, 2020)
180 (Gomez and Gonzalez, 2020)
181 (Gomez and Gonzalez, 2020)
182 (Rubin, 2020)
183 (Rubin, 2020)
184 (Rubin, 2020)
185 (Rubin, 2020)
186 (Rubin, 2020)
187 (Rodgers and Bailey, 2020)
188 (Rodgers and Bailey, 2020)
189 (Rodgers and Bailey, 2020)
190 (Rodgers and Bailey, 2020)

191 (Rodgers and Bailey, 2020)

192 (Rodgers and Bailey, 2020)

193 (RymanWagnerO'DellCrow, 2018)

194 (RymanWagnerO'DellCrow, 2018)

195 (RymanWagnerO'DellCrow, 2018)

196 (RymanWagnerO'DellCrow, 2018)

197 (Trevizo and Schwartz, 2020)

198 (Trevizo and Schwartz, 2020)

199 (Sacchetti, 2020)

200 (Sacchetti, 2020)

201 (Cavanagh, 2020)

202 (Cavanagh, 2020)

203 (Cavanagh, 2020)

204 (Cavanagh, 2020)

205 (Cavanagh, 2020)

206 (Cavanagh, 2020)

207 (Krugman, 2020)

208 (Krugman, 2020)

209 (Fong and Mohs, 2020)

210 (Krugman, 2020)

211 (Krugman, 2020)

212 (Krugman, 2020)

213 (Krugman, 2020)

214 (Krugman, 2020)

215 (Krugman, 2020)

216 (Krugman, 2020)

217 (Krugman, 2020)

218 (Krugman, 2020)

219 (Krugman, 2020)

220 (USATodayTrump, 2016)

221 (Blackwill and Rappleye, 2017)

222 (Trump, Republican primary debate, 2015)

223 (Blackwill and Rappleye, 2017)

224 (Blackwill and Rappleye, 2017)

225 (Trump, Trump Tweet, 2015)

226 (Blackwill and Rappleye, 2017)

227 (Trump, Presidential Memorandum, 2017)

228 (Blackwill and Rappleye, 2017)

229 (PewResearch, 2020)

230 (DeRienzo, 2020)

231 (CochrneFuchsVogelSilver-Greenberg, 2020)

232 (Biskupic, Amy Coney Barrett joins the Supreme Court in unprecedented times, 2020)

233 (Lutz, 2020)

234 (Narea, 2020)

235 (Tapper, Jake Tapper: GOP "led by the gang that couldn't sue straight", 2020)

236 (Tapper, Tapper: Trump can lie on Twitter, but judges need facts. State of the Union, 2020)

237 (Tapper, Tapper: Trump can lie on Twitter, but judges need facts. State of the Union, 2020)

238 (Kang, 2020)

239 (Kang, 2020)

240 (Kang, 2020)

241 (Platoff, 2020)

242 (Lucas, 2021)

243 (SchmittHabermanSangerCooperJakes, 2020)

244 (KesslerRizzoKelly, 2020)

245 (KesslerRizzoKelly, 2020)

246 (KesslerRizzoKelly, 2020)

247 (KesslerRizzoKelly, 2020)

248 (KesslerRizzoKelly, 2020)

249 (KesslerRizzoKelly, 2020)

250 (KesslerRizzoKelly, 2020)

251 (KesslerRizzoKelly, 2020)

252 (KesslerRizzoKelly, 2020)

253 (FunkeSanders, 202)

254 (FunkeSanders, 202)

255 (Woodward, 2020)

256 (FunkeSanders, 202)

257 (FunkeSanders, 202)

258 (FunkeSanders, 202)

259 (FunkeSanders, 202)

260 (FunkeSanders, 202)

261 (FunkeSanders, 202)

262 (QiuSheare, 2020)

263 (QiuSheare, 2020)

264 (QiuSheare, 2020)

265 (QiuSheare, 2020)

266 (QiuSheare, 2020)

267 (QiuSheare, 2020)

268 (QiuSheare, 2020)

269 (QiuSheare, 2020)
270 (TenoveMcKay, 2020)
271 (TenoveMcKay, 2020)
272 (TenoveMcKay, 2020)
273 (TenoveMcKay, 2020)
274 (TenoveMcKay, 2020)
275 (TenoveMcKay, 2020)
276 (TenoveMcKay, 2020)
277 (TenoveMcKay, 2020)
278 (Dale, 2020)
279 (Dale, 2020)
280 (Dale, 2020)
281 (Dale, 2020)
282 (Dale, 2020)
283 (Dale, 2020)
284 (Dale, 2020)
285 (Dale, 2020)
286 (Dale, 2020)
287 (Rothkopf, 2020)
288 (Rothkopf, 2020)
289 (Rothkopf, 2020)
290 (Rothkopf, 2020)
291 (Rothkopf, 2020)
292 (Rothkopf, 2020)
293 (Rothkopf, 2020)
294 (Sykes, 2017)
295 (Sykes, 2017)
296 (Sykes, 2017)
297 (Sykes, 2017)
298 (Sykes, 2017)
299 (Sykes, 2017)
300 (Sykes, 2017)
301 (Sykes, 2017)
302 (Sykes, 2017)
303 (Sykes, 2017)
304 (Green, 2020)
305 (Green, 2020)
306 (Green, 2020)
307 (Green, 2020)
308 (Green, 2020)
309 (Green, 2020)

310 (Green, 2020)
311 (Sykes, 2017)
312 (Sykes, 2017)
313 (Sykes, 2017)
314 (Sykes, 2017)
315 (Sykes, 2017)
316 (Sykes, 2017)
317 (Sykes, 2017)
318 (Sykes, 2017)
319 (Sykes, 2017)
320 (Sykes, 2017)
321 (Sykes, 2017)
322 (Sykes, 2017)
323 (Boot, 2018)
324 (Boot, 2018)
325 (Boot, 2018)
326 (Boot, 2018)
327 (Boot, 2018)
328 (Moore, 2020)
329 (Boot, 2018)
330 (Boot, 2018)
331 (Boot, 2018)
332 (Boot, 2018)
333 (Boot, 2018)
334 (Boot, 2018)
335 (Boot, 2018)
336 (Boot, 2018)
337 (Boot, 2018)
338 (Waldman, 2020)
339 (Waldman, 2020)
340 (Waldman, 2020)
341 (Waldman, 2020)
342 (Waldman, 2020)
343 (Waldman, 2020)
344 (Waldman, 2020)
345 (Frum, 2020)
346 (Frum, 2020)
347 (Frum, 2020)
348 (Frum, 2020)
349 (Kilgore, 2020)
350 (Kilgore, 2020)

351 (Pettigrew, 2017)

352 (Pettigrew, 2017)

353 (Pettigrew, 2017)

354 (Pettigrew, 2017)

355 (Boot, 2018)

356 (Sykes, 2017)

357 (Sykes, 2017)

358 (Sykes, 2017)

359 (Rubin, John Kelly is wrong. These were not good people., 2020)

360 (Rubin, John Kelly is wrong. These were not good people., 2020)

361 (Rubin, John Kelly is wrong. These were not good people., 2020)

362 (Rubin, John Kelly is wrong. These were not good people., 2020)

363 (Rubin, John Kelly is wrong. These were not good people., 2020)

364 (Rubin, John Kelly is wrong. These were not good people., 2020)

365 (Rubin, John Kelly is wrong. These were not good people., 2020)

366 (Nichols, Engaging With Trump's Die-Hard Supporters Isn't Productive, 2020)

367 (Nichols, Engaging With Trump's Die-Hard Supporters Isn't Productive, 2020)

368 (Nichols, Engaging With Trump's Die-Hard Supporters Isn't Productive, 2020)

369 (Nichols, Engaging With Trump's Die-Hard Supporters Isn't Productive, 2020)

370 (McElvaineChisholm, 2021)

CPSIA information can be obtained
at www.ICGtesting.com
Printed in the USA
LVHW030325211121
703996LV00004B/4